op 5ou

Praise for *Ticket to Exile*

"Lyrical at times, incisive at others, humorou: sentimental or hyperbolic....We are accompa indomitable, always inquisitive, ever playful n obstacles, refuses to back down."

— Jane Anne Staw, author of *Unstuck: A Supportive and Practical Guide to Working Through Writer's Block*

"*Ticket to Exile* is both a tender and revealing biography and a sober social-historical document of a time and place that summoned some among us to quiet, but extraordinary, dignity and courage."

—Peter Buttross, Jr., author of *Natchez Cantos: Poems*

"Adam David Miller keeps his ear to the ground and a keen poet's eye on the world around him in accounts of his life from birth to manhood. How he struggles to obtain a ticket out of those environs is like nothing you've ever heard."

—Mei Nakano, author of *Japanese American Women: Three Generations, 1890–1990*

"In the course of Adam David Miller's exploration of the meaning of his own past and of the subtleties of black-white relations, he illuminates historical trends essential in understanding his region and this country."

—Phyllis Bischof, co-author of *Bibliographies for African Studies, 1987–1993*

"In a world where we are accustomed to sound bites uttered in nano-seconds, *Ticket to Exile* provides an opportunity to slow down, settle in, and share in the life of another person."

—Luisah Teish, author of *Jump Up: Seasonal Celebrations from the World's Deep Traditions*

"A coming-of-age tale with a singular bite."

—Gerald Haslam, author of *Haslam's Valley*

"*Ticket to Exile* is a shining light, a glowing beam of human experience and inner truth cutting through the bitter fog of racism, the vein of fear and cruelty that has shrouded American history."

—Joyce Jenkins, editor of *Poetry Flash*

Also by Adam David Miller

Dices or Black Bones: Black Voices of the Seventies (editor)

Neighborhood and Other Poems

Forever Afternoon

A Sampler of His Poems

Apocalypse Is My Garden

Land Between: New and Selected Poems

ADAM DAVID MILLER

TICKET TO EXILE

a memoir

Heyday Books, Berkeley, California
BayTree Books

BAYTREE

This book was made possible in part by a generous grant from the BayTree Fund.

Library of Congress Cataloging-in-Publication Data
Miller, Adam David.
   Ticket to exile : a memoir / Adam David Miller.
      p. cm.
   ISBN 978-1-59714-065-2 (pbk. : alk. paper)
   1. Miller, Adam David--Childhood and youth. 2. Poets, American--20th century--Biography. 3.
African Americans--Segregation--Southern States. I. Title.
   PS3563.I37414Z46 2007
   811'.54--dc22
                              2007018226

Cover photo by Jackson Davis, courtesy of the Papers of Jackson Davis, MSS 3072,
      Special Collections, University of Virginia Library
Map of Orangeburg, S. C., November 1929 by Edward Howes, C. C. Berry & Company,
      Orangeburg, S. C from the Orangeburg Historical Society
Author photo, page 241, by Cathy Cade
Cover Design by Lorraine Rath
Interior Design by Rebecca LeGates
Printing and Binding: McNaughton & Gunn, Saline, MI

Orders, inquiries, and correspondence should be addressed to:
      Heyday Books
      P. O. Box 9145, Berkeley, CA 94709
      (510) 549-3564, Fax (510) 549-1889
      www.heydaybooks.com

Printed in the United States of America

10 9 8 7 6 5 4 3 2

To my mother, who never gave up and who taught me to laugh

CONTENTS

ACKNOWLEDGMENTS

I would like thank the many people who contributed to the making of this volume, without whom it would not exist in its present form.

Malcolm Margolin, publisher of Heyday Books, for his commitment to the manuscript, and his highly competent and enthusiastic staff for their attention to every detail of the production.

The readers of the manuscript before it was submitted include: Jane Anne Staw, *Unstuck;* Joyce Jenkins, *Poetry Flash;* Mary Berg, KPFA-FM; Peter Buttross, Jr., *Natchez Chronicles;* Elise Peeples, Art Between Us; Los Seis writing group; Fresh Ink poetry group.

The Vermont Studio Center, where the first words, "I hurt," came to me and started the process of remembering.

Phyllis Bischof, Librarian for African American and African Collections at the University of California at Berkeley and Professor Robert Petersen, Middle Tennessee State University, for their early support by sending me books about the U.S. Southern experience. Also for their early support, Michiko Petersen and Ken and Linda Clements.

For their help with fact-checking and valuable material resources: Mrs. Evelyn Weathersbee, Orangeburg Historical Society; Mrs. Barbara Raysor, Receptionist, Claflin College; Mrs. Doris E. Johnson, Library of South Carolina State University; Mrs. Jane (Crum) Covington; Mrs. Joyce (Knight) Baptiste; Mrs. Geraldyne Zimmerman; Mr. Ezra Livingston and his daughter, Mrs. Dolores

Acknowledgments

Johnson; Mr. Gene Crider, *The Times and Democrat,* who steered me to human sources; the Orangeburg County Visitors and Tourism Guide; the Baldwin Directory Company for 1941 information on Wilkinson High School; Lucille and Richard Coleman for their help with fact-checking downtown New York City.

Ms. Lisa Rothman, Ms. Andrea Lewis, and Ms. Susan Stone, of KPFA-FM, who presented excerpts; Avotcja of KPOO-FM, who did the same. Frank Bette Center, Poetry Express, the Bay Area Writing Project's "Writing Teachers Write" series, and Kim McMillon's Jazz and Poetry Series at Anna's Jazz Island, where excerpts were read.

Gayle Wattawa, my text editor, and Jeannine Gendar, my line editor, at Heyday Books, for their perceptive and patient work.

Frances Goldin of Goldin Literary Agency, Inc., for agreeing to represent the work and doing a stellar job.

I give a special thanks to my wife, Elise Peeples, for her computer savvy and for her shepherding of the entire process.

INTRODUCTION

Beyond the verse that opens Part I of the book, I had not planned an introduction to what seemed (to me, anyway) to be a straightforward narrative of my life in Orangeburg, South Carolina, up to the incident that resulted in my jailing and exile. Reactions by some of those kind enough to read my manuscript convinced me that a few words from me might go a way to helping readers appreciate what they find here; further explanation is in order.

Ticket to Exile is a work of memory. As closely as I could, I kept my account within the context of the Teller's scope and vision, which meant avoiding the temptation to use hindsight and the wisdom of my great age to analyze events. I tried to show people and events for what they were, trusting readers to judge them as they would, with the minimum of comment from me. I made only such comment as I thought would help prevent misunderstanding.

I was hit by trauma so severe that my memory was frozen. I could not visit that event for many years. But I have an eidetic memory: it was particularly strong when I was younger. Having such a memory enabled me bring up many scenes with great clarity. I also remember conversations, what they contained and how they sounded. When I was finally able to revisit what had so disoriented me, many images were still fresh.

Time did dim some memories, lose some, and distort others, but on the whole, I believe those of my generation who know of the events I relate will agree that I've violated neither their substance nor their spirit. The Great Depression from its underside, the violence of poverty, the crushing of hope, but also the fortitude of ordinary folk are here. Here you will find depictions of race, class, and caste, gender, and what the French called (when I visited France), Système D, how citizens get over and around an oppressive bureaucracy. And occasional fun.

One reader said she was angry about what happened to me and felt that I should have expressed more anger. Perhaps. I wrote what I felt then, not what I feel now. My aim was to give voice to what I felt as events were occurring rather than what I have felt at various times since. To do so would have violated the voice of the Teller. Some readers have said I succeeded. I hope you will too.

Adam David Miller
January 30, 2007
Berkeley, California

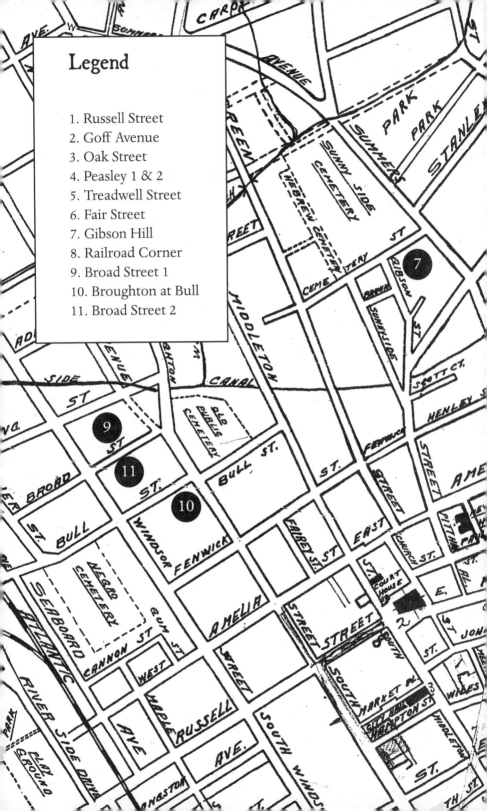

Legend

1. Russell Street
2. Goff Avenue
3. Oak Street
4. Peasley 1 & 2
5. Treadwell Street
6. Fair Street
7. Gibson Hill
8. Railroad Corner
9. Broad Street 1
10. Broughton at Bull
11. Broad Street 2

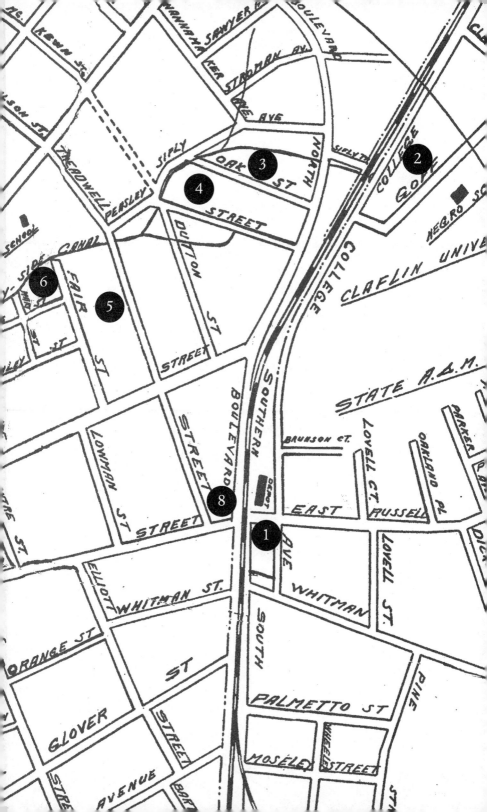

PART I

Illumination

It read: burn this
burn this, it read.

They would not let her.
They snatched it, what I had handed her.

Evidence, they called it.

Trapped between them and me
being one of them,
her smile of friendship cracked.
Deerlight terror flashed in her eyes.

Burn me, it said.

Before her eyes the store began to swim.
She clutched the counter, Hold on now.

She had no place to run.

Carry this message in your heart.
Reduce the written words, their searing innocence
to ash: I would like to know you better.

Everything we know says No!
You must go. Outsider inside with us,
nice nigger, kaffir, untouchable,
today, you run, or you burn.

I hurt. Though I did not realize it then, at nineteen, the first part of my life was ending.

I had typed that note, *I would like to know you better,* after work the evening before, on my thirty-dollar used Underwood, a machine I had bought on five-dollar monthly installments with money I earned as a carhop Friday and Saturday nights and all day Sundays at Carter's Tea Room drive-in, near the northern edge of town. During the week I worked as a cobbler's apprentice at a black-owned shoe repair shop in town.

My job at Carter's, shared with Dambee, round and nappy-headed, was to serve patrons in cars parked in dark areas of the lot, who ate Dora's locally famous chicken dinners: two pieces of crisp brown chicken, hot buttered rolls, homemade potato salad with sliced tomato on lettuce, coffee or tea. Inside my shirt during daytime, under a napkin at night, I also served sealed pints or half-pints of bourbon, for which the tea room was hardly known at all.

Liquor was legally sold in South Carolina only in licensed state stores.

Once I saw Mr. Carter give a man in an Orangeburg police uniform money and a bottle of liquor. And one night two policemen parked their car on a far corner of the lot. Mr. Carter took a couple pints of bourbon, tucked them under his apron, and told me when I started for the car, "That's all right, A. D., I'll get them." While "police pay-off" was not a term in my vocabulary, the manner in which these particular customers were treated allowed me to feel that we had nothing to fear from them.

Dora's chicken was sometimes not Dora's chicken alone but also Mrs. Carter's, who, during a rush, stood elbow to elbow at the giant woodstove with black Dora, her tan bouffant constantly being pushed back out of her eyes. During rushes, which happened after football games or church, even Evangeline, the Carters' heavy-busted, slow-moving daughter, who was beginning to sway like her mother when she walked, was called from her movie magazine to cover the dining room.

Money from Carter's Tea Room was as much as seventeen dollars a weekend. This was in contrast to four dollars for a full week's work in the shoe repair shop. And this four dollars was an increase from the two dollars and fifty cents I earned when I worked after school until seven and all day Saturdays. Without the tea room money, I could never have bought my Underwood or any of the other things, such as new trousers, that I as a nineteen-year-old was beginning increasingly to require.

Money from this weekend job enabled me to pay for my first new suit for graduation, partly in cash, the rest on time; to pay for my first watch, from the young white salesman who supplemented his income at the jewelry store around the corner with an occasional theft of the store's wares; to pay for new shoes from the drummer from Kentucky who came through periodically, measured our feet, and fitted us properly, important in contrast to how we would be treated in a white-owned shoe store, especially important for Fes, the shoe repair shop owner, who wore 10-½ AAA. And money was important for membership in a Christmas Savings club, which money I wanted to use to buy a lot on Goff Avenue over near the high school. I wanted to build a house for my mother, to get her into a better part of town. This house was to be for my mother, not for me. Even then, I must have had leaving somewhere in the back of my mind, though I had no ticket to travel.

As I opened the shop as I usually did, at 7:00 a.m., two hours before Fes came in and an hour before Charles, the journeyman helper, I had time to go over the note, to retype it until it was error-free. Not bad, I told myself, after only three months of practice. The sellers of the Underwood, white teens my age, amused that I would buy a typewriter before I knew how to type, threw in the typing manual they had used in high school. There had been no business courses at Wilkinson, the high school for colored that I had attended.

"Like buying a car and not knowing how to drive, har, har."

But with a difference, I thought. With a typewriter I couldn't run into anything if I didn't know how to stop. I thanked them for the book, took it back to the shop, and immediately started staying after work to labor over my *asdfg, asdfg...*

There was no place in our crowded house for a typewriter, no suitable table, nor a suitable light to read by. So I would stay in the shop, going over lessons until I was too hungry to continue.

The sellers of the typewriter were showing off their school photos one day when I went in to make a payment. Their family owned a photo shop. The children took care of the front during summer. As they had several sets of everyone, they asked me if I'd like a few.

"Put them in your school album."

I could not tell them I had no school album, no graduation picture.

When I got back to the shoe repair shop with the photos, Fes and the others were eager to see them.

"They gave them to you?" This from Fes.

"Didn't steal them."

"And that's a white girl in that one." This from Charles.

"A. D., you sure know how to deal with those white folks," Fes said.

"I was just in there to pay them for the typewriter, and one of them had just graduated. They were real friendly."

"Well, you just want to be careful, that's all. Never know when they'll turn on you." This from Fes.

"I'm not going to keep these pictures, no way. Won't even take them home. Just wanted you all to see them, that's all." I had no further contact with the typewriter sellers after they were paid.

Mid-morning, I folded the note, enclosed into its fold two wood matches for her convenience, to burn it with when she had read its contents. With the note in my pocket, I told Fes and Charles that I was going around the corner to the dime store.

She appeared pleased to see me but surprised when I handed her a note, which I did quickly. She was not alone in the store, but there was no one near her when I handed it to her. I had come into the store dozens of times over the years, always to buy something. My coming into the store would invite no comment; an extended stay, without buying anything, would.

Had I bought an item, or asked about one "for a friend" or "for my mother," I might have been able to slip her the note at the cash register unobserved. She could have said "yes" or "no." Her decision might have remained between her and me.

Something in her face (was it distress?) gave me my first misgiving. All the way back to our shop I wished I could take it back. I had not thought this through enough. Having taken no one into my confidence, I had no one to confide in. With growing apprehension, I realized that I did not know her. My note said as much. She had come into our shop on Broughton Street with her shoe repair needs: a pair of lifts, new soles, a shine, perhaps a half-dozen times over several months. On the two occasions we were alone in the shop, we had been open and friendly with one another, our talk personal but not intimate. We talked of nothing that would bracket us in any way, except our common dissatisfaction with our situations. Something in her reminded me of country rather than city; I didn't think she was an Orangeburg girl.

I had talked to her and she to me, but we had never talked about *us*. Our fingers had touched once, briefly. That touch had seemed to send slight tremors through us both. And I had held her feet in my hands after we had put lifts on her Cuban heels. While I was smoothing out her socks, she lay back in the chair with her eyes closed. But I had never said to her, "Gee, I think you're a nice girl." Never had she said to me, "You're a nice fella."

I do not know what she felt when we talked or what she felt as she walked around the corner to her job, if her step was lighter. She was just entering the world of work and womanhood, high school graduate, eighteen or nineteen, more healthy and strong than pretty, face lightly freckled, filling out into the woman's body she would keep until her first pregnancy. I liked the way she moved.

"I don't intend to spend the rest of my life fondling lingerie and folding baby didies, that's for darn sure," she had told me one day when we were talking about "that dime store job."

Our restlessness struck a common chord. Neither of us was being fulfilled by the jobs we held. We both wanted something more. Since I had never accepted racial superiority in anyone, I could feel no condescension in her manner. Her smile as she left was genuine. She always looked directly at me. We were about the same age. I thought our finger touching had jolted us. I could have been imagining things, but I'd swear the atmosphere was charged each time she came into the shop. I wanted to know her better, but I did not know her.

She put the note in the pocket of her smock and looked around her, to see if she had been seen. She had. One of the older women clerks asked what it was I had given her. When she handed over the note, it was immediately taken back to the male manager, who called the chief of police. Hardly had I settled into work when the chief and his lieutenant came to the shop looking for me.

I had been planning to buy a suit the chief had outgrown, for nine dollars, as soon as the women in his house finished altering it to my size. For a fleeting moment, I thought that he was bringing it or news of it when he came into the shop; and would have held that thought were he alone. But I knew it did not take two of them to bring me news of a suit.

I knew why they had come and prepared myself to accompany them. Both Fes and Charles were in the shop. Fes, face in shock and outrage, snatched off his apron and was about to start towards the front of the shop, the customer area. Except to bring work, police had never come into his shop. He could not imagine them coming then and certainly not for me.

"What did he do?" Fes asked the chief.

I had taken off my apron, folded it, and laid it on my workbench, had put my key to the door on the counter near the cash register. I looked at Fes briefly; I could not look long. It was warm so I had no jacket. I wore a shirt and trousers. My wallet was at home with my Sunday clothes. There were a few coins in my pocket that hit the counter where wrapped shoes were kept as I passed, and a balled-up handkerchief.

"He know what he done, don't you, boy?" They waited in the front of the shop, their bulk suddenly filling the entire space.

Just up on Windsor Street from where I lived on Broad Street, whites and blacks lived side by side. A black man and white woman, both of lower class, rumored to have a love relationship, were forced to leave town, but nothing violent had been done to them.

One of the daughters of a respectable white family had eloped with the son of a prominent black family, a man light enough to "pass" for white. At the country club where I caddied on Sundays, we caddies heard the golfers' candid opinions because they talked among themselves as though we weren't there. This news never made the local paper, but was passed between golfers. The golfers marveled that the courtship and elopement could take place under everyone's noses without their having an inkling of it.

Several years before, a black resident farmhand, in a work situation amounting to peonage, had impregnated a girl said to be the daughter of a retired sheriff. The farmhand had been jailed and charged with rape. There was no other charge possible for him, since any intimate contact between a black man and white woman could only be rape, as no white woman in her right mind would allow any such contact. This, white men wanted white women to believe.

There was talk on the golf course before the case went to court. "Can't be no rape," one of the golfers in my foursome had said. "After all, she didn't accuse him."

"Don't he live on the place?"

"She's pregnant."

"That's the one that's kinda crazy, ain't she?"

Before the case broke, I had not heard of anything happening on the sheriff's farm. Some events were never talked about, or, if talked about, were mentioned only in code. Certain words were used, certain phrases. As a seller of boiled peanuts at the courthouse, I had witnessed this man's trial from the black gallery. The Court had provided him with a lawyer.

A judge was hearing the case. No jury.

"How do you plead?" the judge asked.

Standing next to the lawyer was his client, a slightly built chocolate-colored man of forty, who had lived on the sheriff's farm his entire life. He was shorter than his lawyer, who was not a tall man.

"We plead guilty, Your Honor," his lawyer said.

"Ten years." Judge pounded his gavel, "Next case."

Erect prior to his sentence, on hearing it, the condemned man slumped. From my side view he looked like a hand with the fingers bent from the palm.

Chief may have been thinking of this other "nigra" gone bad. Must have perplexed him.

"Come on, boy," as I dawdled, not realizing I was doing so. "We ain't got all day."

Charles kept his eyes on his bench with his ears cocked. He did not look up, but laid his hammer to the right of his shoe last, still in his hand.

Fes took a step towards the front. "Is it bad?" He asked the chief. He stopped, right foot held suspended.

"'s bad as it gits…"

"Oh my god! Well, I just wanted to know." There was sadness in his voice, a sound approaching a sob.

Fes still seemed to be waiting for something from me, some explanation, some qualification, even denial. But I had no denial. I had no explanation for myself. I had thought unthinkable thoughts and committed an unthinkable act. When I didn't contradict the chief he said, "You better go, then."

He set the foot down and hung his left arm over the wire wood-topped barrier that ran the length of our workbench, a place where friends stood and gossiped while we worked.

I had trouble negotiating the distance from my workbench to where they were waiting, patiently I thought, as I bumped into the pile of wrapped, "will-call" shoes and steadied them and myself. I was not being slow or clumsy on purpose. I traveled that distance dozens of times a day. This morning my feet were intolerably heavy and forced me into things. A distance of a few steps seemed a long, long way. When at last I had reached them, Chief took me by my right elbow, lightly.

"Let's go, boy," his lieutenant said.

I went with them to their car, a black '42 Chevrolet four-door sedan reflecting the bright sun, its high polish the work I'd seen prisoners do. The day was going to be warm, even for late March.

They drove me past the Market Street city jail, a two-celled affair with its "black" cell on the street side. I had stood on that sidewalk one bitter cold gray Sunday afternoon, and told my mother through the heavy wire and iron bars that I would go ask my boss for the ten dollars required for her bail.

Two policemen had walked into our house around noon that day, into her bedroom where they found her and a visiting male friend fully clothed. They had been charged with adultery, having been fingered by the "holy roller" Sanctified jack-leg preacher whose church was next door to our house, and whose late-night shout-and-sing sessions made early sleep a fiction for me and the other four people who lived on that side of the house.

My mother had protested that they were simply sitting. In that small four-room home inhabited by six people, her bedroom was the only space where she might have any privacy. While this fact might hold water for some, the cops had been called by a minister of God and told that she was an adulterer, on a Sunday morning at that.

Having come, they were going to take *somebody*. My mother's protest only made them more certain that if she and her friend weren't doing anything then, they either had done something or were going to do something, given the nature of black folk to do "it" every chance they got. So they were taken to jail.

There is no way to say how angry but helpless I felt watching the police take my mother to the city jail, following them on my bicycle and talking with her through the screened and barred window of her cell on a side street where the city housed its black prisoners. Or riding across town to Treadwell Street, where Fes lived, telling him what had happened to my mother and asking for bail money.

It had been a sticky cold day, with ice in pockets of shade. I had no gloves. The family (Fes, Bertha, Sara, and the baby) had just returned from Sunday church services, and were about to sit down to midday dinner. After saying that he would take it out of my pay, Fes lent me the money for my mother's bail. My mother's friend had not been so lucky. Next morning at Magistrate's Court he was given thirty days on the chain gang (which meant thirty days free labor for Orangeburg County). I never saw him again.

I knew that white people could, if they wished, do anything they wanted to black people for any reason, or for no reason, at any time, at any place of their choosing. And that blacks could do nothing to prevent them. And I was black.

"Be a minit, Barney," Chief said.

I didn't hear what the lieutenant answered.

I could feel they were fulfilling a duty that was painful to them, the more so because they had no clue to my actions. I had crossed a line that was once staunchly held but was now becoming increasingly frayed, a line that in our lifetimes would be snapped.

What was happening to me was surreal. Broughton Street was deserted of passersby as I climbed into the police car, as was Market, the street the jail was on. Except for my coworkers and the men in Mr. Pendarvis' barbershop, located diagonally across the street, which may have been occupied, no one I knew had seen the police take me away. I do not remember thinking at the time of who might see me. I do not remember thinking at all.

The drive to the county jail, a more secure structure in a building all its own, was three short blocks, hardly time to realize what was happening. No one spoke. I was allowed to let myself out of the car, as I had been allowed to let myself in, and walk the long walk to gray stone steps. Chief escorted me. Lieutenant lit up a cigarette and rolled down the window. I was being arrested for the unadorned fact that I had handed a prospective friend a note requesting further acquaintance, the note saying: " I would like to know you better."

"Sign your name here, boy." The sheriff pushed a heavy gray rough-grained ledger to the edge of the counter. He looked at me as though he were seeing a stranger.

Something in me wanted to say to him, to them all, to insist, to shout, to scream if necessary, "I'm the same person I was yesterday, this morning, the same 'A. D.' my family and black friends call me, the same 'Brownie' white golfers call me, the same 'Kelly.'" I had recently named myself after Kelly Miller, the black Reconstruction assemblyman who, after Governor Cole Blease told him that if he repeated what he had just said, "I'll eat you alive," replied "Yes, and if you do, you'll have more brains in your stomach than you've got in your head." A. D., Brownie, Kelly, the same, the very same. "Don't look at me like that," I wanted to say to them, "Don't."

But was I the same? Didn't I declare, by my act, otherwise? Was I not saying to them, to everyone, "I am not the person you thought I was"? I am no longer predictable. I am no longer a good nigra, no longer safe. How does a good nigra become a bad nigra? The hate in their eyes was adulterated with something else. Was it *fear*?

The first floor of the jail housed the sheriff and his family. As there were few prisoners, the family hardly knew the cells over their heads were there. We had played with the sheriff's son in his backyard during my early teen years. We had strained to see the prisoners on the upper floor.

"What we gon charge him with?" Sheriff asked.

A brief pause.

"Attempted rape, I reckon. That's the only thing I can come to, Ernest," Chief said. "Boy, who was in with you on this thing?" Sheriff held up the note after writing something in the ledger. "Who helped you write this note?"

I was surprised to see him holding my note to her. I felt something dreadfully wrong I had no word for. I wanted to say, "That's my note. *Ours*. It wasn't sent to you. I don't want it fouled by your goddamned hands."

I don't know how much of my anger showed. My face must have passed muster as I answered, "Nobody, sir. I did it on my typewriter. It was my typewriter there in the shoe shop."

They both seemed to weigh this information, received with some incredulity. "You sure there wasn't nobody else, now? Nobody in the shop or nothing?"

Chief lowered his voice, as though he wanted me to believe he wouldn't tell anyone or hold it against me if there were. He seemed to want there to have been a conspiracy.

I didn't understand why I would need someone to help me write a seven-word note. I was tempted to say as much. It wasn't as though I were a chimpanzee or anything.

"Nobody put you up to this, nobody in the shop?" Chief again.

"No, sir. Nobody knew I'd done it. Nobody but me."

"Did she give you any indication?" the sheriff asked.

When she had first come into the shop six months before, and I had taken her order for lifts and a shine, her eyes had smiled at me, more than her lips. They followed me about the shop as I went to the shelf to get the lifts, and to the counter to show her the polish we'd use. And when I went over to the counter to get the tag to sign her in, I turned to find her right at my shoulder. The air in the shop had changed in a way I couldn't define.

"Indica…, she, oh, *no* sir!"

They both looked at me as though they were looking at a new species, with amazement, but also downright puzzlement—a being they were not at all sure what to do with. Everyone who worked for any length of time downtown had seen or run into everyone else at one time or another. As an iceman helper for a week, shoeshine boy, boiled peanut vendor, newspaper boy, shoe delivery boy, caddy, I had been in and around town enough and long enough so that anyone who wanted to see me had seen me. I was familiar to them, in and out of the stores. How can you be selling someone a suit one week, as the chief was, and be charging him with attempted rape for writing an innocuous note the next? That must have required some chewing on.

"Take him upstairs, I got to be headin on back. I'll call you." With this, Chief started to the door.

"I'll take care uv um. Come on, boy."

I followed the sheriff down the hall to where a heavy barred door led upstairs to the top floor, where the jail cells were.

Up to the moment of the closing of that heavy door behind me, and the shutting off of light, the reality of my being jailed had evaded me. I had done nothing to warrant jail. Or so I thought. Chastisement, a warning maybe. But jail? Jails were for people who had committed crimes, or so I reasoned. I had committed no crime. Been foolish, dreadfully so. Had committed a monstrous indiscretion. But no crime. Passing a note requesting acquaintance might be vain, might be foolhardy, but no crime.

The cells looked to be six feet square. They were arranged along the walls of one long room that took up the entire floor, except for one cell in the center. This center cell was larger, with its own toilet and stronger bars. I was placed in this center cell. There was only one other person in jail during that time, a boy about my age. He tried to find out what I had done. I didn't tell him. One, because I didn't know for sure what I had done, and two, because he was someone I didn't know and I didn't want to talk about it to a stranger.

I knew I had done something dangerous, but because of who I thought I was, I didn't see it as a life-and-death matter. Since I had acted alone, had involved no one else, not even the girl, couldn't I be told of the error of my ways, have my boss told to keep an eye on me, and be allowed to take up my life where I had left off?

I had had no intention of challenging the social order by this one act. I had no concept called "social order." I had simply wanted to do what I wanted to do, as though I were somehow living above, around, away from, below, somewhere the social order couldn't find me. I moved and lived pretty much as I wanted, and for the past year I had been pushing things.

I had already done things those people set in the social order would not like if they knew. That held for both sides of the racial divide. I had never accepted the racial divide. There were times I had been forced to acknowledge it, sometimes with great pain, but never had I accepted it, ever.

Nor had I accepted the idea that anyone was better than I. More money, better house and clothes, more privileges. Privileges because of money, position, class, race, but not because of person. I had never accepted that anybody's person was better than mine. Some people were smarter, stronger, better looking, had more power because of the group they belonged to; but although these things, which I acknowledged and sometimes envied, established a difference between us, they did not make those people better than I. In my eyes I was as good as anyone.

I had been made to feel bad by black folk as well as by white folk, had been treated generously or miserly by both. If someone took my labor and paid me too little for it, it would be the same pittance regardless of whether that person was white or black.

I had seen too many miserable white folk to imagine that their race made them superior. I had worked, played, fought with individual white boys and white girls, had been treated kindly or cruelly by individual white folk. Rarely was the treatment distinguishable by color. The venom of the snake, whether white, black, or mulatto, stung. Race, class, or caste, I couldn't tell the difference between their venom.

"They no better, they jus' white," or "they think they better 'cause they white," people said, the implication being that just because whites thought something didn't mean it was necessarily so.

This attitude was reinforced by discussions in the shoe repair shop. Interminable ones. We had seen too many white drunks and failures, no-good whites, "just like we got," especially during the Great Depression, to think them superior. Whites' power had been gained and maintained by force, fraud, hypocrisy, and deceit. Hence it was not legitimate; it did not prove they were superior. "They no better, they jus white" was what most black folk I knew believed. This had been the tenor of part of our talk.

Give black folk opportunity and some of the promised resources, e.g., forty acres and a mule, then let's see who's superior. "Look at what we have done with the little they allowed us, and what we continue to do with all they throw in our way." We never thought of ourselves as inferior, only trapped by a system that whites controlled to their advantage. "What they lay on our backs is worse than a mule. A mule, hear me tell it, a mule."

Talk in the shoe repair shop could be free and wide-ranging, especially on Monday morning when the events of the weekend would be dissected barbershop fashion, or when a professor from one of the black-run colleges came down. Talk might cover such events as the visit by the Harlem Globetrotters, a professional basketball team, or Hitler's latest triumphs in Europe. Once introduced, a topic would be chewed on and over until its substance was exhausted. Take the University of Carolina–Villanova football game at the county fair. We were treated to an analysis of the teams' respective strengths, their records, predictions of the game's outcome. To everyone's surprise and delight, underdog Carolina tied mighty Villanova, score 6-6. It did not seem to matter to anyone that most of Carolina's best players were recruits from northern and eastern schools—in short, mercenaries, brought in through special admissions to play football, who would be dropped as soon as their athletic eligibility was exhausted. All that seemed to matter was that a Southern school had bested a Northern one. "We showed those damn Yankees who think they're better than us." The fervor in our shop rivaled that in the white barbershop and restaurant across the street.

I did not notice a comparable interest by whites in the activities of blacks, college or otherwise.

Talk about movies that had colored characters in them was likely to generate a lot of heat. *Amos 'n Andy,* a popular radio comedy, was played by two white actors. The program gave shop talkers yet another example—minstrelsy being one—of white men making a good living ridiculing Negro life while Negroes received no economic benefit from it. The men found themselves in something of a bind. In one way, they were glad when Hollywood did give some colored actors work. At the same time, they hated the demeaning roles those actors were required to play. And they were incensed at the Tarzan movies on two accounts: one, they portrayed Africans as savages, and two, white men in cork face were hired to play them. By analogy the men in the shop felt demeaned, *and* denied the opportunity to make a living. They laughed at Tarzan swinging through the trees, saying that white men's hairy bodies placed them closer to the apes than black men who had little body hair.

They hated Hollywood's slavish catering to white Southern racial attitudes. They saw through the careful staging so that whites and blacks did not appear in the same scenes, unless the blacks were in roles subservient to whites. There could be nothing in the scenes to suggest that there might be peer contact. The brilliant Bojangles Robinson, tap dancer without peer, could dance with the child Shirley Temple, but not with adults Fred Astaire and Ginger Rogers. Even the incomparable Paul Robeson had to sing "Ol' Man River" from behind a bale of cotton while the white lovers sat on the other side enjoying the river, oblivious of his presence. Only his voice they heard; his body they did not see.

Fes complained that Hollywood movies always showed blacks eating when they were not doing some manual labor—"tote that bale"—while whites were shown drinking at cocktail parties. That distinction passed over my head, as did Fes's dislike of "loud" Count Basie music as contrasted to the softer music of Duke Ellington. I liked them both.

I was personally offended by the portrayal of colored women in *Gone with the Wind.* My mother and sister and women I knew were or had been household servants. Hollywood lost a good customer in me with that movie. I've probably seen a couple dozen Hollywood mov-

ies since, and these only after several trusted friends had seen them
first and vouched for them.

With all the range of talk, conversation in the shoe repair shop
never got around to slavery or its aftermath, Reconstruction, except
when Kelly Miller was mentioned. Nor did they talk of the black
peonage that persisted into our own time. Jim Crow discrimination
was groused about, avoided whenever possible, but on the whole it
was accepted as a given. "White man ain't gon change. Nothin nigger
can do to make him." "Nigger where he is 'cause white man got his
foot on his neck. He hold nigger in gutter, he got to stay there too."
"Now ain't it the truth!" Or the contrary. "Nigger where he is 'cause
he jus like the white man say. He lazy. Give 'em an inch, they take it
all. Would you want them people from Red Line in your house, with
your wife and daughters? No, you don't."

Such talk did not give me a solid picture of folk or a clear sense
of black-white relations. My neighbors were desperately poor and
ignorant but they were not stupid. Boys I played with could outrun
me, had better hand-eye coordination, and could beat me at checkers.
They were better judges of character, especially of white folk, and
had a better grasp of their place in the world. I appeared smarter
because I had language and was glib, but I had no better judgment
than they had. I had more information but no more smarts.

So when some black person, my boss Fes in particular, commented
on how well I got along with white folk, I liked the praise, accepted
it as my due. But there was more to it. The comment should have
been expanded to say that I got along well with most people, white
and black. Fes's comment, coming as it did from a black person, had a
double edge to it. It was said for praise, out of envy, and with a need
for caution: okay to get along with white folk—necessary if you want
to live—not good to get along too well, if you wanted to live.

I was well mannered and respectful of my elders, and so well
thought of by some mothers that they allowed me to take their
daughters out to movies, and bring them back home after dark.

I had actually had two movie dates, with different girls. Both had
ended in a similar kind of social disaster. Mrs. Benton, who lived up
the street from us on Treadwell Street during one of our short stays

there, had watched me grow up. When a niece of hers came down from the North for a summer visit, I was asked to take her out. That same summer I took Earl Jurgen's sister to a movie (Earl knew me and said I was all right—could be trusted). In both cases, we walked across town to the movie, sat in the Jim Crow section through a double feature, and walked home again. We stood for a short time talking at the door.

Ignoramus that I was about female anatomy, I did not have sense enough to ask, "Don't you want to run in for a minute to powder your nose or something? I'll wait here for you."

At our movie house, the Carolinian, rest rooms were labeled "White Ladies," "White Men," and "Colored." I didn't know the condition of the white toilets, never having been in them. No colored woman of my acquaintance ever used the one assigned to her race. She held her water, and suffered. And if her date was ignorant, as I was, he allowed her to suffer until she had an "accident." As my dates had had. "Good" girls did not discuss their bodies with boys, so my dates could not tell me of their bodies' needs. And as a "good" boy, I was to ignore that they had bodies. A losing proposition all around.

That Earl and Mrs. Benton had trusted me meant a lot. To me, to our world. "All them boys want to do is get under your dress, and get inside your drawers," mothers said. And there were the senior high school and freshman college pregnancies as proof. That they thought I was interested in more than that had made me feel good.

For it was true. I was more interested in how a girl thought and what she was able to talk about than how she looked. If a girl was smart and pretty too, so much the better. I found out, though, that girls could be smart and pretty and still not be willing to hang with my long-winded talk of world affairs. They wanted to be admired.

Virginia, one of my classmates, fixed me up with a particularly fine friend of hers. "You two brains should hit it off," she guaranteed. Well, we did, almost. Ruth, the friend, was looking her best. I noticed this but said nothing to her about it. On our way home, after much meandering on my part, she blurted out, "Don't you know anything to talk about other than books?"

• • •

I was taken upstairs to my cell, a barred cage larger than the others. A single lightbulb, encased in wire, hung from the ceiling. No chair, no table. Sink, toilet, and bunk completed the appointments.

The meals were brought up from the kitchen downstairs. I drank the water but sent the food back untouched. For a reason I can't fathom, I refused their food. At first the turnkey took it away without comment. My not eating did not become noticed until the day before I left. I was determined not to eat for as long as I was in there. Since I didn't know when I would be let out, I had no idea what I was letting myself in for. The idea of fasting was unknown to me. A fast in protest was the farthest thing from my mind. For some reason I cannot explain, I did not feel like eating.

I kept thinking. I thought and thought hard. I could have been a journalist. The Simms boy, my age group, graduated about the same time as I. He had worked on his school paper and the city paper his folks owned. He was apprenticed to a paper in North Carolina to start his career.

I had worked on my school paper, which turned out better than the paper at the black-run state college. Many early mornings I had slipped into the back of the local paper's office to read the news as it came over the wires. I loved watching the typed pages as they poured out of the AP and UPI machines. I would not have been allowed in the front, where white newsmen worked. Having no advisor, I had no one to encourage me in what was clearly an interest in how news was made. This interest got buried.

My good buddy white Charlie Suggs, comic book artist as a boy, had gone off to summer CCC camp on the coast and came back with stories, including some end-of-summer sexual exploits. The adventure of the camp not available to black boys—working, going somewhere—intrigued me.

When Charlie went off to CCC camp I did try to join the army. Two recruiters with their table, signs, and forms camped for a week on Russell Street, center of all foot traffic downtown. "We not taking no coloreds now," one of them told me. "Why don't you try the navy? 'Member the movie, 'Join the navy to see the world.'" He laughed at his attempt at singing.

He had it all wrong.

I could have told him the song he sang was in a movie that purported to spoof the armed services but whose real motive was to prepare us to accept war if our rulers started one.

But I didn't tell him. And I didn't tell him I wasn't joining no man's navy. I had shined enough shoes on the streets of Orangeburg. Personal service was not my cup of tea. The navy could get someone else to make their beds and cook their meals. So my attempt to leave by joining the service got put on hold.

• • •

I slept fitfully my first night. The slightest sound woke me up. The scurry of rats. The muffled sound of the occasional car. Light from one that seemed to aim its beams at the window. I think I also woke up thinking there had been a sound when there hadn't been one. I welcomed morning.

I spent all of my first full day expecting to be let out, since I did not feel my indiscretion warranted jail time. Surely everyone would see that. I still saw myself walking and riding Orangeburg streets, delivering shoes. I saw myself collecting tips and banking them. As the day progressed and no one had come for me, I began to feel uneasy. Where was Fes? What was he doing? He must have told my mother. I lay on my bunk much of the afternoon. After the evening meal had been taken away uneaten, and for the second evening the pale yellow light of the setting sun had filtered through the bars and heavy screen, I was beginning to wake up to my predicament. I was in jail and might not ever get out. But I would get out, I thought. I *would.* Though I couldn't say how, couldn't say when.

I had been at the edge of trouble many times before this and had so far avoided falling into it. For instance, one day I was shopping for Fes's wife at Sandy's meat market. Sandy treated whites and blacks differently. White customers' meat was placed on a thin waxed liner before it was put on the white butcher paper. Ground beef was scooped with a trowel, never handled with fingers. Especially with ground beef, Sandy was known to low-weight colored folk. He would do this by putting his hands on the scales while talking to you. He was clever at it. He would lay the meat on an open paper. The paper extended beyond the scales. With his left hand he would place the meat on the scales. If he put on too much, he would take it off with his left hand; too little, he would make up the difference with his right hand, which, under the extended opaque white butcher paper a customer could not see from across the counter.

When I ordered the ground beef that day, Sandy pulled his sleight of hand, low-weighting me. An impulse in me decided not to let him get by unnoticed.

"That's not the right weight," I told him. "That's not enough."

"What you mean, not enough, can't you read the scale?" The color was rising from his neck through his face. His eyes tried to stare me down. I wouldn't bend.

"Then take your hand off it," I said, not raising my voice, but putting my hands on the counter. There were no other customers in the shop.

His right hand shot up as though hot oil had been splashed on it. As he did the scale pointer swung left then settled right, a few ounces short. He scooped a handful of hamburger, slid the paper off the scale, slapped the meat on the rest, wrapped it up and slid it towards me on the counter. All this without a word. He was seething.

When I told Miz Bertha what had happened, she opened the package and weighed it on her kitchen scale.

"This time it's too much," she said, smiling. "About time somebody called him on it." She continued smiling, and asked her housekeeper, Sara, to make me a glass of lemonade.

I was high all the way back to the shop, where a different reception awaited me. Fes was just ending a phone conversation with Sandy as I was leaning the bicycle against the wall under the front window, just outside from where the phone was inside.

"Yes, sir, I'll tell him," was what I heard as I entered the shop. He put the receiver on its hook and turned to face me.

"What am I gonna do with you, boy?" His face, though smiling, showed concern. "You got the white folks mad at you, again."

"What'd he say, Fes?" Charles and Blas had open ears.

"He said, 'You better keep his black ass out of my shop. Don't send him back here no more.' He was hot enough to pop a cap."

"He tell you what I did?"

"Said you sassed him, that you better mind your manners."

"He tell you he had his hand on the scale?"

"You don't expect him to tell me that, do you?"

"Don't expect him to lie."

Charles laughed out loud and Blas, our college-age worker, clapped his hands. "Everybody know Sandy got his hand heavy on the scale."

"You know the white man'll lie to get his way. Was anybody else in the shop?"

"Nobody but me and him."

"Well, I don't know. You been getting into a mighty lot here lately. Whistlin with your hat on, walking through the front of Tony's Restaurant. Telling the bank teller he didn't count right when I sent you around there to get change."

"But if he was right, then I was stealing. And I don't steal no dime."

"Just hold on now, nobody accuse you of stealing. You coulda dropped it on the way."

"He coulda looked in the tray as easy as I could. Easier. But he wanted to say he couldn't make no mistake. Hadta been me."

"All right, that's done settled and over with. And then there's the grocery store not delivering everything on Bertha's list."

"And Miz Bertha jumping down my throat about it. I just take the list. I got nothing to do with what they put in."

"I know all that. But something's wrong. I don't know. It seems like you just don't *understand the eternal fitness of things.*"

Then there was the Saturday night when I was coming in from my last delivery and saw two white men attacking a black man in the empty lot at the corner of Broughton and Russell, the dividing line beyond which middle-class whites would not cross for services. I ran the bicycle between them, kicking the one nearest me, running into the other with the heavy basket on the front of the bicycle. At the same time I shouted to the black man, who was staggering and muttering, "Wha...wha..."

"Run, you stupid bastard, run."

He straightened up and turned down Russell. The white men were trying to help one another up and "black sonofabitching" me. I was halfway down a dimly lighted street. There was no way they'd catch me. I took the bicycle inside until I closed up. Then, when I felt certain they were gone, I took an indirect way home.

And the time Dambee warned me after I sopped the Coke from the lap and legs of one of our Tea Room customers so she wouldn't be embarrassed when her date came back from his pee and gossip with his buddy at the back of the lot.

"If they see'd you doing that."

But they hadn't. And I was certain they wouldn't. The lot was dimly lit on purpose, to prevent identification of lovers, as they sat with their dates and their illegal bourbon. Furthermore, their car was shaded by a tree. She was from Pasadena, a place I knew from the Rose Bowl. They still had on their swimsuits and their California tans. He was at the Air Force training base, the Hawthorne School of Aeronautics on Highway 21 south of town. She was visiting before he was transferred. I was part of a mini-conspiracy between us two. She may have thought, "Help me get this drink wiped up before he gets back."

I could smell the alcohol and lipstick when I bent over her. Our faces almost touched as I wiped the front of her down to her legs. Wherever there was liquid, I mopped. Though I was as deliberate as I dared, spending more time on some places than was strictly necessary to remove moisture, she was dry in seconds.

"Much better," she said, as I straightened up and folded the towel. "Thank you. Here, wait," she said, as I started to walk away. She reached into her date's fat wallet, which he had left with her so she could pay for their order, and handed me a five-dollar bill. The dark didn't let her see my eyes, but it didn't hide my smile.

"Thank you, ma'am," I said, as I pocketed the bill and headed to a car that had just pulled in on the other side of the lot.

Later, when I retrieved their tray, there were two more dollars stuck under a plate. "Nice chicken and service," he said. "Come back again, sir," I said. I did not look at her, she did not look at me. Our mini-conspiracy had been successful.

Or one Sunday night a mulatto female who was later to be my lawyer and a similarly light-skinned man from the state college came to the darkest part of the lot. Another conspiracy, this one unspoken. The Tea Room did not serve colored. I gladly served them and received a large tip. Sin and lawbreaking come high. I did not acknowledge her that night, nor did I ever tell her that it was I who had served her and her date at the Tea Room. So I will never know if she recognized me, or the chance I knew I had taken.

When we got a breather later that night, Dambee was steamed. "You know you shouldn'ta done that."

"Man, that's over and done with. You makin somethin outta nothin. Them people home by now."

"That's all right by you. Now what'd she gi ya? I seed her gi you sumpn."

"Five hundred and ten dollars," I told him.

"Nigger, you lyin. I know you lyin. You betta watch yo step."

• • •

That night, Friday, there was some kind of commotion at the front of the jail. There were several cars outside, from the sounds of their engines and the way their headlights lighted up the street. I could distinguish different levels of voices but could not make out what they were saying. Then came a lull in the voices. A strong voice said something. A voice answered and the strong voice repeated itself. Car doors were slammed and the cars were driven away. I never learned if the commotion had anything to do with me. I wondered if it had. I wondered about *her,* whose name I never knew. What did they do to her? Could she explain that my note was not solicited by her, that it caught her by complete surprise? And would they believe her? She had been innocent. Surely they could see that. Or could they?

My thoughts were plentiful, but inchoate. I knew what I'd done, I didn't know what I'd done. I had never accepted the place whites assigned and blacks accepted for me. Anyone who had followed my life at all carefully would have seen it. What I realized was that I had somehow slipped under everyone's attention. Some may have spotted bits and pieces, but no one spotted enough to make a case against me. I had been characterless in a way, even in my use of language. "You from around here?" asked one of the customers at the Tea Room.

"Yes, sir."

"Your talking, thought you might be from Africa or something."

I *knew* I had done a dangerous thing. Because of who I thought I was, I didn't see it as a life-and-death matter. I had no conscious intention of challenging the social order any more than I already had—by never accepting it, ever. I find it hard to explain what my social experience was like. Take social class among blacks. The well-off blacks had more money behind them, but I could talk to them because I was well spoken, had language, read a lot—newspapers, books, magazines when I could get them. But in many ways I lacked experience. I had been nowhere, seen nothing but one town.

I had no political awareness or understanding, had not been taught to think, though the constant arguments between Fes and his buddies in the shop had given me a feel for rhetoric, and some reasoning. And I could tell when I was given two contradictory positions. I was ripe for a solid course in philosophy or political science. We were fed a lot of loose thinking in the shop, some anti-communist: "Reason they say they like Negroes is because they don't have none in Russia. You wait till they get some, you'll see how fast they'll change." The "Commies" I'd seen were not those in Russia but a visiting panel of white Northerners at the state college, who had made a young black with them who was not much older than I the centerpiece of their presentation. I didn't have the knowledge necessary to critique their ideas, but his manner with his comrades suggested peer status, an experience I found exciting.

Or, "Jews got all the money. Look at Harlem and who owns all them stores and buildings, the Jews, that's who. New York, they say, 'The Jews own it, the white folks run it, and the niggers enjoy it.'" I knew that while the Jewish people who owned businesses on Russell Street were well off, the family who ran the corner grocery store in our neighborhood were not. And as for enjoying it, one of the most miserable Negroes I had ever seen was a Harlem boy who'd spent some time in Orangeburg.

I had read none of the black Northern newspapers seriously, like the *Amsterdam News* and the *Baltimore Afro-American*. They spoke of a world I had not experienced. While the North was held up as being better when compared to the South, once there, all your troubles would not be over. Fes cautioned, "It ain't all no bread and roses up there, not all peaches and cream. You work like a dog for every dime you get. Most of them live worse than we do down here." This he had seen with his own eyes when he and Miz Bertha went there for vacation. Vacation: New York, the Caribbean, any place but the South.

• • •

For the second night I tossed and tumbled, balling up my bed sheet and holding it at my chest. When Sheriff came after breakfast Saturday to tell me that I had visitors, he omitted reference to the events of the night before, the noises and the lights. Curious as I was, I saw no way to ask him about it, unless he brought it up.

Mama and Aunt Maude were seated in the small waiting room. Sheriff closed the door and left us to ourselves. "Call me when yawl done," he said. Hardly had he left when Aunt Maude lit into me.

"See what you done done to your mama?" She pointed to Mama, who had a package in her lap and a handkerchief to her eyes. Tears had smeared her powder. She, too, looked at me as though she was looking at a stranger. I was thrown back to the moment when Chief had brought me to Sheriff, when Sheriff had looked at me as though he didn't know me. For the first time this additional magnitude of my action hit me: I had caused my mother suffering. I did not want to see her suffer. Why, oh, why hadn't I thought this out? Who else would suffer because of my impulsive act? That note, that crazy note. What had seemed so simple and clear as I pecked it out seemed not at all simple now, as I sat in the chair next to her.

"Mama, I...Mama. I...I..." My words stuck. What could I say? What could I say that she would understand, that anyone would understand?

I remember when my mother was told to warn me after I had delivered shoes next door to the Methodist parsonage downtown.

There had been some children playing in the backyard and as I passed I waved. They waved back. Their cook, Miz Luannie, mother of one of my friends from around the corner on Shuler Street, told my mother that I shouldn't have waved at them. My mother passed the word to me. It must have worried my mother that she had to work and could not exercise closer supervision of her children. She thought she had brought us up right, according to her lights, but she knew also that we were brought up partly by the streets. I did not wave at any more children.

What I had done, few, if any, would believe possible, could believe. The police had acted as though they were eager to have me say I had an accomplice, that I had not acted alone, that I'd had someone to prod me, to share the blame.

Why had I done this thing to them, they must have wondered. Why was I toying with utter catastrophe? I was someone they had seen enough to know, to trust. If *I* were not safe, and my act demonstrated beyond doubt that I was not, then who was? Was this the reason for what I thought was also fear in their eyes? If this could go on while they were watching, what must be going on behind their backs? Who *could* they trust?

But my mother had been partly behind my getting to this point. Though much of my feeling had come from my experiences as a child, some of my feeling that I was as good as anyone else came from her. My mother had come from people who owned land and she had neighbors who owned land. These were people, a folk, who had known chattel slavery, then peonage, the KKK, and the Black Codes. Some of them had experienced that window of freedom and opportunity called Reconstruction. Through the agency of Reconstruction they had acquired land; by their hard work, thrift, and religious faith, they had held onto it.

Living without her own land most of her adult life must have been galling for my mother. Two of her older sisters had married farmers and were established on their land. My mother, too, had married a farmer and lived on the land at one time. I think I sensed this. Which may explain why I put my first extra money in the bank to buy a lot on the eastern side of town. I felt no particular pull for land for myself, had not even thought of home ownership, perhaps because it was so impossible to realize. I must have been thinking about her.

She had never talked of land, or of owning a home, though I knew she detested landlords, the landlord class. But then we never talked much about her aspirations.

"A. D., what did you do? Did you do anything to that girl?" Mama's question came as partial relief. It gave me something I could answer.

"No, Mama, I didn't do nothing to nobody."

"Then...?"

"I wrote her a note. I just..."

"You call that nothing?" Aunt Maude hissed. "You just wrote a white girl a note and you call that nothing. A.D., what you use for brains?"

"A. D., you wrote a *white* girl a note?" Mama seemed to be struggling to hold the idea in her mind. She must have thought, *Why you do something like that? With all our nice colored girls, weren't they good enough for you?*

It was her unstated question, the same question everyone would be asking when they found out.

"Yes, Mama, but I didn't mean..." I thought, *to hurt you all. It doesn't mean I don't like nice colored girls. I adore nice colored girls. I only wish they liked me better.*

Mama was shaking her head, letting what I had done soak in.

"Well, mean it or not, you just got yourself in a mess." Aunt Maude hissed again.

This gave me an opportunity to ask something I needed to know. "What is Fes doing?"

"He come by and told us. Doing what he can. He can do just so much. He be trying to get you out," my mother said.

I was relieved that he was doing something, anything. She remembered the package in her lap.

"Here some clean clothes we brought. Them things you wearin be stinkin up the jail." She laughed. I was so glad she laughed. That was my mama. In the newspaper-wrapped package were clean pants, a shirt, socks, and boxer shorts. I thanked her. We sat awkwardly, no one knowing how to continue our conversation, yet no one knowing how to end it. Mama stood up.

"We better be goin now," she said.

Aunt Maude stood up, still wanting to say something. I didn't give her a chance. "I sure appreciate you all coming and bringing me these things," I said, and took both Mama's hands in mine. My gesture was instinctive, a throwback from the times she took my hands in hers and extracted promises from me to be good. This time I was taking her hands, but I think we both knew that I could be making no promises. I did think I would be seeing them again in a couple of days.

With only the other boy and me as prisoners, Sheriff was casual in his treatment of me. After he had let Mama and Aunt Maude out, he told me, "You know how to get back to your cell. Close the door when you go up." The heavy downstairs door had been propped open with a newspaper. The door to my cell had been left open. When I closed the door, I was locked in.

The clanging of the cell door was always jarring, but this time I didn't feel the shock and isolation I had felt the first day. Someone had been to see me. I was not cut off from the outside world. Fes was doing something. The boy across from me was asleep when I returned, so I didn't have to discuss my reason for going downstairs. He spent most of his time sleeping. He didn't read. I didn't ask him if he knew how. After I had sponged myself off and changed into fresh clothes, I actually felt upbeat for a while.

• • •

I had graduated from high school with nothing to do but continue in the shoe repair shop and caddy at the white public country club on Sundays. I was salutatorian (one number separated me from Doris Isaacs, the valedictorian), and was awarded a partial scholarship to South Carolina State A & M College. The award, thirty dollars, covered tuition for one semester (fees for the University of California at Berkeley at the time were about twenty-five dollars). This was an academic scholarship. Sports scholarships covered everything.

My scholarship award, the work of Misses Jenkins and Thompson, had come as a surprise. Having no school counselors, I'd had no way of learning what my opportunities might be after high school.

We'd had some statewide test, on which I scored among the highest students in the state. I do not remember anyone putting this test into any meaningful context. I was delighted by the scholarship, and for a short time basked in the glow of love and confidence shown by two of my favorite teachers.

I was convinced at the time by Fes that I should not attend the black-run state college. On partial scholarship, I would have to work my way for what was an inferior education in an anti-intellectual setting. Also, it would have been galling to me to watch the spectacle of our president going at budget time each year, hat in hand, to beg from the white racist state legislators, most of whom were from rural counties and were against education for colored citizens. ("Book larnin'll spile the nigra. Make'm f'rgit his place.") I would have been low man on the totem pole of a class/caste-based system of hazing and humiliation. Better that I avoided such experiences at a time when I would have few allies who opposed them.

Fes had little trouble convincing me not to accept this scholarship. Though I was happy to receive it and grateful to those teachers who had helped secure it for me, I was quickly shown how inadequate it was. In addition to tuition I would need books and supplies, clothes, and money for campus activities. Except for my shoe repair shop wages and a few dollars earned Sundays from caddying, I had no money. And I had begun to give more of what I earned to support our household. My brother, John Lee, had not yet begun to earn money. But not accepting the scholarship, with no comparable alternative, did present a hidden problem that would surface as time went by.

College education was the key to upward social mobility. It provided one with entry into the lives of the Daniels girls, who lived across from Fes and who would go to Spelman, the Atlanta private college for women. Or Dr. McTeer's daughter Miriam, who lived next door to them. I could flirt with these girls when I made deliveries or did some work in the front yard for Fes. Or with Annie Mae Tedder, niece of Bill Davis, owner of People's Barber shop, who lived farther up on Treadwell. This flirting took place in their front yard or on their porch. I was never invited inside. Without college, I had no future in their eyes or the eyes of their parents. Without college, the lives of these girls and girls like them were closed to me.

I do not know why Fes didn't suggest that I try to go to Claflin. After all, it was his alma mater. He had graduated with honors. It would have been hard. I would have had to work my way. But it would have been worth it, since Claflin was reputed to be a much better school. Was there a thought in Fes's mind that a college education would have taken me away from the shop, that he had plans for me there? I don't know. I don't know. But this thought has occurred to me, and were it true, it would give credence to my sister's warning: "Fes is not your friend."

Everything seemed new to us in the period leading up to graduation. To begin, we had only been in our new building a year. We were now Wilkinson High School, named for a president of South Carolina State College, instead of Dunton Memorial. We would be the first graduating class. The graduation activities—senior prom, clubs, *The Wolverine,* our newspaper—were all new. And exciting. People tripping over each other in happy haste, rushing in and out of offices. For me a haze covers most of it.

Confusing things still more, the date for graduation had been moved up. Because of the 1939 polio epidemic, all Orangeburg County schools were closing early. The early closing affected me in an egregious way. I was having a front tooth replaced, one that had been chipped when I was eleven and had fallen on my skates. Dr. McTeer, having extracted the broken tooth, had scheduled the replacement in time for the original graduation date. He would not replace the tooth in time for the early ceremony. When, as salutatorian, I opened my mouth to greet the assembly, everyone in the front rows laughed at the hole they saw. Others joined them. The auditorium seemed a sea of laughing faces.

My astonishment at their laughter was so extreme that I do not remember ever finishing my greeting or any other part of that graduation. This, and the fact that the girl who had accepted my invitation to the prom changed her mind too late for me to respectfully ask another girl, leave sour memories of that period.

My consolation date was Miss Jenkins, one of the chaperones, who lived in my neighborhood. This turned out to be not a bad tradeoff, as I got to go with someone whom I admired, and respected, an elegant woman who was also an excellent dancer.

I was excited leading up to the prom and by the prom itself. There was the warm night, the live music, girls in long pretty dresses, some for the first time. Girls, each with a different hairstyle. Girls wobbling on unfamiliar high heels. Boys in dress suits, boys with slicked-back pomaded hair, boys with twinkling shoes. Jitterbug, fox trot, slow drag, waltz, chaperones like hawks, circulating, posted against the walls, sensitive to their charge from parents, *no monkeyshines on the dance floor*. A gentle tap on the shoulders of the couple who were spinning on a dime too long. Sitting on the porch in moonlight with Miss Jenkins after the ball and seeing a fellow caddy's girlfriend, Lynette, come out of the undertaker's back door. I recognized her but didn't let on to Miss Jenkins that I knew her.

Then there was the senior year Future Farmers Fathers and Sons Banquet. I had no father. My best friend's father, Reverend Fridie, refused to attend. We were required to wear white shirts and dark trousers and shoes. Nathaniel Fridie and I sat next to one another as we graduating seniors received inspiration to become better farmers. Hand over his heart, our professor gave a heartfelt rendering of Kipling's "If," and someone sang an equally inspired rendition of Edgar Guest's "Trees." Nathaniel and I had no intention of becoming farmers. In truth, we were playing at becoming farmers. Maybe we were also playing at getting an education.

After pork chops, mashed potatoes with gravy, butter beans, string beans, sweet potatoes, buttered biscuits, and lemonade, and a closing prayer by a minister whom I didn't recognize, Nathaniel and I went out into a soft zero zero Orangeburg night (it was impossible to see an oncoming person until they were right in front of you). He went home to his tarpaper tin-roofed shack, and I across town, down Peasley, along The Ditch, across Sunnyside, along Fenwick to Broughton, to Broad, and to bed in my slightly more substantial house.

Mama and brother John Lee were asleep. I undressed, hung my clothes on nails on the wall, and slid into the bed John Lee and I shared, pushing him out of the middle. He grumbled sleepily, but did not wake up. The walk home had been good for me. I had sung many of the latest hits, including my current favorite, "When You Were Sweet Sixteen." With a minimum of tossing, I slept.

Only one person came to see me graduate. Not my mother, who worked twelve hours that day. Not my boss at the shoe repair shop. Not John Lee, who was in school on the other side of town. Not my sister, who was Up North. Only Miss Grace Long, who lived on Peasley Street, in the house next to where we had lived. She brought not only her kind self but a box of handkerchiefs as a graduation present as well. I had not seen her for many years. We had moved a half-dozen times since we had lived on Peasley Street. She herself was a teacher in a school somewhere in the county. I found it then and still find it amazing that she would not only have remembered me, a feat in itself, but that she would have followed my progress in school. When Miss Grace walked up to me after the ceremonies, I was overjoyed. My graduation had mattered to her. She had shown it by walking all the way from Peasley Street on a hot day to bring me a present.

I don't know why my mother didn't come. She valued education. She had insisted that we go to school, and worked to see that we did. As I don't remember ever asking her why, I can only speculate. It may be that the hospital would not allow colored workers to take time off for such a trivial (in a white supervisor's eyes) event. A death, perhaps. A graduation? No way. But if so, why don't I remember us talking about it, and her disappointment that she couldn't get time off? Or maybe she didn't have proper clothes? Not likely, since she had clothes to wear to church. Maybe she would have felt out of place? After all, no member of her family had ever graduated from high school. Though she liked people and they liked and respected her, she was not a social person. Her work hours did not permit her to become one.

● ● ●

My emotional high that third day in jail did not last the day. Mama's face kept coming back to me. Her *why* haunted me. Because it was also my question. What was it that led me to take such a rash, thoughtless action? I could see all the people I knew asking me, *Why, A. D., why? How could you do this thing to us?* Why *did* I do it? What was it in my recent life that had brought me to this point?

Questions, questions that can never be answered now. Let's go, then, to the long distant past.

PART II

CHAPTER ONE

My Trip

My trip begins
in a slender house
in a thick wood.

Weak light
guides the midwife
as she pulls me out.

Grandma Ozelia shouts,
"Praise the Lord!"

Then Grandma's farm,
its cows, pigs, the mule,
and my rabbit
suffocates
under a pile
of barnyard lumber.

Aunts and uncles
who tend me
when my mother
has to leave
my father,

and who are soon to join
the 20's Migration
North.

"Snake holes"
to stand over,
my first punishment
for theft, of my
youngest uncle's
elderberry wine.

Then the small town,
many houses, each
we live in for
far too short a time.

My sisters' books
from school
amo, amas, amat,
they practice
their Latin lessons
on four-year-old me.

The pre-Depression
store we own
one winter;
my stepfather
gives credit
to his friends
despite my mother's
warning, then
sawmill whistle
lays them all off.

On railroad tracks
kerosene holder
for kitchen stove
drops and smashes
while moving
to cheaper house;
no money
to replace.

Barefoot to Negro school,
white children torment us
as we pass their place;
never to use public
library or any
tax-supported
leisure space;
bright enough
to sense a wrong.

Working from age nine
like my buddies
at odd jobs
after school, weekends;

Eleven-year-old
favorite sister dies;
why, why, why?

Good times, eating
hot candied yams,
butter dripping,
stone-ground
whole wheat rolls

from government-issue
flour, a puppy
one whole summer long.

Reading books,
winning a Bible verse
contest at ten.

Mulatto-run House
for white men
down the street
where I make
good money
shining shoes;
madam mistress
to police chief.

Falling from
every ladder,
fence, or tree
I climb, yet
forever climbing.

"That boy live
to see twelve
will be a miracle,"
my mother swears.

I do live
and in my most
Jesus voice
announce:
"I must be about

my Father's business,
now that I'm twelve."

"You better sit down here
and eat your dinner
before it gets cold.
Father's business
my big foot."

A prophet is never
received well
in his own country,
I remind her.
Like the Rock of Ages
She cannot
be moved.

Year 1922. Freud's ideas about the importance of the unconscious
and repression were making headway, the use of Ford's automobile
had burgeoned, giving freedom to the wanderer and the licentious.
Woodrow Wilson had returned home from The Hague with his tail
between his legs, his idea of world community shot down by his own
Congress.

U.S. whites were entering the Roaring Twenties, the Jazz Age, as
U.S. black intellectuals were introducing the New Negro, who would
give to the world the Harlem Renaissance.

Far from these nation-shaping events, oblivious of them, in the
early morning of October 8, after cleaning out a well the day before,
my mother, Margaret Ann Elisabeth, let me be born. Grandma Ozelia
Butler was there. While Midwife Hagar twisted my head expertly
and set herself to catch me as I tumbled out, Grandma Ozelia let out
a "Praise the Lord!" She thanked her Maker for His gift of a healthy
baby boy.

"Never thought I'd live to see yenna gimmie a boy," as she and Hagar cleaned me up, cut and tied my umbilical cord, and put a tight band around my navel.

"Had to be, with all that kickin in my belly, that or the devil. Bet my insides done tore up." But Mama was smiling as she reached out for me. And her two daughters slept through it all, on floor pallets in their room next door.

I was born in that small farmhouse, deep in cypress swamp country. The cypress and other hardwoods had long been logged out. Farming and logging had degraded stream banks and slash clogged some slow-moving streams. The room was lighted by a kerosene lamp and a small fireplace that sent out more heat than light, but little of either. Hagar had delivered all of Mama's children: her first two girls, Edith and Leola in that order, and me, the first boy. There had also been a third daughter, Mitt, who died in infancy.

Confusion clouds my mind over whether there was another child, "the baby" that I had heard people in the family talk about. I never asked my mother. When I asked my older sister long afterwards, she temporized:

"A. D., I just don't know. I was too little myself. There might have been another baby, I'm not sure. But I think it was Mitt. You shoulda asked Mama, she the one who could tell you." So I let it stand at Mitt.

Three out of five (she had another boy later, and my favorite, Leola, who died at age eleven) was about average for Low Country Carolina black small farm families during the twenties. Her parents' record, ten of thirteen, was better, but achieved on a larger farm at the turn of the century.

I was not to live long in that house. My father, Adam, had lied to my mother about his past. He had told her that his former wife was dead. In fact, she was still alive. When confronted by my pregnant (with me) mother, he said, "Well, she was dead to *me*." My mother always snorted when she repeated his lame tale. Mama was furious at his deception and at his non-explanation. She sent him packing on the spot.

Honest herself, she hated liars. She *hated* them.

"If he only woulda told me, we coulda figured something out," she complained bitterly the few times I got her to talk about him at all.

Mama's youngest sister, Maude, was stronger in her condemnation. She never mentioned his name to me. When she was angry at something I did that she thought stupid, she would say that I resembled his brother, who folk said was a little wiggy. I never learned the name of this uncle, or names of anyone on my father's side of the family.

I was never told what happened to him, where he went or what he did. It was as though my sisters and I had never had a father, that he had never existed.

The family was doubly angry with him, I think, because he had been accepted as one of them. They felt they had been taken for a ride and didn't like it one bit. They had taken my father in, in a way they never accepted John Walker, her second husband. My two younger aunts spoke of Walker with derision.

"Don't see what she want with that little ignorant monkey-lookin nigger."

He was short, my mother's height, about 5'2", and black, but I didn't think he looked like a monkey. My mother might have told them, as they well knew, that when you're drag-ass poor with three children under five to support, you don't have much choice.

Once my father was gone, it took five months for them to settle my mother and sisters with her oldest sister in a town nearby. Grandma took me back with her to the family farm until my mother could put her shattered life together and find a place of her own. The woman who had cleaned out a well the day before letting birth was battered by her husband's betrayal, but would not be beaten down by it.

I was to remain in the care of my two youngest aunts and uncles, the last four remaining at home, until my mother was able to have me with her.

• • •

The Butler farm was in a period of transition. Its elder, Grandpa Isom, was dead. He died the year after I was born. The farm, good bottomland cleared from the swamp, had been owned by the family since what many called the "farce" of Reconstruction. It had supported twelve mouths, twenty-four hands, working year-round.

They did take off for camp meeting time, when the community got together to celebrate the past year and thank God for permitting them to live another one.

They grew cotton for cash, corn as food for humans and animals. Tobacco was later to replace cotton as a cash crop. Vegetables: beans, tomatoes, okra, and the root crops, beets, potatoes, and rutabagas, filled the garden. There were apples, pears, peaches, pecans, and black walnuts in season. Berries and nuts were gathered from the woods, as were scuppernongs (wild grapes) and chestnuts. From the woods also came foxes, raccoons (coons), and opossum, and an occasional rattlesnake. (Using a forked stick, they held the snake so that it couldn't strike. They made rattlesnake filet.)

Cows furnished milk, cream, butter and cheese and flesh. Chickens, ducks, and guinea hens provided eggs. There were hogs and rabbits. All made tasty meals.

Dogs provided security and cats kept down the rat population. Two mules provided power for the plows and transportation when hitched to the wagon.

Pens kept the pigs in. The barn and chicken coops sheltered the fowl, cow, and mules, and provided storage for farm tools and the cured meats and preserves for winter.

While it was a well-kept prosperous farm, it was not a very large one. Not enough land to split six ways. By the time I was born, three of the males and three females had left—the older, more experienced workers.

Two, James and William, joined the 1920s' Great Migration north, James settling in Cleveland, William in Freeport, Long Island (New York). Like many, they had bought into the myth of the North being the Land of Milk and Honey (the Chinese, remember, called the U.S. "Gold Mountain").

Grandma hadn't wanted her young men to leave. When she learned of their decision, she tried her best to have them stay.

"Yenna think you men, now, you can do what you want."

Sullen silence.

"Yenna wanta go, ain't nobody can stop you. Go head on."

"Nothin down here for no colored man."

"Think you can find more up there where you going?"

"Can't find no less."

"I give you over to the Lord, you too much for me."

Joseph bought land in a nearby town. Lucy, the oldest daughter, married a Tobin and settled near Joseph. Rachael married a Berry, her own Joseph, and settled across the branch, less than a mile away.

Grandma found herself trying to manage the farm with four quick-tempered, restless, fractious children in their late teens and early twenties, without the steadying hand of her husband to complement her. With fourteen fewer hands to do the work of keeping up the farm, it suffered. No way could five people do the work formerly done by twelve.

They were not helped by the fighting between the sons, Johnny and Benjy, over who should do what work or in which direction the farm should go. The two brothers could not agree on who would decide how much of what to plant, and they almost destroyed themselves by their decision, over the objections of the women in the family, to buy a car. Buying a car, instead of something more practical like a truck or another mule, was bad enough. It was compounded by the fact that neither of them could drive.

The miracle was that the farm survived at all. But it did survive, with the help of male neighbors and relatives, and two women, Grandma and the second-youngest daughter, Cather Lee. After Grandma's death, Cather Lee held the land until, finally, she gave it to a young woman who cared for her in her last years. More than a hundred years of continuous family ownership ended.

The brothers were right in their assessment of their increasing inability to farm. Government policies and white control were making it difficult to raise the money for the next year's crop. White farmers were lent the money necessary to plant and support their crops, black farmers were not. These policies of racial discrimination were forcing more and more black farmers to lose their land or to leave it for the cities.

• • •

I didn't recognize my mother when she came to visit. It had been such a long time since I had seen her. We were on the front porch, my aunts sitting with me on the chair that moved like a swing, when she came up the steps.

"Why, look at what the cat drug in." Aunt Cather Lee made a mock sneer, hiding the happiness in her voice.

"Well, well, well, see who's here," Aunt Maude added to no one in particular, as Grandma was in the back of the house, the boys in the fields.

"Here, lemme take this." Aunt Cather Lee took her bag and set it near the door. "You must be beat lugging it all over the place."

I stayed with Aunt Maude in the swing.

"Thing like a ton a bricks after a while, in all this heat." The woman wiped her face with a handkerchief she pulled from her purse, which she set next to her bag.

"Who's this little gentleman you got there?" she turned to me.

"Oh, this something Santa brought us," Maude said, as Cather Lee joined her on the swing.

"Santa, hmnn, well let me see." She bent, holding out her arms. "Come on, come on over here."

She was squatting now, about six feet away. My two aunts were holding me, each supporting me on one of her knees and holding me loosely by one arm. When I hesitated, she clapped her hands together, smiled, and repeated, "Come, come on." She said, "I'm your mother."

I looked back to my aunts. They, especially Aunt Cather Lee, had mock frowns on their faces.

"Don't you let her fool you, she's not your mother," Aunt Cather Lee said, shaking her head.

I looked to Aunt Maude. She was no help. She shook her head from side to side. They were both enjoying my indecision. Whether I sensed something familiar about this pleading woman, whom I had not seen since I was five months old, more than a year ago, or whether it was the novelty of a new face, or my sense that my aunts were teasing me, I will never know.

"Come, come."

Her voice was insistent, with more urgency the longer I hesitated. She kept her arms extended, her smile never fading. I took a look from her to my aunts and back, lunged forward, breaking their slight restraints, and wobbled my bowlegged self over to her.

She lifted me as she stood up, pulling me to her bosom.

"That's my baby, that's my boy!" she shouted, hugging me to her.

• • •

"You ain't aiming to take my child, now?" Aunt Cather Lee asked, more serious than not, after they were seated in the front room, fanning themselves with "Brooks Undertaker" fans they got from church. Grandma Ozelia, hearing the commotion, had come in, her apron full of butter beans she had been shelling for that evening's supper.

Mama caught them up on what she had been doing in her absence.

"And how's Lucy'n them over that way? Them chillun." This from Grandma.

"Ev'body's fine. Lucy littlest start school come October."

They were awed. He was a "just a baby" last time Lucy had him over.

"Naw, he almost come up to my waist now." She stuck out her hand to show his height.

"'n Joseph had to get another mule. Ol' thing drop dead right in the middle of plowin."

"Lord have mercy!" Grandma exclaimed. "Hope he got a good one this time."

"Nothing wrong with the other one. Just old. Worked to death."

The room quieted, fans working. I squirmed. Mama let me down and I ran over and held on to Aunt Cather Lee's knees. Mama appeared not to notice.

She looked at Grandma.

"Was hopin I could leave him here till I got everything straight. I got a man helpin me now."

They had heard something of this, in the way that backwoods news traveled. In bits and pieces. They awaited her confirmation.

"John Walker ain't much to look at, but he's steady. Works at the sawmill over there, and lets me keep his money."

"He know you got chillun?" This from Aunt Maude.

"He know bout the girls. He seen 'em. Ain't told him bout this'n yet. Got to tell him though. These days'n times, not many mens take a woman with chillun—'n little ones at that," she added hastily.

"Truth, sho nuff," they acknowledged.

"What about his peoples?" Grandma wanted to know.

"He don't know much about 'em. They from around Augusta. He lived with a granny in Beaufort."

That was not a good sign, a man not knowing about his people. Grandma hoped the positives would outweigh the negative. She said something I was to hear many's the time from Mama when she had doubts about something: "I hope you know what you doin."

"Soon's we get nuff money, he gon help me with a store in Orangeburg. Canned goods, groceries'n like that. He gettin a job in the new mill they open up that way."

"A store," Maude exclaimed. "You sure you don't want your little sister to help you with everything?"

"You gon keep your behind right here on this farm. What you know bout any store?" This from Cather Lee.

"Now, now, you heifers. Jus keep your tails down." Turning to Mama, she asked, "And you'll be taking the boy with you?"

"Well, Mama, that's what I wanted to ask, if yenna could let him stay here a little longer. Till we got set up and all. I can give you a little somethin to help out."

She reached for her handbag. Grandma stopped her.

"He too little to plow," she said with a twinkle, pulling me over to her.

"A. D., you want to stay here with us?"

I nodded my head with a circle.

She looked to Mama.

"I reckon," then added, "Don't be too long, now."

"Or he will be plowin," Cather Lee added, "'n then he b'longs to us."

The deal sealed, Mama left me with them. When I finally joined her in Orangeburg, I found a store in the front room of our house, a new father, my two older sisters, and a new baby brother. And my first look at white people close up.

• • •

My aunts and I disagreed on exactly how I spent my time on the farm until an emergency illness propelled them to send for my mother to come and get me. What we did agree on was that I was forever underfoot and literally into everything.

As there was no other child closer than a swamp crossing, "most a mile" away, I was either in the company of my adults or left to my own childish devices, which were many and which sometimes got me into trouble.

Although I was not a sickly baby, apparently I had a weak back, or poor muscle coordination. It was a long time before I could turn over on my stomach, if you laid me on my back. I stuttered as I learned to talk.

And talk I did, stutter and all. Because I was around adults so much, I quickly picked up their language. Being around adults, I spoke like them. I never spoke like a child, which didn't make me popular with children of my age who did.

Then there were the bow legs. I must have had rickets. Grandma massaged my legs a lot. My bow legs were a source of fun for my aunts and other adults who, at Sunday gatherings, would call me to see me wobble over from one of them to another. Children my age didn't think it funny, as I was the center of attention, not they. Whatever Grandma Ozelia did plus healthy food must have worked, because my legs were completely straight by the time Mama took me to join her in Orangeburg.

My uncles Ben and Johnny brought me a tiny rabbit from one of their hunting trips. They made a box for it and showed me how to feed it and warned me not to let it out. All was well until one day I picked it up to play with and it wiggled out of my arms, dropped to the ground, and cottontailed it to the barnyard. Once there, it squeezed itself into a pile of lumber left over from mending the barnyard fence.

I had run after it. With my wobble and its hop skip, skip hop from side to side just as I reached down for it, no way was I going to catch that bunny. I had occasionally caught chickens, but they ran straighter than this animal.

When it disappeared into the lumber, I sat on the pile, winded and wondering to do. What would my uncles say when they found I had been careless with their gift? I hoped the bunny would come out. I tried calling, "Come, bunny, come on now." Nothing. There was no one to help. All but Grandma were in the field chopping cotton, and she was far away in the kitchen.

In desperation, I started pulling at the boards. One shorter flat one slipped, and there below it was a quart Ball jar filled with a reddish liquid. I wrestled the top off, stuck my finger in, and tested it. The liquid had a sweetish taste, not at all disagreeable. I sampled it, first a little, then more. My appetite sated for a while, I secured the top and went to sit in the porch swing.

I had uncovered Uncle Ben's secret stash of elderberry wine. He was not supposed to make it, no one was supposed to find it. I had. After the effects of the first drink wore off, I went back for a second sampling. And back to the swing. I was asleep in the swing when the four came in from the fields at sunset, but was jarred awake by their talk and their stamping of the field sand off their feet.

The other three went into the house, but Benjy went out to the lumber pile to check his stash. I had put back the lumber a different way from how he had left it. He must have known something was amiss. Pulling the flat board aside, he saw a greatly diminished supply of his wine. And he guessed the culprit.

I was pretending to still be asleep when he grabbed my arm, shook me awake, and began pulling at me, half dragging me out into the yard away from the house.

"I'll teach you! You little bowlegged..." He said this in a stage whisper.

"I-I didn't mean it, Unca Ben. I-I'll never do it again. I didn't know it was yours. I didn't know it was yours." I knew it was wrong to take what wasn't mine, and I was frightened of what he would do to me. I had seen him take a whip and lash a balky mule one day when I was following him in the corn row he was making.

"Hush up!" he kept saying in that strange whisper. When we got

beyond earshot of the house he let go of me and resumed his normal
speaking voice. We were under an old oak near a clearing where
several snakes had been recently killed. I had seen one of them laid
out. It was longer than I.

"I didn't know it was yours," I said again.

"And I'll make sure you don't," he said, yanking me under the oak.
"See them two holes?"

He pointed to two round holes about two feet apart, about half the
diameter of a golf cup. He pushed, then dragged me when I tried to dig
in my heels to slow him. He was so much stronger, I was no match.

"I don't w-want to stand over them holes, Unca Ben. S-snake might
bite me."

He held me.

"You just stand right there. And shut up."

I was still, sniffling. And terrified.

"Now you ain't gon tell nobody you found any wine, heah?"

"I won't tell nobody, Unca Ben. Unca Ben, c-can I go now?"

He held me a short while longer, then shoved me in the direction
of the house. He went back to the barnyard. I went back to my
swing, where I promptly fell asleep.

Aunt Cather Lee woke me up to wash up for supper. As she was
scrubbing my face she noticed my caked tears.

"What was that ruckus I heard out there?" she queried.

"L-lost bunny rabbit gone."

"Gone, gone where?"

"I-n the lumb—in the shed."

"Don't worry about it." She hugged me. "Uncle Ben'll find it for
you in the morning. Let's eat."

I was usually a good eater for a small child, but that night I ate only
some sweet potato and corn bread. And immediately after dinner, I
retired to my cot on the side porch and fell asleep again.

This upset the chickens, as I had neglected to feed them, one of my
two chores. The other was filling the wood box behind the kitchen
stove. By ones and twos the chickens all came chick-walking up the
steps, onto the porch, and rested on the window or any other flat
surface on the porch. One even rested on the rail at the foot of the

cot. "What in the Lord…" Grandma Ozelia cried. "Look what they doin to that boy!" They saw, and were suitably amazed. All but Uncle Ben, who knew that there was nothing wrong with me a good night's sleep wouldn't cure. He had had his hangovers. "Ain't nothin wrong with that boy. Just been playin too hard. Them chickens jis hongry. I'll feed 'em. Shoo!" He shooed them out to their feeding box and gave them their supper. Most of them went to their various roosts, but several of them, who used to follow me around the yard during the day, came back to the windowsill and spent the night there. Uncle Ben didn't try to remove them.

• • •

Despite my theft of his elderberry wine, or maybe because of it—we were partners in crime—Uncle Ben and I became close. He allowed me to follow him about the farm. I struggled along row on row as he geed and hawed the mule. Occasionally I would try to wander away but he would call me back. There were snakes in the fields, like mines waiting to be plowed up or stepped on. There were black snakes, rattlers, and where the land edged towards the swamp, an occasional water moccasin. This was especially true during the spring plowing, when winter rainwater had settled over much of the land.

I loved squishing the soil between my toes, collecting small stones, and biting off a bitter weed, chewing and spitting it out.

Uncle Ben carried me when he went to visit other farms and on excursions into the woods to pick blueberries, huckleberries, and chestnuts. Once we tried to outrun a summer squall. We lost, and came home drenched and laughing.

He showed me how to feed the chickens, how to scatter the grain so that each chicken got a share, but none more than another.

He did not show me about cows, as the milking was done by my aunts. I had to learn about cows the hard way. I watched one or the other of my aunts sit on a stool and pull on the cow's teats, squirting milk into a bucket wedged between her knees. Aunt Kate rested her head against the cow's side and rained foaming milk into the bucket. Occasionally, she would direct a stream in my direction. There's no taste quite like warm milk direct from the cow, even if it meant some of it splashing over my face. When her bucket was full, she always patted the cow and gave her a little scratch behind the ear. After she had finished, the calf, standing by during the milking, took over and had her breakfast.

One morning I decided I would nudge the calf aside and get me some more milk. Though the calf was not much bigger than I, it resisted my attempt to interrupt its meal. I nudged, the calf nudged back. Then as I reached for a teat, I found myself on a pile of straw in a corner of the barn.

Stunned but unhurt because the straw had cushioned my landing, I realized that I had been kicked by the cow. The calf resumed her feeding, while its mother seemed unaffected by the incident, switching her tail as before. When I had recovered sufficiently, I ran into the kitchen crying. Aunt Cather Lee was separating the milk from the cream.

"Aunt Kat, Aunt Kat, cow kick me."

She swung around from the table, took me by both hands, and looked me over. Seeing no bruises or scratches, she pulled me to her.

"Hush, now. What did you do to cow for cow to kick you?"

"Nothing, Aunt Kat, I just pushed the calf."

"Ohhh, I see," she said, as she picked me up and carried me out to the barn, where she saw the calf still pulling on her mother's teats.

"Oh, so you wanted to be a calf."

"Aunt Kat…" sniffles.

"Now now, don't cry, it's all right. Cow won't kick you no more. Longst you don't push on her calf, hear?"

Then there was the huge white hog that appeared near dusk one evening, out near the pigpen, rooting. It was not a local hog, they were much smaller and usually dark. This was a prize hog, Uncle Ben and Uncle Johnny knew, probably from the county hog farm. How it got so far was a puzzle to them. He had to be got back there, for the white county agents would be out looking for him.

"First thing we gotta do is get this sucker in a pen." This from Ben, after he was through admiring him. "If we don't, he'll 'stroy everything."

So they did, calling the dog, Kaalo, for help. They pushed and shoved him towards an empty pen. He resisted, slipping away just as they thought they had him headed in the right direction. They kept waving me out of the way. Finally Kaalo took over, snapping at his legs and rump each time he veered, until at last he was safely penned in. They hadn't wanted to put him with the other hogs, for fear he might attack one of them.

All night they worried about how to get word to the county farm agents. They didn't want to keep the hog, for if they did they'd have to feed him. And they couldn't free him to root out their crops and those of their neighbors.

"'n you know county ain't givin us doodly. Might even say we tryin to steal him. Anything not to pay us." This from Uncle Johnny, as they sat smoking after supper.

They need not have worried. Next morning when they went out to feed their hogs, Big White, as I named him, was gone. The same strength and ingenuity that had allowed him to break out of county farm and find his way all the way to our place had made short shrift of our pen, which had been built for much smaller hogs. They spoke admiringly of him, especially Uncle Ben, but were glad he was gone.

• • •

Winter storms were preceded by high wind, summer ones by stifling, stifling weather.

I remember rain, the early heavy separate drops whipped up by the wind, then the incessant drumming on the tin roof as the rain gathered force, the staccato hail balls, pounding, pounding; water falling in sheets off the shed porch roof, the slap of the wooden window someone left unlatched, the shriek of the wind in the chinaberry tree outside my window.

There was the chill in the house despite the roaring fire, fire that sputtered when water collected at the top of the chimney and drained down. Water collecting and standing in the yard. Chickens coming onto the front porch and nesting on its railing.

The worried looks of the adults, their talk in whispers though the wind was screaming. The house always leaked, sometimes water dripped on my bed. There was the musty smell of dampness. The darkness, the kerosene lamps being lit, casting weak yellow flickers.

The orange flames from the fireplace with its red background, flames curling around the logs, the wet wood steaming until dry, steam pouring out both ends of the logs. People huddled in front of the fire. A dog in a corner near the fireplace, allowed in because of the storm. The house shuddering.

A dash through the short covered walkway that connected the main house to the kitchen, water gushing between the two buildings.

Years later I saw this separation of main house and kitchen in West Africa, a practice that protected the main house from a fire in the kitchen.

After the storm, there was the opening of windows and doors, the emptying of pans of water set to catch the rain, the wringing out of clothes used to plug the bottom of doors, the hanging out of wet bedclothes, the raising of voices.

The watch for snakes, rattlers, that liked to snuggle under the house at the base of the chimney. And water moccasins, flushed out of creeks and swamps by the rain. Fortunately, there were the dogs, Gyp and Kaalo, good at treeing coons, who were death to snakes, so that none that came onto the yard ever lived to bite anyone.

• • •

I don't know how long I would have remained at Grandma's farm, but for the incident that forced them to send for my mother. It happened a few days after Uncle Ben and I had almost outrun a summer storm, Uncle Ben whipping the mule in our vain attempt. We had reached sight of our house, just around the woods, just across the branch creek that flooded and blocked the road after each heavy rain.

"Dang!" Uncle Ben swore, as the poor mule struggled, knee-deep in water, to get us over the creek.

The day before, I had been playing in a fallow field, marveling at what was left of a pine tree that had been struck by lightning and set ablaze, oblivious of the broom sage stubble that dotted the field. A piece stuck in my right foot, infecting the area between the fourth and fifth toe. When Ben and I returned from our wild ride against the storm, I was fretting and feverish. Grandma went into the nearby woods, as my mother was to do later in my life, dug up some roots, brought them back, washed and boiled them. The tea made from them was bitter, and I had to be forced, screaming, to drink it. The first night I slept, but next day the fever came back. More tea, some relief, but the fever would not be broken.

Then they noticed my foot. I had been favoring it as I walked, more noticeably when I ran. By the time Aunt Cather Lee and Grandma called me to look at it, the infection had penetrated deeply into the foot, eventually forming a pus pool on its top.

Alarmed, they put me to bed, but not before bathing my foot, putting some foul-smelling salve or ointment on it, and wrapping a rag around it, I suppose to catch the pus.

I slept much of the time, which they did not like. And they liked less the reaction of my fowls. Again they came up on the shed porch at night, and refused to be shooed away. Shoo them, they would go a short distance. When backs were turned, they'd be right there at their posts on the windowsill, head of the bed, wherever they could grasp a toehold. After a while, my folk stopped trying, but the conduct of the fowls troubled them as much as my increasing illness. There was something they couldn't explain, hence something not quite right about it. Nothing to do but send for my mother.

My mother came on a Sunday, the only off day for the owner of the Studebaker she had rented.

They were apprehensive about her coming, and they were right to be so.

"What yenna done to my boy?" she lamented, when she saw me on the shed porch, and felt my forehead. I had fever but not as much as the day before.

Aunt Cather Lee pouted, "We done the best we could. Where was you?"

"Ahnh now, yenna stop that. Ain't no need squabblin over spilt milk. Git that boy where he kin git some right attention. Nothin mo we kin do here."

"It too hot for foolishness and carrying on. Dinner most ready. You gon have to eat somethin fore you git back on the road," Grandma concluded, hushing what might have developed into a futile game of blame casting.

My mother knew she had left me with them longer than she should have. While they liked having me around, I was more a burden to them than help. With all hands and eyes needed for the spring planting, they did not need a sick child. And I was her responsibility, not theirs.

Uncles Ben and Johnny were out in the yard with Mama's driver, admiring the Studebaker, which was a curiosity not only to them but the farm animals. One cat leaped on the hood, then off when she realized how hot it was. A hen that settled on one running board was shooed away. The dogs, after initial growling, settled down in the shade of the chinaberry tree. Uncle Ben was later to just escape breaking his arm when the engine he was trying to crank bucked before it started, wrenching the crank out of his hand. Only his instinctive jerking back saved him.

That was our only auto incident except for a flat tire halfway to Orangeburg. While the flat was being repaired, I saw my first white people up close as they drove by. My other sighting had been the distant ghostlike figure of the mailman as he put mail in our box, Route 1, Box 26, out on the main road. If the Sunday-dressed couple and three children tooling along in a shiny black Model T Ford noticed us, they didn't show it. They did not stop to offer help. If my relatives around our car noticed them, they didn't show it either. It was as though two universes, known but not recognized, separate and unequal, were sharing the same space for a brief moment.

CHAPTER TWO

My Dog When I Was Seven

The year was 1930
When my family produced nothing
To add to the GNP

Out of the money economy
We were both underfed and skinny-legged

He came in from the street
I fed him part of what I had
The rest he scrounged in outhouses
Reached before the city's honeybucket men.
He drank from a scum-filled ditch
At the bottom of our yard

My buddy

We ran up the dirt sidewalk a way
Then back home
I was happy to have someone my own size

That day in July his eyes took fire
Foam at the mouth, his piteous yelps
As he zigzagged through his madness

At the end,
Body caked with dust and sweat
His coat a mud gray, he lay, teeth bared
In a hideous stiffness

My stepfather warned "don't touch"
But through my tears buried him
Where he lay

Orangeburg was the seat of Orangeburg County, an agricultural
region between Columbia, the state capital, and Charleston, once the
largest port on the East Coast. Cotton was king. Not far from where
we lived was a cotton gin, where farmers brought their wagons piled
high with the freshly picked stuff, to be turned into bales for market.

Orangeburg had a population of about ten thousand, evenly
divided between blacks and whites. In addition to several Jewish
families, there were a few Eastern Mediterranean families, who
owned small businesses, and one Chinese family, owners of a hand
laundry.

County seat. County jail, county courthouse, county library, into
which neither I nor any other known black was ever to set foot except
to clean it and the county hospital. A few miles outside of town was
the county farm, home of the prison chain gang. Men from it were
used to clear roadside brush, repair roads, and do other maintenance
work the county needed. This while wearing chains on their ankles,
long enough so they could walk but not run. A white guard with a
gun accompanied them at all times.

Orangeburg, founded 1704, was well situated on the Edisto, once
a partly navigable river. A crossroads, it was served by two railroads,
the Southern Railway and the Atlantic Coast Line; two highways, one
route from Charleston to Columbia. General Sherman came through
the town on his historic March to the Sea during the last days of the
Civil War. There is a picture of him crossing the Edisto River. It was
rich farming country, between the Low Country and Piedmont.

Orangeburg was unique for Southern blacks in several ways.
It boasted of not one but two black-run institutions of higher
learning: Claflin, a Methodist University; and South Carolina State
A & M, a state-owned agricultural and mechanical college. Reading
promotional speeches by the white Young Men's Business League,
you would not know that a single black person resided in the town or
the surrounding area.

Claflin had an excellent high school for those families who could
afford it, and the elementary school needs of these same families
were served by Felton Training School, one of the many schools
throughout the South set up by the Julius Rosenwald Fund. This
school was located on the state college campus. Next door to the state
college, separated only by a wire fence, was Claflin University, where
a Methodist-sponsored grammar school was available to those black
families who could afford it. A few well-off families sent their children
to Mather Academy in Camden and to Robert Smalls in Beaufort.
For poor blacks there was only Dunton Memorial, which provided six
years of schooling with agriculture and manual arts training.

In the Orangeburg of my boyhood, relations between the races
seemed settled and stable, the last known lynching rumored to have
taken place in 1926. The tree on which he was lynched, Jack's Oak
to blacks, stood only a block from the last two houses we lived in,
on Shuler Street near the corner of Waring, the west side of town,
near the Edisto River. Not much of a tree. Looked to me like any
other oak, until you looked at it up close. Not nearly as majestic as
the one near the corner of Russell and Windsor Streets, where we
gathered Saturday mornings for serious marble shooting. Yet there
was something about Jack's Oak that occasionally arrested me.
Standing alone on a red clay plain, some of its branches missing, it
had never reached its full height. Where were those branches? Which
branch had held Jack as his fellow citizens shot and mutilated him?
These were questions I never heard discussed. The tree disappeared
sometime later, between my intermittent visits to the town. It was
not talked about, its loss was not mourned.

Racial stability had been viewed by outsiders as racial harmony,
which was a false reading of how white people actually felt. Their
true feelings emerged after *Brown vs. Board of Education,* in 1954.

Because of the surface tranquility, outsiders, as evidenced by the Northern press reports, assumed that Orangeburg would be an ideal place for integration to succeed.

They were dead wrong.

Whites fiercely resisted not only attempts at school integration but also integration in places of public accommodation. So much so that at a campus rally after students had attempted to desegregate a downtown bowling alley, white highway patrolmen shot and killed three black South Carolina State students, *the first to be killed* during attempts by college students nationwide to affect public policy through campus-based protest demonstrations. Jack Bass, in his excellent *The Orangeburg Massacre,* documents these state murders.

Local blacks, having lived these many years under repression, subtle and not so subtle, were not surprised by such hostile white reaction. For starters, they would remember their attempts to establish a Catholic church and school on Russell Street, across the street from where we first lived.

Whites, thought by blacks to be Klansmen, burned down the first two attempts. Blacks had not succeeded until they built on Treadwell Street, in the middle of an all-black block, where the construction could be under constant surveillance.

There was an element of religious as well as racial bias present if they were Klan burnings, since the KKK was known to hate Catholics. No one was ever prosecuted for these arsons, as no one was prosecuted for the many black churches burned during the 1990s.

Orangeburg of my boyhood was unique for a town of its size in the number, quality, and location of its black businesses. Blacks owned the bicycle shop and the tailor shop. A black man owned the finest grocery store, Maxwell's, whose customers were wealthy whites and blacks. Blacks owned a barber shop for whites and the town's two shoe repair shops. These, except for Maxwell's, were all within the "white" business area downtown.

Orangeburg was also unique in the amount of construction done by skilled black craftsmen. John Dorman, a black architect and longtime teacher at the state college, though unlicensed for a long time, designed houses for many white families.

It has been a given throughout the U.S., enforced formerly by racially restrictive covenants in property deeds, actions of white real estate brokers, and racially biased lending practices of white banks, that public space and downtown belong to whites. That blacks had established and maintained businesses in what was "white" territory was a substantial accomplishment.

In addition, there were black businesses that catered to blacks, such as a movie house, a café, two restaurants, a dry cleaner, a candy factory, and one then another undertaker.

One restaurant, Charlie's, owned by Charles Summers, attracted some white customers, who were screened off from other customers. Eating behind a screen!

Many whites would patronize black businesses or employ black skilled craftsmen if it was convenient, if it was for an essential service, if what was offered by blacks was of high quality and not readily available elsewhere, and if, as was often the case, they saved money—and if their patronage did not imply either friendship or social equality.

• • •

After we arrived in Orangeburg, my mother collected her three other children from a neighbor woman and set about curing my foot. She bathed it in warm water, poured hydrogen peroxide into it. I was curious about the foaming it made. Then she gently spread a salve over it and wrapped it in a clean cloth she had heated in a pan on the stove.

My foot did heal, though it took a while, and left a scar at the center of my foot that still shows today.

Her husband was not at home when we arrived, nor did he show up until a day had passed. But we had the new baby—my brother— and the two girls my mother said were my sisters, Edith and Leola, four and three years older than I. And we had the store.

With my mother occupied with the store and my brother, who was still nursing, my care was taken over by my sisters, who seemed glad to have me to join them. John Lee, the baby, was too little to be played with yet. As I liked having someone to play with, even though they were older, I melded easily into the household.

Leola, the younger of the two, was especially helpful when I showed interest in their schoolbooks. *Amo, amas, amat* is what I remember from their attempts to teach me Latin as they practiced their lessons. They would follow one another around the house spouting phrases. I would try to follow them. Latin was long gone as part of the curriculum at Dunton Memorial by the time I reached their grade.

• • •

The house, first of twelve (one twice) that we were to live in before I got myself driven from town fifteen years later, was on a corner. It faced Russell, an east-to-west street that ran through town, starting at the eastern edge and snaking its way to the Edisto River, its western edge.

Not only were we on a main street, we were a block from the Southern Railway station, which was located on Highway 21 that ran from Charleston to Columbia. Across the street from the station was the black business block known as Railroad Corner. At Russell and Highway 21 was the town's Esso gas station and garage.

While the location would seem to be dangerous for children, actually it was not. The Southern Railway passenger train ran twice a day, morning and evening, with an occasional freight. Not many people owned cars yet. Most people walked. Horse and mule traffic could easily be avoided.

I liked the street and was in it whenever I got a chance. Young office workers on their way to work would pat me on the head, call me cute, and give me nickels, much to my mother's chagrin. I was talking without my stutter unless agitated, and would chatter away to anyone who would listen. I wonder which of these young white women would later run away with a son of our black grocer.

"You git in this house. Let me catch you out there on the street, beggin…"

"But Mama, I didn't ask them for nothing."

"I don't care. You hush up and stay in *this* house, you hear me?"

Ah, but if only I had listened.

• • •

Orangeburg proved to be a place of excitement for me. On sunny spring mornings I watched the Esso worker wash down the front of the gas station, lugging a heavy hose that roiled and bucked as water under pressure scoured oil and debris from around the pumps, down the driveway, into the street. He liked to squirt water in my direction to see me skip, laughing, out of the way. I never told my mother about this excursion.

Nor did I tell her about crossing Russell Street, a "no-no," to meet the morning train from Charleston. I was thrilled by the huge steam engine, whistle blowing, bell ringing, huffing and puffing smoke as it rolled into the station.

Station workers pulled trucks loaded with baggage to where they knew the baggage car should be. Passengers streamed out of the two waiting rooms, one for blacks, another for whites. The blacks positioned themselves up front, near where they thought the engine would stop. Whites moved towards the rear, where they would find the dining car and sleepers, prohibited to blacks.

The white engineer, long bib cap, striped overalls, oilcan in hand, descended majestically from one side of the cab. The black fireman, covered with soot and grime from shoveling coal into the boiler, descended, in blue overalls, from the opposite side.

On routes where the railroads had not converted to a cleaner burning coal, firemen (or stokers) were still black. Once the job became cleaner, and safer, black firemen were forced out of their jobs, some through intimidation. Others were shot. So the job of running the railroads, in the South as well as throughout the nation, was made lily white.

As a four-year-old, I didn't care who ran the trains. I was fascinated by them. On cold mornings I was warmed by the engine's heat as I stood near front wheels taller than I was. The huff-de-chuff made by the train as it had pulled into the station now silent, it made merely an occasional hmfph, hmfph! as it adjusted itself for pulling out, once the engineer finished his oiling and the passengers were all inside. I longed to join the people on the train as the conductor sang out, "Allll aboooard!"

A year later I did get a chance to ride the train down to pay a visit to Grandma Ozelia. I let a nickel I was holding slip into the window casing, and I remember my mother's "I told you to put that nickel away" as I sniffled about my loss.

I also remember that our car, the first one behind the engine and the baggage car, and the only one allotted to black passengers, was crowded. Some men stood, giving their seats to older people, women, and children. There were always several cars for whites, including a diner and a sleeping car, often with empty seats. Those seats stayed empty.

Some families, like my mother's, were dressed up in their Sunday best, girls with patent leather shoes, boys with long pants, women with striking hats. Families carried shoeboxes tied with string. These boxes were stuffed with food: crisp fried chicken, potatoes, collard greens, biscuits, and pound cake. These family boxes were supplemented by large platters held high by dexterous waiters who wove their way up and down the aisle. Those platters contained small mountains of fruit and soft drinks. The smell of food merged with those of bodies and boxes and bags of goods, in the aisles and at either end of the car.

Some men wore their work clothes, and carried their toolboxes. Others, dressed in their Sunday suits, tried in vain to protect the spit polish on their shoes and the knife-blade-thin creases in their trousers.

There was no way for the gentlemen to protect their suits and white shirts, nor the ladies their pretty dresses and outrageous hats. Soot and ash streamed into windows from the smokestack of the moving train. Windows had to be opened to prevent suffocation. Heat, plus sweat, plus soot and ash resulted in black passengers becoming disheveled and frustrated.

• • •

My mother would not have learned about my crossing the tracks to walk the black business district, Railroad Corner, had I not had yet another accident.

I was charmed by the black movie house. Though I couldn't go inside, I gazed at large posters of well-dressed black women and men, many of whom looked white. One day when the door was left open, I got a peek inside. Standing in the foyer I could see a long dark space, at the end of which was a lighted area where figures were moving. And I heard some of the music I had heard on the Victrola at home before the ticket taker shooed me away.

Behind the row of businesses was an alley strewn with empty bottles, broken cartons, other debris no one thought to clean up. It was a play space for kids, like me and others, who couldn't get to the college campus, where there was green grass. I learned later that playing on the campus lawn was forbidden.

One day, chasing someone and being chased, I stepped on what was left of a broken Ball jar. My now-healed right foot was gashed across the instep, so severely that my foot hung like a hinge.

To my cries and those of the other children, some of whom ran to their houses, Sheldon Berry, a homosexual who lived in a back room on the alley with his partner, dashed out to see what was the matter.

"Oh, child!" he shouted, when he saw what had happened. Scooping me up, holding my severed foot together, he took me into his room. He knew me from having watched out for me on occasion when my mother had business and couldn't take me along.

"Lord, Lord," he fussed. "What's Miz Maggie gonna think?"

The cut was so clean, as if made by a super-sharp blade, that I don't remember there being much blood. He gathered me in his arms and took me home.

"Lord, have mercy!" was my mother's response. "What I'm gonna do with this boy?"

After thanking Sheldon, she took off the cloth he had bound my foot with, cleaned it up with the ubiquitous hydrogen peroxide, put a slab of fatback on it, and bound it tightly.

It healed. My foot came together with only a raised seam along my right foot extending from the bottom to near my ankle. These two marks, the one left from the infection and this one, are visible on my right foot today, almost eighty years later.

"What I'm gonna do with this boy?" was soon joined by the question "What I'm gonna do about this marriage?"

• • •

Grandma had been right to be skeptical about my mother's marriage to John Walker. Even granting its emergency nature, which she had been willing to do, it was the wrong way to get married. To begin, you don't marry someone when you don't know his people. Marriage was not something just two people did. It was the joining not just of two people but of two families. Hence, it was the community's business.

For my mother to go away and marry, and simply report it to her family, was a huge breach of marriage etiquette, a slap in their face. Foreshadowed by a question mark because of the breakup of her first marriage, this new step moved my mother further outside of the closeness that family cohesion required.

Her actions, though, were more evidence of the disintegration of the Butler family after Grandpa Isom's death. Acts unthinkable during his lifetime were now the order of their experience.

In addition, a woman married a man who was clearly her equal or superior. Mama had not done that. Except that he was healthy, a hard worker, a non-drinker, and willing to accept her with her children, John Walker had little to offer.

For one thing, he was unlettered. His training was sawmill work, a dirty, dangerous, poorly paid occupation, one doomed for elimination as forests were cut down. His friends, such as they were, were similarly situated, low-paid, uneducated sawmill workers. Like him they would all soon be out of work and on the streets.

So Grandma had been right to question the wisdom of their union. It had been a union made out of desperation, great need on Mama's part for support, a need on John Walker's part for what must have seemed like a family to him. But never having had one, I don't think he realized the weight of a woman and children, even a woman willing to shoulder more than her share of the load.

His male friends did not like him marrying my mother.

"What you doin marryin that woman think she so much? Got them chillun. Man, don't see me in no mess like that. 'n you gi her *all* your money. Man, you a fool. Never ketch me doin nothin like that."

They didn't like it that he could no longer run with them. That he gave his pay to my mother to run the house and put into the store. And the women he had known resented my mother's taking a man, temporarily as it turned out, out of their reach.

So their marriage was being pulled at least two ways: from the Butler side that thought she had married beneath herself; and from John Walker's friends who thought he would be deserting them for a woman who "think she better than us." With their personal differences, which became more apparent the longer they lived together, the looming Great Depression, and their lack of friends in common, their marriage had little chance of success.

His being unlettered put him in a position of inferiority impossible for me as a child to imagine. It was only a dozen years ago, after reading a profile of an unlettered French woman that detailed the dodging she had to do to negotiate her life in Paris, that I got a sense of the enormous psychic—and emotional—burden he was laboring under.

It locked him into a shadowy prison of suspicion and mistrust, not only of those in the outside world, but of us inside his household. What a crusher it must have been to him to have me, a four-year-old, do what he, a grown man, could not. My sisters had taught me my letters; I had taken them and run.

• • •

The store, at first a success, began to be a source of tension. A small operation in what should have been our front room, it filled a need for people, like ourselves, who were not welcomed in Maxwell's. My mother ran the store. My brother was on the floor in a basket. She insisted that people pay cash for what they bought. This practice worked well during the summer and fall, when folk had more money, but not well during the winter. There were fewer jobs for them in winter. Difference developed between my parents because my stepfather insisted on giving credit to his friends, despite my mother's warnings. When the sawmill shut down that winter, laying them all off, we had to close our store.

There was still some stock in the store, and it helped us through the cold months. I remember my stepfather and friends shaking frozen Cokes, and the spray when they took off the caps.

I also remember the smell of roasted rats that my parents used to supplement our diet. Rats would be trapped, skinned, and roasted over a skimpy fire. The smell was unique, unlike any I remember since.

It was during this time that my stepfather had the first of his several leavings, and the only one in which my mother sought to intervene. I remember her standing with my brother cradled in her left arm, holding me with her right hand, at the door of a woman's house where she had been told she would find my stepfather. Responding to her second knock, after a wait, a dark-skinned, heavy-set woman cracked the door. Seeing us there, she opened it a bit more but stood in it, with her hands folded under her apron.

"Just lookin for John Walker."

"Ain't no John Walker heah."

"That ain't what I heard."

"Well, you heard wrong. Ain't no John Walker in heah."

My mother didn't move. The woman pushed the door open more with her foot but stood blocking it. She kept her hands under her apron.

"You think he in heah, you come see for youself."

My mother was no fool. She knew the peril of entering someone's house.

She had contempt for women who fought over men.

"You tell him I was here. Tell him his wife was here."

The woman, as glad as my mother at not forcing a showdown, snickered, "If I see him, I'll tell him."

Not long after this, my aunt Maude came up to help us with the first of our dozen moves, to Goff Avenue, where I would begin school.

Once we were settled, John Walker left his woman and joined us. He came into the house through a back window on a day we had gone to Grandma's farm. He had put a two-by-four ramp to the window, forced it open, and entered. He did not take down the ramp. Seeing it there, I tried to climb it. As it had not been secured, it fell, smashing my face as it did. Except for some blood and a loose tooth, I escaped serious injury.

Mama let him come back, as she was to do for many years. I never knew why she allowed him to do as he did, when there was work and when there was none. Any help he gave was welcomed, especially during the Great Depression, even though this help was meager and sporadic. And it had its costs. Almost to the point of costing her her life. Was it because of the social weight of not having a husband? Why she was so stubborn in letting him back into our life, after so many transparent failures, remains to me one of the mysteries of couples, why people stay together when every visible index indicates they should have long been separated.

• • •

We moved from Russell Street to Goff Avenue, across the street and just down the block from Dunton Memorial School, the public school for blacks.

Goff Avenue was where I first became aware of my little brother as a rival for family affection, and one who was fiercely defended by my aunt Maude when I snatched back something of mine he had taken. "He jus' only a baby. You should be glad to let him play with it. You wasn't using it nohow." Well, I wasn't glad, just a jealous five-and-a-half-year old acting out against his eighteen-month-old brother, who was still being suckled.

I was one of those children who are the despair of those who have to watch over them. I was curious to the point of being nosey. Many is the time my hand was swatted away from something I was not supposed to touch, like a newly starched tablecloth or a new dress. And I was forever climbing, and falling. That I escaped maiming—or worse—before I was twelve, the age my mother set as the outside date for my survival whole, is a miracle of near misses which followed me throughout my life in Orangeburg.

I wanted to do what I saw others do, forever trying things I should not. This penchant got me into more trouble than one could shake a stick at, my mother said. I've told of how I was kicked by the cow and of falling from the two-by-four my stepfather left on a window sill.

I envied my two older sisters and their friends when they played "spin the top" in the street, a game where one participant would start the other spinning. The second one would continue spinning until it was necessary to stop, usually through a threatened loss of balance. I never saw one fall. They never let me play. "You too little. How come you all the time trying to do what you see us do?"

My brother was too little to be of use to me as a playmate, so I often found myself creating my own amusement. I decided one day when I was alone and wanting for something to do that I would try "spinning the top."

My first few spins went well. My early success made me giddy and bolder. I loved to see trees and houses blend into a blur as I whirled myself, twirling away, oblivious of how to stop.

When the girls tired or felt themselves losing balance, they would throw out a leg and lower their center of gravity, gliding to a stop like a great blue heron. I had picked up none of this from watching them. Thus when I tired and began to lose balance, I found myself tripping over my feet, even then too big for my age.

Dazed, I lay on the ground, the world continuing to spin, this time in colors. I don't remember how long I lay there. Again I was lucky, in that, short for my age, I hadn't far to fall. And that the road was dirt, not cement. Lucky, too, that no one in my family had seen me fall. It would have meant a switching. "When're you ever learn you can't do everything you see people do?" rings in my head even as I write.

It was from the Goff Avenue house that I started school, having begged my mother since we lived on Russell Street. After all, if Edith and Leola, my sisters, were going, why couldn't I? "I can read," I insisted. And I could. I had repeated their Latin lessons after them, and had pestered them to teach me the alphabet. I memorized the multiplication table from the back of the tablet they used for their writing. I had an eidetic memory, almost total visual recall.

School meant learning to deal with people other than my family; books, reading, letters and numbers; basement classroom, cement floor; children who wet their pants rather than ask to go to the bathroom. We were afraid of the teacher, who was the first big person we had seen outside of our families who had absolute authority and complete control over us. I, like the others, had been admonished, "Mind your teacher. Do what she tell you. Teacher give you whipping at school, come home you get another one." And they weren't playing. "I send you to that school to learn something, not mess up." "Don't you go there and shame me now, like I ain't taught you no manners, no how to behave."

School also had inside flush toilets, a marvel to me, and water fountains with no "colored" signs on them, though this last meant nothing to me yet.

I took to school like the proverbial rabbit to the cotton patch, a cat to catnip, a duck to water. School was made for me and I for school. There was a place I could show off what I had learned at home. In addition to the letters and numbers I had learned from my sisters, there were the long narrative poems my mother had recited to us that mesmerized me, that I memorized, parts of which I can still recite.

I remember "Poor Deacon Brown," who had lost his "loved and beloved wife" and had been rebuffed by the gruff farm mistress Savannah Simpkins, whom a sly neighbor had sent him to court, and Benjy, the hapless inventor, whose long-suffering wife lived through his many useless inventions: "...locks and clocks and rowing machines, reapers and all such trash / why Benjy invented heaps of them / course, they don't bring in no cash."

Because I had an excellent memory, I easily learned the counties and their county seats, and the states and their capitals, and my side usually won in the weekly Friday spelling bees. My sisters and I played games spelling names of states, countries, and cities that were polysyllabic or had some trick in their pronunciation. We broke them into syllables, and made easily remembered pictures of them. Mississippi, for example, was "Humpback I, crooked letter crooked letter I, crooked letter crooked letter I, pee pee I." Learning was exciting. It was fun.

Because I could read and count, having memorized some numbers from the back of my sisters' composition books, I was moved out of the basement class into a grade on the first floor. I made such rapid progress there that at Christmas they wanted to move me up another grade. My mother wouldn't allow it. She came to the teacher who wanted to move me and told her, "He too little (I was small for my age) to be in there with all them big chilluns."

I agree with her decision not to move me the second time. As it was, I found myself hanging on to the teacher far more than most of my classmates. I remember at a class picnic I had to be directed by a teacher to "Go play, they won't hurt you."

I don't recall my mother ever coming to school again, not even for my high school graduation.

I didn't notice then but remember now that our textbooks were never new, nor our erasers for our chalkboards; that our school had no regular janitor, our schoolyard no play equipment, swings or sliding boards; that our recess play area was packed dirt, not grass; that our play was mostly unsupervised; that there was no school nurse, no doctor to come around at the beginning of the term and test students for communicable diseases, like tuberculosis, and give inoculations. I was busy learning. It would be several years later, when as a ten-year-old I had to walk every day past a newly built school for white children, and see its magnificence when compared to ours, and be taunted by those children, that I began to sense a gross inequity. I hadn't that name for it then, but I had its feeling.

Mr. H. D. Sharperson was the principal of Dunton Memorial. Along with his position as principal, he also taught algebra, which I took when I started high school. From his algebra class, which he taught by rote, what I remember is his repeating, like a mantra, "x times x equals x to the second." I don't remember any discussion of number theory or how algebra might be useful in my life. When I began my higher education at Whitman College many years later, I had not been taught that you couldn't divide by zero. I learned it there.

Mr. Sharperson was what polite folk called a "white man's Negro," while others called him "de buckra's nigger." "He all the time tomming (from Harriet Beecher Stowe's Uncle Tom) de white man, bowin 'n scrapin every time he come 'round." This to the disgust of all who witnessed. His being very dark and round, with skin that shone with perspiration and small eyes, didn't help. He was not a pleasant man to look at.

Mr. A. J. Thackston, the superintendent of the Orangeburg Unified School District, whose office was in the Orangeburg High School (white) building, paid an occasional visit to our school. Had we a band, I am certain it would have been brought out for these occasions. Lacking this, we were made to stand at attention, recite lessons, and sing happy songs. Think of African children going through similar motions when a district colonial administrator visited a school.

Our principal, hired by whites with no say from anyone black, was responsible to them, not to us. Whites had no interest in us having more than a modicum of learning.

"Too much book larnin'll spile th' nigguh. Make'm fit fer nothin. F'rgit his place."

This was the attitude of whites, who wanted loyal, polite, docile, reliable, uncomplaining servants or workers, willing to work long hours in all weather for whatever their masters or mistresses were willing to pay. And it was the attitude of that handful of blacks of the professional class who could afford servants. Too much learning just might help people to begin to sense a different, better order, and to demand it as their right. Such a demand was to come, but later.

Mr. Sharperson was an ideal white man's principal. He kept his teachers in line. He conspired with the superintendent to keep their salaries low. He even refused a raise from ninety dollars a month to one hundred. "Oh, no sir, ninety dollars is fine with me. I can get on nicely with what you pay me." With their principal blocking them, how could *his* teachers complain, though they were paid on average half to two-thirds of what their white counterparts with comparable or less training were paid?

I wasn't aware of any of the contrast between white and black schools at the time. I was too young, had not been out of my neighborhood yet. What I did see was that the red-faced, sandy-haired, smiling white man who visited our school was treated like a god.

Goff Avenue was where my aunt Maude, who was visiting, first warned me against too much reading in the chimney corner by firelight. "You'll be blind as a bat, you keep that up." She threatened to take my book if I didn't put it away. She was right about straining my eyes by reading in dim light, but that was the only kind of light we had after sunset. And I insisted on reading. When in my mid-teens the school finally tested students' eyes, mine needed glasses. For how long they had needed them, I'll never know. What if I had been tested earlier and it was found that I needed glasses? Probably nothing. No money. I remember bending over my school desk to write, my table to eat, and holding my book close to read; but many children did the same. Did we all need glasses? Probably.

Goff Avenue also provided my first contact with the Williams family, whose younger son, John C., was to figure prominently in my later life as "Fes," the boss of the shoe repair shop where I would work. They lived in the house next door, on the side towards the school. There were four of them: the father, daughter Blondell, and sons Joshua and John. The mother had left the father, "gone North," a move not sanctioned by the community, and left them as objects of pity, and by some, contempt. This was the talk we heard.

For a man's wife to leave him, there must be something wrong with him. For a woman to "desert" her three children, shame on her. So despite that they were light-skinned, light enough to "pass" for white in the dark, and that Mr. Williams had put both his sons through college, daughter Blondell having gone North to live with her mother, they never were fully accepted by the elite light-skinned blacks on the "Gold Coast," a section in the far eastern edge of town inhabited by mostly black professionals and "old money" blacks established in business or industry.

John felt this lack of acceptance in an especially cruel way. After graduating with honors from Claflin University, he tried to marry Maxine Sultan, his college sweetheart and daughter of one of the Gold Coasters. Her father was said to own, among other holdings, a lumberyard. The young lady was willing, her parents were not. Respecting her parents' wishes, she married a man acceptable to them, and moved away.

The Williams children were good to our family. As they were in their mid-teens, they were not playmates, but they spoke to us and chatted with us. And on Christmas Eve, they surprised us with a most welcome large bag of fruit, nuts, and toys. In the bag was our first board of Chinese checkers.

I remember the Goff Avenue house as the place where I got my first look into the world of sex, by way of my sisters and other girls their age playing "doctor" and "husband and wife." In the latter play, sister Edith would roll up the front of her dress into a simulated penis. Though I was allowed to be audience, I was never allowed to play.

"You too little," was the answer I got when I asked.

So I had to wait.

Claflin's women's dormitory was between our house and the university. I watched young women cross the street in the mornings and return in the afternoons and early evenings. It was my first sustained look at people that age.

CHAPTER THREE

My Finest Shoes

Aged nine years already my feet took
a small man's shoe. "Steamboats,"
my companions derided; "battleships," I countered.

That Carolina winter I walked to school
barefoot, bragging hollowly that my boats
were tougher than those of my schoolmates
whose shoes had soles on them.

Widowed and wizened Mrs. Gissentana
saw me pass her house.
Explosive, five-two like my mother,
alert to her young neighbor's plight.

Came to our house with hands
in her apron, "That boy feet cold."
"He want to go to school."
"What you go do, you go let him freeze?"
"I'mmo put me on his feet?"

Alone, burdened with four (rheumatic
fever hadn't freed my other sister yet)
under twelve, what was she to do?

"I'mmo take him with me to Silver's."
My mother threw a look at me,
saw my eagerness to go downtown.
Tear proud she nodded her agreement.

Mr. Silver (changed from Silverstein) sold
used clothing from New York. Noticing
Mrs. Gissentana examining a pair
of walking shoes, he hurried over.

My boy,
back to college
left these
hardly worn.
75 cents too much?"

Mrs. Gissentana snorted.

My finest shoes had been worn
by a small Jewish man.

My childhood could well be told as a "Tale of the Houses," each
with its own story. It would not be an overstatement to say that my
family moved a lot. From Goff we moved to Oak, from there to
Peasley, where we lived in two houses, Treadwell to Fair to Gibson
Hill...Moving so often had its headaches, and its heartaches. There
must have been something good in it but I remember mostly its down
side. Like when we moved from Oak Street to Peasley Street. Though
a mere block away, it meant piling our household goods on a wagon
rented to us by friends of my mother—as my stepfather had no
friends he brought to the house—battling mushy cold, and possibly
losing my friends from down the far end of our block. Plus breaking
something valuable, our kitchen stove.

From Reverend to Reverend to Doctor. From Reverend Taylor's house on Oak to Reverend Simons' on Peasley to Dr. Rowe's shotgun on Fair Street. All in all, we lived in seven houses in less than three years.

In none of these houses was there electricity, an inside toilet, or inside running water. Our Gibson Street house shared a spigot with three houses. The closest we came to inside water was a spigot at the back porch of our second Broad Street house. We lived on paved streets three times, on Railroad Corner, Treadwell Street, and Broughton Street. In colored neighborhoods unpaved streets with no sidewalks were the rule. And few of the houses were wired. An outhouse out back was the standard toilet.

During the depth of the Great Depression we moved not to better houses but to cheaper ones, to places where the landlord either took pity on my mother and her children or believed her when she said that she would somehow make the rent.

Reverend Taylor of the Oak Street house and my stepfather had a falling out over rent after my stepfather told him he would have it at a certain time, then didn't show. When my stepfather finally did pay him, they made up, temporarily.

Reverend Taylor was a generously proportioned light-brown-skinned man, my stepfather short, slight, and dark. On the day they made up, my stepfather apologized for having lied. His rent safely pocketed, the reverend attempted to console him by admitting, "Everybody tells lies sometimes. Even me."

My stepfather looked incredulous.

"Oh, I've told some of the biggest lies," the reverend assured him, and reared back and let out a huge laugh. Not long after, we moved to Peasley Street.

But our Oak Street house holds memories of my brief foray into four-letter words; my hearing the Harlem accent of a boy down for the summer and adopting the accent so well for the next school term that I told my playmates, "I spent the summah in Noo Yawk," and they appeared to believe me.

I had learned the cuss words and was displaying my knowledge of them on the way to school one morning, trying to outdo my schoolmates, when a passing teacher called a halt. A chorus of boasting, swearing boys was instantly reduced to a choir of little black and brown angels. We knew that if Miss Addie Winningham stopped on her way home and told any of our parents that we had been using foul speech, they would set our tails on fire.

I liked wandering around the grounds of Claflin University, especially on Saturdays, when no students were on campus. Peering into the window of what must have been a science laboratory, I saw my first skeleton. It came as a shock, those bleached bones. I didn't feel any connection between them and me.

One Saturday morning I ran into the campus electrician, with a large strand of wire coiled over his left shoulder, a smaller one in his right hand. He was wearing a canvas belt from which hung many tools. Handing me the smaller coil, he asked if I'd like to be his assistant. He was putting some wiring in the gymnasium. For the dime I'd earn, I eagerly accepted. I was to hand him tools and run errands.

This job, like many I was to have during my boyhood, was short-lived. Before the morning was over, I was in the infirmary, with the nurse putting Vaseline on a scar under my right eye. I had stood under the ladder looking up while my electrician was soldering a light connection, and a drop of liquid solder had fallen on my cheek. Except that the burn hurt, the electrician had been more upset than I. He knew that another fraction of an inch would have seriously damaged my eye. So did Mama when he carried me home. When the circumstances had been explained, she thanked the electrician for his concern, and forbade my wandering the campus "until you get sense enough to know what you doing."

One more near miss stands out on Oak Street. I fell out of a pecan tree at the fence between our house and that of landlord Reverend Taylor. I missed the fence but not by much. Some scratches and soreness were the sum of that incident. My poor mother applied Vaseline to the scratches and shook her head. I would not make twelve alive, she was sure of it.

But the incident that stands out most in my mind from the Oak Street house happened the night my stepfather attempted to shoot my mother.

He had moved over with us from Goff Avenue. The highway division was tarring US 21 through Orangeburg and north and west towards Columbia, the state capital. Black men were hired to do the digging and heavy lifting, supervised by whites. Some of these men lived in a rooming house around the corner on Railroad Avenue.

My mother, ever on the lookout for ways to provide for us, took in some of the men as boarders. She fed them dinner and packed lunches for them when they worked too far away to come to the house. She provided them plentifully with good solid food—she'd had experience feeding her brothers on the farm—and they were grateful. It was always Miz Maggie this and Miz Maggie that, "Miz Maggie, you sho can cook." They paid promptly and well. She was pleased. Her girls helped with preparation and serving, with an occasional boost from Aunt Maude, who by this time had married and moved to Orangeburg.

It was a busy but happy time. We all had enough to eat. My sisters were promised new dresses for school. A happy time for all but my stepfather, that is. It bothered him to see my mother so much the center of attention, surrounded by all these strange men, so independent of him. Because he couldn't express himself, he sat on the back steps and pouted. I can't imagine his fantasies, but they must have been huge. And they were enhanced by a romance that developed between one of the highway workers and one of my mother's friends, Mrs. Edna Berry, wife of Felton.

Mrs. Berry was Yoruba handsome; the man she selected equally so. I figured in their liaison as message bringer. One night after dinner she gave me a quarter to take a note to him, "and wait for an answer." When she bent over to hand me the note in the soft dark, I could feel the heat of woman flesh and smell the aroma of cinnamon.

My stepfather did not drink, so he had to be stone sober the night he made his botched attempt on his wife's life. She was in the front room at her ironing board. I was asleep on my pallet in a corner against the wall. She was ironing by the usual dim light, which cast a weak shadow on the wall beyond her. I awoke to voices. Apparently they had been going on for some time. He was standing just inside the door, holding a bright object that he was pointing at my mother.

The weak light only showed me part of his face. As he was black in the gloom, I couldn't make out his features. I lay still, watching.

"Woman, I got unuf uh you'n yo foolishness. Tryna make a fool outta me."

My mother was calm, as calm as I'd ever seen her.

"I been tryin to tell you. What you gon do, you go ahead and do. You play the fool."

I heard a click. No sound. Another click. Still no sound. He took the pistol, looked at it, shook it at her, and left. Reprieved, she continued with her ironing. How long I stayed awake after he left, I don't remember, but eventually I slept.

Next morning, playing under the house, I found the pistol, a nickel-plated .38 caliber. He had hidden it near the chimney. Though I don't remember ever having seen a pistol before—my uncles had rifles—my haste to get it to my mother blocked what would have been my normal curiosity. I didn't examine it, but carried it by its barrel directly to my mother. She took it without a word. How she disposed of it, I never knew. She did have friends who knew about guns. I never talked with my mother or with anyone else about that night.

As an adult, I put it in a note, to be developed should I ever write about my life or about my mother's. Other than that, it has lain buried until now. It is possible that because I was so young, between seven and eight years old, and had been asleep while their argument was developing, I did not receive the emotional impact of what was taking place. Neither of them shouted, perhaps not to awaken my two sisters, asleep in the next room. Mama had not shown fear. I had never seen a pistol, had no clue to what they did. I had no sense of what it meant to kill a human being, had never seen one dead. I had seen headless chickens run wildly and drop, rabbits skinned and gutted, a hog stunned with an ax, a dead snake next to its hole, but never a dead human. I did not know that humans died. This I was to learn too soon thereafter.

During the summer of 1930, when she was cooking for the men who were tarring the highway, Mama had bought a new kerosene stove. Blue-black shiny, it glistened. With its oven and two burners and gray-green upside-down glass tank, which held the kerosene, it was something to behold. I loved watching the fuel work its way down from the top into the well that cupped it, making a musical gurgle, a soft gurrump as gravity pulled it to its flaming death.

None of the several men helping noticed that the tank was detachable, so no one took it out or secured it. The stove had been put on last, at the rear of the open wagon. I was seated on a mattress near it, my cold fingers dug in. On the first bump after the wagon started, the stove jiggled, tipping out the tank. I watched, frozen, as it fell, in seeming slow motion, first to the flat bed, then a little way to the newly surfaced road below.

The men blamed each other for their oversight and were fearful, knowing my mother would be furious over their carelessness. And she was. She didn't swear at them, as that was not her way. But she chided, "I thought yenna was going to take care uh my things. You know I ain't got no money to buy no more."

"Miz Maggie, we sorry…"

"Sorry don't git it. Sorry don't buy me no stove tank."

The magnitude of the loss she experienced can be realized if we remember that she had spent the money she got from feeding the men on new clothes for her four children, better food for them, a few new pieces of furniture, and that very stove. Her husband had just lost his job at the sawmill, she had no training in anything but housekeeping (and farming, a skill useless in town). It was in the dead of a nasty winter.

As was typical of her, she had spent next to nothing on herself, this despite the urging of her fashion-conscious friend, Mrs. Edna Berry:

"Girl, you better get something for yourself, now. That road gon be built before you know it."

"Got to take care of these chilluns," was all Mama would say in answer.

She didn't have money to buy a new stove tank (nor had the men), as we were literally out of the money economy for the next two years.

Loss of the stove tank created a job for eight-year-old me, feeding the stove. While before I could happily watch the kerosene move onto its well, it was now my job to stand at the stove and feed it as needed. If I daydreamed, allowing the well to go empty, the stove went out. If I held the oil can wrong, oil spilled, drawing sharp words from the cook. I learned to hate this job, and by extension the men whose carelessness had made it necessary.

I would like to say that Oak Street was the end of my stepfather's involvement with our family. It was not. Through what means I have no idea, my mother and stepfather made it up. He joined us at Peasley I, remained with us through both Peasley I and II, was away through Treadwell, Fair Street, and Gibson Hill. Joined us again on Railroad Corner, the year I became twelve. For all practical purposes, Railroad Corner was his last contact with us. He made an aborted attempt at the first of our Broad Street houses several years later.

• • •

Peasley I was located on the lower side of the street, across from the house of the landlord, Reverend Willie Simons. Reverend Simons was a widower. He no longer commanded a parsonage, but occasionally carried his gospel message to country churches throughout the county. At the west edge of the lot was the Ditch (the only name I heard it called, though its formal name was Sunny Side Canal), which wound from somewhere north and east beyond Goff, was culverted at Railroad Avenue, open at the bottom where Oak dead-ended, open and covered at various streets as it snaked its way, wider in some places and narrower in others, to a point above the public white people swimming pool in the slow-moving Edisto River.

Reverend Simons' was the first house I had access to where there were books other than the ones my sisters read to me. I am sure there were books in the Williams' house on Goff Avenue, but I don't remember entering it. The only book in our house, other than my sisters' schoolbooks, or any house I remember entering, was the Holy Bible. The reverend's library consisted of several Bibles, other religious texts and pamphlets, tracts on how to succeed and how to make money. These last were yellowed, musty, and stained, suggesting age and use.

What intrigued me most were the Bibles, with their gilt-edged leaves, and the books of Bible stories. These latter contained full-page color illustrations with scenes of pink people wrapped in white sheets with one shoulder bare. They had wings growing out of their shoulders and seemed to be suspended on clouds. There were rays of light all around them, coming from someplace in the clouds. In one scene there was a man with long hair holding a long stick with a crook at its end. In front of him were a small sheep and a kneeling woman. In another, there was a man who looked like this first one but with big nails in his arms and wire wrapped around his head. He was nailed to this post shaped like a capital T, and blood was dripping from his arms. Some women were kneeling in front of him, too. I wondered who these pink people were, and how they could fly.

There were scenes of horses pulling a flying wagon, and a huge ship with a plank, with animals I had never seen walking up the plank in twos. I especially liked what I later learned were the giraffes, because of their tall legs and long necks. I wondered how the animals and people were going to fit on that ship, even one that big. And I wondered how the man could breathe inside that huge fish.

My questions were answered after a fashion when as a ten-year-old I was sent to a summer Bible school. I was told that it was not a small sheep but a lamb, and that the man holding it was Jesus, who loved us so much he died on the cross to save us from our sins. The kneeling woman was his mother, Mary. The man sitting on the big steps covered with all those blankets and the light behind him was God, and those pink people with streaming hair and sheets and wings growing out of their shoulders were God's angels. The Holy Bible was the Word of God. What we read there was the gospel truth, to be taken on faith.

"But Mama, what is faith? 'n where God is?"

"God in heaven, that's where…"

"But Mama…"

"Hush up, A. D., and mem'rize your verses. You ast too doggone many questions."

I had a dog one summer. He appeared from nowhere, a scraggly mongrel, older than a puppy, a young dog. He adopted me and I accepted him. Mama said I could keep him if I kept him outside. I ran with him up and down the street, happy to share with him what

I had. I hadn't thought of a name for him yet when he became rabid, foaming at the mouth and running in crazy patterns over the yard. When he died, my stepfather wouldn't let me touch him, but buried him where he died, down near the Ditch. There was never another pet in our house.

•   •   •

My exploration of Reverend Simons' library was for rainy days; sunny days were spent playing in the street, especially with marbles. I shot well for my age, holding my own with other eight- and nine-year-olds. I began to think I was pretty hot stuff. There was a flat walk between our front steps and the street where we played. One afternoon when I was alone on the front steps, a twelve-year-old girl swaggered by, on her way home from Claflin University's private elementary school. She was Dr. Rowe's daughter Grace, she told me, from Treadwell Street. One of her dress pockets was nearly full, she wanted to play. I had never seen a girl who shot marbles. It was a boy's game. Despite the evidence in her dress pocket, I took her on. So we played.

Well, she played; I watched. She won every round, from all distances. In less time than I cared to know, she had cleaned me out, completely. Losing that way was a new experience for me, and a painful one. I had few pennies to buy marbles with, depending on my winnings to keep me supplied. I was left with not even a single taw to trade. As she confidently pocketed my last agate, I detected a sneer of contempt. As though I had been a fool, which I had been, to challenge her. As she swaggered away with her tomboy walk, I turned toward the steps, doing everything I could to keep from crying.

I never played her again. But I did improve over time. Marbles were one way to get acquainted. On almost any street, there would be a boy willing to play. Race was not a barrier. When I quit playing as I entered my teens—I had discovered "Famous Funnies" and "Tip Top Comics"—I had graduated to the big boys' circle under the giant oak at the corner of Russell and Windsor Streets. In head-to-head matches I never ever cleaned anyone out without leaving them with at least a favorite taw.

• • •

There were no ghosts in any of our houses. But there were many in my head and in my dreams. They came from stories by the fireside told by men—it was usually men—who recounted harrowing encounters with sperits and hants that shrieked on rainy nights. Almost always it was a wild rainy night, unless there was a full moon. Sperits of superhuman strength that cast aside the most ferocious of hunting dogs like they were puppies, sending them away yelping with their tails between their legs. I wondered if they would do the same to Gyp and Kaalo, our dogs at Grandma's farm. I didn't want them hurting Gyp and Kaalo. The sperits arrested a double team of mules and the occasional horse as they attempted to cross a stream deep in the woods. Mighty were those sperits. So mighty that only a silver bullet or a Bible verse could vanquish them. The storyteller was always alone during these encounters.

Hants inhabited cemeteries, sperits the woods and fields. A typical scene: winter night's oak fire. Parched peanuts, with sweet potatoes buried in the ashes. Anyone holding forth:

"'n I was riding ol' Henry down Goose Branch way. That thing grab Henry, shake him lak a raggedy doll. Henry rear up on his hind legs. Nigh turned around. I took out my .44 'n empty it."

"You git um?" chorus from listeners.

"Ain't hurt that durn thing a lick."

"What you do?"

"Jesus wept!"

"That'll git um ev'ry time." A sigh of relief from the chorus.

They knew the story, knew about the dogs being "shook like a pile o' rags." They knew the ending, the only possible ending, since none of them had a silver bullet. They also knew to use the shortest verse in the Bible. Pure theater.

But it was all new to me, balled up in a corner of the hearth, entranced by the stories, hating to leave the dwindling fire, shivering and shaking, to go to a cold room and a pallet on the floor, my little brother sleeping with Mama. To a cold pallet and my dreams.

I would be in this dark house with high ceilings (none of our houses had high ceilings) that extended beyond where I could see. I would be wandering through rooms in this house until I came into an area suffused with light, the light shimmering. I knew that this was the *hant*. Or, I would be walking through a wooded path, going downhill through high bushes. Suddenly one of the bushes on the right side of the path would begin to shake and become bright with this light. Again, the sperit. Frightened, I always woke up immediately after these encounters.

In my waking life, between the back of our Peasley I house and Railroad Avenue, there was an abandoned white cemetery, a shortcut between Peasley and Railroad Avenue. Some of its graves dated from before the U.S. Civil War. One stood out: "Melissa Higgenbottom, 1832–1864, In Loving Memory." While I could make out the "Melissa," it took big sister Edith to get the family name for me. We played hide and seek among the tombstones and the oaks during the daytime, among decayed slabs, grass-covered headstones, and a baby grave, but steered clear of it at night. So fearful was I of its hants and sperits that one night, after spending the afternoon until dusk at Aunt Maude's, across town, I went four blocks out of my way to avoid it.

I did learn to use the shortcut, after Edith, four years older than I, forced me to walk it one night to show me "There ain't nothing in there to hurt you. Them white people dead, A. D." First she walked through it with me. Then she made me walk it alone. I was free of hants until once in my mid-teens I was walking home by the colored Orangeburg Cemetery, founded 1889, on Bull Street one warm windless night. I came upon something white moving slowly along the ground in front of me. I felt no breeze, how could this be? My skin crept up my neck. I stopped. The Thing kept moving. Something of my sister Edith must have rushed through my brain. I leaped on the Thing. It was a piece of toilet tissue! The air near the ground was cooler than the air above, enough to create a slight current, just enough to push the tissue along. It was with much relief that I continued on home.

• • •

My unlettered stepfather's curiosity about what was in my mother's letters from her relatives finally got the better of him. One day when she was away at work, he held out one of them to my sisters:

"Here, tell me what in this."

When neither of them reached for it, he handed it to Leola, the younger one, saying, "Read it!" Leola, her head turned down and away, handed it to Edith. Edith took it by its edges, pulled out a single sheet, and smoothed it out on her dress. The letter was pencil written. I recognized Aunt Cather Lee's big-loop down-slanted cursive script.

She peered at it, as though trying to make it out.

"Tell me what it say." He was looking intently at her.

"'Hello all. We got a lot of rain. Be good everybody.'" She stopped.

"That all? Nuthin bout me in there?" he asked, with a rising voice.

Shaking her head, she handed the sheet to him, as though to say, "If you don't believe me, read it yourself." She knew full well he couldn't.

When she handed it to him, I realized that she had been holding the paper upside down. Even upside down, I saw many more lines than what she read. I think he, too, thought so, but was powerless to say what he thought. With a puzzled look he put the letter back in Mama's drawer, the three of us with our six eyes looking at him.

"Yawl kin go play."

We immediately broke for the outside, the girls to the front yard and hopscotch, I to the outhouse in back to relieve myself of the pressure on my bladder. What he hadn't known was that I would have read the letter to him. I loved to show off my skill at reading and, unlike my older sisters, had developed no sense of privacy, of "Mama's things."

• • •

Aunt Cather Lee had come up bringing some welcome meat, vegetables, and eggs from the farm, stay awhile and be introduced to Reverend Simons. With the Great Depression extending itself, resulting in almost no money coming in, we needed every mouthful of food we could find, from any source. The U.S. government had begun distributing surplus foods, the kinds and amounts varying with sections of the country. In the South, food was distributed according to race; and within race, according to class and caste. Whites, who received all of the food and controlled central distribution, gave themselves more, as did the elite light-skinned blacks who controlled distribution for us poor blacks.

Mama, too proud to stand in the half-block-long lines at the black-run state college, our distribution point, sent Edith and me for the government-issue flour and the occasional tin of beef. Some people had walked miles for the food. Mr. Rhodes, the mulatto man in charge of distribution, seemed harassed by the sheer volume of work the handling entailed.

It was the *best* flour. Unbleached, the entire wheat kernel had been ground with all the vitamins intact. No need to take out and add anything; it was all there. It made true wonder bread. Wonderfully delicious. We loved its taste hot from the oven.

Reverend Simons, being a minister, was allowed a freedom in our house not granted ordinary acquaintances. He could enter even when Mama was absent. It was on one of these occasions that he seduced, or raped, Aunt Cather Lee, with a predictable result. He made her pregnant. When she told Mama, Mama was angry. But what could she do? This was a Man of God. To whom could these two poor black women make their claim? And to what end?

Aunt Cather Lee had come to Orangeburg, at a time when my stepfather was not with us, "to help you with these chilluns." She was an open, gentle woman, with a sly humor, a comic sense of herself and the world. She could make people laugh. Orangeburg was not to prove kind to her.

"I didn't know nuthin bout no man," she tearfully told Mama.

"I believe you, child," my mother said.

Within a week we had moved up the street to Peasley II.

• • •

Peasley II was a few houses up the street on the same side, on slightly higher ground, with the Ditch forming the back boundary to the property. Peasley I had been set back from the street, with that flat space where Grace Rowe had cleaned me out of marbles. Peasley II was only a few yards from the street. You walked up three steps to a shallow porch, then entered the front room. The property was on a slight slope, as had been the Oak Street property, so that there was space under the house to play. Or to do one's business, if it was too cold of a morning to go to the outhouse, situated near the Ditch.

I remember Peasley II for a lot of reasons. It was there that I began to go out into the wider world, and earned my third money, another quarter. A white widow woman on Amelia Street paid me this and magazines she had read for mowing a small front lawn and combing and brushing her hair. I was proud to bring money into the house. A quarter could buy five pounds of rice. This when the only money coming into the house was the seventy-five cents a week my older sister earned from work in a white woman's house after school. I was nine years old, my sister Edith was thirteen.

Our destitute state no doubt contributed to my out-of-work stepfather's stealing a chicken from our well-off next-door neighbor. This mulatto family lived behind a high fence, so that few ever saw them. I remember peeking through the fence and seeing a very pale, white-haired woman at a window. This woman sometimes let out a piercing scream, which is what attracted my curiosity about what was going on beyond that fence. The neighbor missed his chicken, a Rhode Island Red hen, and suspected my stepfather of the theft. He even came to our front door and asked if we had taken his chicken.

Of course my stepfather denied it. And my mother, to her mortification, could not contradict him. While she herself would never steal from anyone, she couldn't turn in her husband for trying to feed his family in the only way he saw open to him. It was winter, a cold one. The neighbor had a big yard full of chickens. I don't know how he would have felt had my stepfather been more selective. But I suppose darkness and the need for haste didn't allow this. In any event, the neighbor let us off with a warning that he was "keeping an eye" on us, and that any other theft would result in unspecified dire consequences. I am almost certain that this episode contributed to our moving to Treadwell Street. That and a string of deaths. In some regions of West Africa people bury their dead inside the family compound and mark the spot with an upside-down bowl. When enough bowls appear, they vacate the compound and establish it elsewhere, as we did after the deaths started to pile up.

A then-pregnant Aunt Cather Lee had moved with us to Peasley II. She was the first of several pregnant women my mother allowed to stay with us until their time. Aunt Cather Lee was never to know motherhood. Some months into her pregnancy, she started bleeding. Despite my mother's efforts, she aborted her fully formed fetus. When she had recovered sufficiently, she retreated to the farm, to her mother and younger brother, Uncle Johnny having married and moved away. Except for an occasional visit, she never returned to Orangeburg. And she never had another child.

During that time the teen-aged daughter of a neighbor two doors away was dying of tuberculosis. We children were not told that it was contagious, so we played in and out of their house. I remember Authorene, the daughter, as having thin arms and large eyes. She had a slight cough, with sputum she spit into a cup she set on a stool near the head of her bed.

At the opposite end of the weight spectrum was the neighbor who died of dropsy. We children would see Mrs. Bell sitting on her front porch, usually asleep, no doubt because the porch was more comfortable than the tiny rooms of her house. Once in a while, she would ask one of us children to get her a cold bottled drink from the store.

"Be sure to get me a Nehi, now. You remember?"

"Yesm, Miz Bell."

"Now hurry on back, now."

We'd be on our way before she finished speaking.

We would do it, because an adult neighbor asked us to, but reluctantly. Her swollen body repulsed us. We wondered if by close association we might not become like her. We too might catch what she had and swell up and die.

From Peasley II I remember not only the dying but also the playing. In the streets mostly, especially in the cool of early summer evenings. One evening at dusk I was sent to tell my sisters to come in. In the group of children there was a bigger boy who wanted them to keep playing. They lingered. I told them I was going home and would tell Mama that I had told them. This made the boy mad. When I got across the street in front of our house, he picked up part of a brick and threw it at me, striking me on my left knee. Lucky for me, much of the energy of the brick's flight was spent by the time it reached me. "None uh yo damn business," he shouted at me, then ran away. My knee was sore but not damaged. My sisters got a dressing down from Mama.

Another bigger boy talked me into attempted sodomy. He told me he'd give me a nickel if I'd let him do something to me "that won't hurt you." Eager for money, I agreed. He told me to lie face down and he would get on top of me. I expressed apprehension. "You want your nickel or not?"

"Course I want my nickel."

"Then lay down and hold still."

I lay still for a short while, then moved. Angered, he got up and accused me of "messing with him," and threatened me. I was confused. I hadn't asked him to do anything. I had never heard of what he was asking me to do. Finding me unsuitable, he never asked me again. I don't remember being sorry, except for not getting the promised nickel.

Years later, while I was a golf caddy, the older of two deaf mute brothers was sent to state prison for sexual molestation. Sodomy. The case was murky. We could never get anything clear about it. I remember feeling dreadful when the sheriff took "Dummy" away. He looked like he didn't know what was happening to him. As orphans the two brothers had only one another. To take one was like taking a bird's mate. "Big Dummy," the younger, was lost without his older brother.

● ● ●

Once on Peasley Street, to my surprise, our stepfather took me fishing with him and two of his friends. That had not been his habit. Always happy to go somewhere, I sat out on the edge of the street, near a tree, to wait for them. I sat too near an ant's nest. Hardly had I seated myself when ants were crawling over my legs, in my pants, and up my back. I danced around, beating myself with my hands, trying to shake them off. My stepfather came out.

"Boy, you ain't got sense enough to stay outta ant nest. Git on back in the house."

After my mother had shaken the ants out of my clothes and put Vaseline on my stings, I followed my stepfather and his two friends into Edisto swamp were they fished. I don't remember their catch. I remember stepping over roots, spongy moss underfoot, pushing aside branches, swatting mosquitoes, and keeping an eye out for feces on the path. While the men were fishing, I wandered away, fascinated by a brightly colored water snake traveling near the riverbank. It disappeared under some tree roots that extended into the water. My stepfather did not take me anywhere with him again for a long time.

It was on Peasley II that Mrs. Gissentana, a neighbor woman older than my mother, took me downtown and bought me a pair of shoes. I had been going to school barefoot. One morning when I passed her house, she had asked me where were my shoes. I had hedged, wanting to tell her that my shoes were in my house. She had apparently seen me before. On my way back from school, she accompanied me home.

With the barest of greetings, she got to the purpose of her visit.

"You let this boy go barefoot in this weather."

"What I'mmo do, he wanta go to school."

"He got to have shoes. It too cold out there."

"I'mmo put *me* on his feet?"

"Well, he can't be out there like that. I'm taking him to Silver's."

Mrs. Gissentana lived alone. Behind a low fence her yard was full of flowers, and there was always something growing in her garden. She shared what she grew. Vegetables were one thing to accept. These the two women could exchange. My mother too kept a garden. But shoes? Her brothers on the farm had gone barefoot to school during the winter. Shoes were saved for Sunday and church. She also knew that people in town wore shoes when it was cold. I think she didn't want to have to admit that she was unable to put school shoes on her child. She hesitated. I tugged on her apron. She looked down at me. Saw I wanted to go.

"All right. You kin go. But you mind Miz Gissentana, you hear me?"

I skipped along with Mrs. Gissentana, sometimes running ahead, so eager was I to go downtown. Silver's was a Jewish-owned used clothing store. My shoes, worn by a boy in New York, cost seventy-five cents. When we got back to my house, my mother appeared to have made her peace with herself.

"The Lord will add a star to your crown," she told a smiling Mrs. Gissentana, who was not one to smile often.

• • •

My sisters played with me but also liked to tease me. When it rained while the sun was shining, they told me that if I took a smoked glass and looked between a crack in the door, I could see the devil beating his wife. I dutifully did as I was told. Something must have been wrong with my eyes, said my laughing sisters, when I told them I didn't see anything. And they would shut me out the back door at night, telling me that the ghosts out back would get me. I would have to bang on the door loud enough to attract adult attention before they would let me in.

Leola was my favorite sister. She was funny and generous with whatever she had. She always shared with me. I could talk with her. She was the one person in the family who took the time to try to understand me. When they teased me Leola was first to stop. "That's nuff now," when Edith persisted. "Why are you such a silly boy?" she would sometimes ask me, her eyes twinkling. "Why are you such a silly girl?" I would ask her. This was always a signal for a race around the house. When she caught me, as she always did, she would grab me and whirl me around, laughing as I squealed with pleasure.

Ten times smarter than I was, or so I thought, Leola would plop herself on the floor and drag me down to show me things in whatever she was studying. She would point out places in her geography book, making me name countries and rivers, and products various places were known for. All in different colors. There were pictures of people standing on their countries, sometimes holding fruit.

Indirectly she got me realizing that the five races whites taught us in their books were a lot of hokum, a failure of the white men's eyes to see what was before them. "Miss Jenkins got Indian in her and she not red, she almost black as me." Leola was middle chocolate brown. "Mr. Lee (who owned the laundry), he brown, 'n his wife whiter than them white folk. They red-faced." I remembered the pink people in the Bible stories, "white" people with wings. I had not worked for the white woman over on Amelia Street yet, but I had seen a white-faced old woman next door. They were a "colored" family. That fact threw me a curve that I struck out on, but it started me looking at people around me more closely.

Leola got sick with rheumatic fever when she was eleven years old.

My mother worked over her several days into the night, trying what she knew of herbs and roots, making broths and poultices, sponging her feverish face and chest; praying when it seemed other remedies were failing her.

As she had run out of remedies, Mama sent me for Dr. Crawford. He was one of four colored doctors: he and Drs. Green and Rowe, medical doctors; and Dr. McTeer, a dentist. Four doctors for more than four thousand town people, plus those country folk who were able to get into town. If you were in the countryside needing medical care you couldn't get from a midwife or traditional doctor, you cured yourself or you died.

Colored people could go to white doctors, of which there were many more; but those who went had to wait for hours, sometimes days, while the white doctors served their white patients. And they had to wait in a separate waiting room, entered by a separate door, with a sign saying "colored waiting room in the rear." The waiting rooms for whites were furnished with stuffed sofas, coffee tables with magazines and newspapers, those for blacks with a few plain straight-backed chairs. Despite the inconvenience and the indignity suffered, some colored people still went to them, even preferring them to the black doctors, whom they felt didn't know what they were doing. Some even thought the black doctors to be "stuck up." Mama was not one of those.

Dr. Crawford came at once, at the end of a long day of work. A young, rotund, bespectacled, light-skinned man, Dr. Crawford was the most recent of our doctors to set up practice. He was newly out of medical college and, with his family, a welcome addition to our medical corps. He was cheery despite his hard day.

He poked at Leola, listened to her chest with his stethoscope; and after asking my mother how long she had been suffering, diagnosed her illness as rheumatic fever.

"Will she die, Doctor?"

Dr. Crawford took off his spectacles, wiped them with a handkerchief he took out of his trousers pocket, and looked at Mama. "With the help of the Good Lord, Miz Maggie, we'll pull her through."

With that bit of optimism, he wrote out a prescription, laughed a little laugh, then left. As Mama had no money with which to fill the prescription, it lay on the fireplace mantelpiece.

And Leola lay there, small and frail, looking with trusting eyes for Mama to save her, to make her well.

"Leola s-s-neep, Mama?" I stuttered from my pallet, as she sat with head bowed, holding my sister's hands.

"Yes, baby, Leola sleep."

• • •

Death was not a subject poor people talked about. Perhaps the reason was that there were so many deaths, often of children. People cried at funeral services and at gravesides. Maybe they felt that was enough emotion to show. Not even Edith, and the two sisters had been inseparable, ever said to me, "Do you ever miss Leola? I know I do." I missed Leola dearly.

I could not fathom the permanent absence death brought, and for a long time I expected Leola to appear from wherever she had gone. Sleeping in the same room with her during her illness, I was intimately involved in her passing.

I was devastated. Not so much by her death, which I still did not fully understand, but her absence, which I did.

Deaths were becoming a frequent occurrence. In short order, there had been Aunt Cather Lee's stillbirth, Mrs. Bell's dropsy, Authorene's tuberculosis, now Leola's rheumatic fever. Deaths due to the diseases of poverty and ignorance. She was only eleven years old when she died. I was eight. Little was known then about a disease that today is hardly more serious than bronchitis. Few people die of it now, but this fact did not save my sister.

Mama was alone with us three children, Aunt Cather Lee having gone back to the farm, our stepfather on one of his times away. We moved to Treadwell Street soon after.

CHAPTER FOUR

Night on the Town

Public space belonged to white folk.
Big black folk knew this and cleared
out of it at night. Little black folk
didn't know it yet, and, by keeping quiet,
slipped under the radar of whites' scorn.

"Cute little nigger," they sometimes said.
They gave me a penny as they rubbed my head.
(Lore had it that "rubbing a little nigger's head"
made dice fall seven-eleven. A *little* nigger.)

We had no electric lights where we lived,
the nearest were five blocks away
on a white people street. So, for me,
sneaking into bright downtown at night
was like creeping from a deep forest
into a savanna. Lions and leopards
may lurk there, but oh, how gaudy!

My mother knew about public space.
Her "Stay out from under white folk's feet"
circled between my ears on warm nights when
I wandered streets where lighted windows
held electric trains perpetually

entering and exiting tunnels,
scoop that swung down, picked up sand,
dumped it on red truck's flat bed,
then swung back for more.

I feel a rip at my shoulder as a finger pulls at
an unmended tear in my shirt. I see a reflection
of two white men behind me. My older sister works
after school for one man's wife, cleaning,
washing and ironing clothes by hand,
handing her things she can well get herself.
I do not think he knows me, but I see him
evenings when I go to their house
to walk my sister home.

I feel hot air, hear laughter
as they walk away, turn to see one
punching the arm of the other.

"You are eight years old," I can hear my mother
through my tears. "You old enough to know right
from wrong. How many times have I got to tell you,
stay out of them streets at night. You know I got
no money to buy thread to fix that shirt."

I look around at the big white people with their
families. They look at me with sympathy, turn
quickly away, grip the hands of their children
tighter.

Treadwell Street was different from Peasley Street in several ways.
One, it was paved; Peasley Street had not been. Its residents were
comparatively well off. Three doctors, teachers, other professionals,
and store owners lived there. John Williams, my former neighbor and

future employer at the shoe repair shop, was to build his house there. Outside of the "Gold Coast," it was the "best" black neighborhood. And it morphed into a "white" street. Beginning at Russell Street it wound its way north, across the Ditch and up the hill for another block. There it crossed Ellis Avenue, changed the color of its residents, and changed its name to Wilson Street.

Summer is how I remember Treadwell Street. That spring before, I had had a leading role in a play at the Trinity Methodist Episcopal Church. "Jack in the Pulpit," it was called. I was Jack. What I remember is the night of the performance, being backstage among other children and adults, the confusion of trying to keep us all still long enough to put on costumes and check lines and entrances. I had memorized my lines and said them, but my memory of the audience reaction is a blur. I was greeted with a hug when I came off stage. This did not begin a stage career for me. My next stage appearance was the year I finished high school, in a play I myself directed.

Summer was the time for vacation Bible school. I was up for anything that had school in it, especially since it meant Bible stories and memorizing verses. I loved the stories though their theology escaped me. Our teacher, a matron older than my mother, was as ineffectual as my mother had been in bridging the gap between what my senses showed me and what I was supposed to believe. My confusion was submerged in the Bible verse competition. This was memory work, something I understood and excelled at. By the end of our session, I had memorized more verses than anyone, and received my very own Bible as reward.

Summer evenings meant roaming downtown, looking in shop windows, especially lighted ones. My mother did not approve of this practice. (But what did a mother know?) Downtown was white folk's territory, especially at night. As there were no street lamps in our neighborhood, I usually made it home by dusk. On one Sunday evening in late summer, I was struck by a window that had a lot of toys, including a toy train that ran through a tunnel under a mountain, and a dump truck with a scoop that picked up and emptied dirt.

So attentive was I that I did not notice two young white men walk up behind me. They stood briefly looking at the display, then one of them stuck a finger in the rip in the back of my shirt and widened it. I turned to see them walking away, the one who had ripped my shirt punching the shoulder of the other. They were both laughing.

My shirt was clean but torn; clean because my mother had washed it, torn because she had no money for thread for her needle. Sometimes white men rubbed small black boys' heads, said it gave them luck, especially if they were gambling. I don't remember any of them ripping boys' clothing. My mother used safety pins to hold the parts of my shirt together. She didn't whip me for disobeying her, as I was sure she would, but did remind me through my tears that I had been warned about going downtown at night.

• • •

Mrs. Embly lived just up the street beyond the Ditch, just where the street began its ascent towards Ellis Avenue. Although she already had three children of her own, she asked my mother if she could have me. The Emblys lived in a two-story house. Mr. Embly owned a café on the west end of Russell Street. I would become her second son, she said. Her first, Gent, was a problem teen, seemingly bound for nowhere, except perhaps for trouble. Her girls, older teens, were doing well. One was in high school, the other in college.

Mrs. Embly would see to it, she said, that I was housed and fed, could continue school, would be treated just as her other children were. My mother, struggling with three children, obviously unable to provide adequately for all of them, would be relieved of the burden of one of them. One less body to buy clothes for, one less mouth to feed.

This was Mrs. Embly's line of reasoning. Given black Southern culture and a practice that had its roots in West Africa, she was making my mother a reasonable proposition. But one reasons with the heart as well as the head. She could not have picked a more inappropriate time to make such a request, or a less appropriate person to make it to. In short, she made the right request at the wrong time to the wrong woman.

We had just lost Leola. Whether we said so or not, we were still grieving her death. I know I was. Not only did I expect to see Leola in rooms in our house, but also on the streets at night. I played with her in my dreams. Leola's death tore an emotional rent in our family that it would take time to heal. Having just lost one child, my mother was not about to give up another.

There was also a deep abiding reason my mother, were she so inclined, would never give me up to Mrs. Embly: class and caste. The Emblys were a family of light-skinned people, I was brown-skinned. Caste barriers within the black race were as severe as those between races. There was no way I could escape these exclusions. My mother had been oppressed by landlords who had light skins. She developed a dislike for the well off, those she saw as no better in their treatment of those below them than whites. She never made any effort to join them, to socialize with them. While she was courteous to Mrs. Embly, all their discussions were carried on out in the street.

My mother grumbled about the prospect of me as being little more than a servant to the Emblys. This happened, especially when the person brought into the family was from the country, hence less sophisticated, or of a lower class or caste. My mother was having none of it. Shortly after Mrs. Embly's proposition, we moved into one of Dr. Rowe's shotgun houses on Fair Street. They were called "shotgun" because one could shoot a bullet that would travel from the front, through the house, and out the back without hitting anything.

• • •

Mercifully, we lived in the Fair Street house for only a short time. The four of us were crammed into three rooms set one behind the other. Actually, there were two small rooms and a tiny kitchen. Dr. Rowe, father of the Grace who had cleaned me out in marbles, owned several of these houses. Ours, next to the Ditch, was directly behind his own two-story house on Treadwell Street (shades of Oak Street, where we lived in back of Reverend Taylor's two-story house!).

Where the Ditch was culverted, as with Peasley and Treadwell Streets, water had made depressions as it exited, the size and shape of these depressions depending on soil composition and speed of the water. Pools of various depths and shapes were formed, some deep enough that small children swam in them after heavy rains.

Storms raised the water level to near flood stage, increasing the likelihood that water moccasins would be washed out of the Edisto River swamp. One afternoon returning from school, we saw one laid out along the path we made along the banks. A long one. Someone had smashed its head in and stretched it out as warning to us.

A bullfrog lived in a cave backwater had created at the culvert on Peasley Street. I took a long stick and worried it out of its lair. Its legs made a welcome addition to our otherwise bland fare. I didn't know at the time that frogs' legs were considered a delicacy. Like the rats of an earlier time, they were added protein.

We moved from Fair Street after only a month. Over rent. Mama had told Dr. Rowe she would have his rent on a certain date. He told her he didn't believe her. They argued. My mother didn't like having her word doubted. She'd been raised to honor her word and when she could, did so. She resented his assumption that because she was poor and had no husband she was a liar and a cheat. When he came on the date she promised, she gave him his rent. And notice. He tried to palliate her, explaining that he "didn't mean no harm." He just didn't see how she could get money since "you didn't have no job" (and no man).

"So many of these people…" He let his voice trail off when he saw she wasn't listening to him.

He was right in what he had started to say, that many of his tenants, many tenants, couldn't pay rent. Some landlords, especially with good tenants, those of long standing, simply took what rent they could get and put the rest on the books. Better to have someone living in a house than to leave it vacant. Houses left standing vacant were fair game for vagrants and vandals. Siding and windows, for example, would be stripped for firewood. But he was speaking to my mother, who was not just *any* tenant. So we moved to Gibson Hill.

● ● ●

Gibson Hill was not much of a hill, but since there were no real hills in the town, it qualified. Most of the town was of a rolling flatness, with a raised bump here and there. Pie-slice shaped, Gibson Hill was such a bump, preceding a drop-off to the north where whites were establishing themselves, where new white power would reside.

Gibson Hill was black, a throwback to earlier ownership patterns, a white-owned Big House with small houses nearby that blacks lived in but did not own. Wedged between paved and lighted Summers and Stanley Streets, it provided servants, once farmhands, to whites of the town. And during cotton-picking season, trucks still gathered at the bottom of the hill to take its residents to outlying fields.

Our Gibson Street house was larger than the one on Fair Street. No cramping. And it had both a front and side porch. I remember sitting on the side porch combing and putting Vaseline in the rows of Mama's hair. This was a job sister Edith would have, but she was on her first trip to the North, where Aunt Maude had taken her with a group to find work in service: "Kin make more in a month there than you kin here in six."

I didn't tell Mama I'd had experience combing hair of a different kind. I had told her I got the quarter mowing a white lady's lawn. She was concerned that I had gone all the way over to Amelia Street without asking her. Mama's hair was just beginning to streak (gray hair came early in our family), the other's hair was mostly white. Mama's hair was short and wrinkly, the other's longer; Mama's soft, the other's more brittle. Mama wanted her hair plaited; I had brushed the other's hair straight out.

• • •

In our moves so far we had started at Russell Street, across from the Southern Railway station, and moved north beyond Claflin University to Goff Avenue, half a block from Dunton Memorial school.

We had started to move west, one block at a time, west and along the Ditch, either alongside it or within sight of it. Gibson Hill was no exception, our farthermost point west, but the Ditch was less than a block away down the hill. We walked along it on our way to school, where we passed the new white grammar school, far enough away for us not to disturb the children, but close enough for us to see their play yard equipment and the yellow buses that brought them in from outlying areas. Each move west got me farther away from our school.

And school and books were becoming more and more important in my life. Unable to use the town's public library and having no library at our school, I was fortunate in discovering the children's section in the library at the state college. I remember being curled up on the floor between rows of books until the library closed. My inner world was enriched by such stories as *The Arabian Nights, Ali Baba and the Forty Thieves, Aesop's Fables,* and *The Arkansas Bear.* I admired the cleverness of the third little pig, laughed at the literal-mindedness of Epaminandas, and identified with Gluck in Ruskin's *The King of the Golden River.* Gluck, the youngest of three brothers, had, in contrast to his two older brothers, risked thirst by giving water to successive famished beggars along the way to the gold of the river. I admired his compassion and wanted to be like that.

By my eleventh year, I had read all the books in the children's section. There was a hiatus in fiction until I discovered comic books in my early teens. My book reading had its down side. Few of my playmates had done this reading. I didn't play with the children of the two private schools who had. In my brief contacts with some of them, they expressed surprise. They resented that I seemed to know as much as they knew, as though their privileged status should give them exclusive right to knowledge. So I was boxed in. I had no Leola. How I missed Leola! Because of their ignorance, I couldn't share what I'd read with my playmates; nor could I share it with children who had knowledge, because of their resentment. Caught between a rock and a hard place, I found myself keeping much of my inner life to myself.

● ● ●

School. Haven. Refuge. Comfort zone. Place of order. Status giver. Social life. Extended family.

I liked school, I liked books, I liked most teachers. I thought they were all good. It was only later, when I learned what they had not taught us, that I realized how incompetent, how poorly prepared many of them were. To their credit, some of them, especially those who taught high school, took advantage of summer classes in northern universities to improve themselves. They worked hard to make up for what their South had denied them.

I was especially thankful for Miss Alfreda James, our history/social studies teacher, who brought new information and new teaching techniques back from her summer study and put them into practice in her classroom. We had a class subscription to *Scholastic* magazine. I remember one piece in it about the odds in various games of chance. The article so impressed me that I decided then and there to keep my money in my pocket. The games were not set up for players to win.

Miss James brought her small radio to our classroom, so we received breaking reports of U.S. and world events. And two newspapers. I remember one story that compared Roosevelt's New Deal to National Socialist programs in Germany with a chart that illustrated the similarities. We knew of Hitler's march into the previously demilitarized zones. We saw pictures of Ethiopian civilians being bombed by the Italian air force over Addis Ababa. And of German and Italian planes bombing civilians in Spain.

I was interested in these foreign events, but as there was no follow-up or in-depth treatment of them, I received no real understanding of them. We were an island in a school of indifference. No one expressed interest in what was "white people's business." There was no support outside of class for what I was being exposed to, so my learning became an abstraction. I can pull up now what I couldn't talk about then.

Our high school English teacher was top rate. I remember stories she read to us when she was our third grade teacher. We loved those stories, especially on rainy days. I can see even now a beautiful black-haired heroine being destroyed by a flaming torch that came out of nowhere to burn her to a crisp, as she sought to escape retribution for some terrible thing she had done. We students had been holding our collective breaths, wondering if the heroine would make it.

Then there was her constant attention to our pronunciation and articulation. Sloppy speech pained her. Sloppy speech, sloppy dress, sloppy anything. I remember clearly her injunction: "Do not drop your 'g.' Now say it, 'run-ning.'" She practiced what she preached. Her dress was impeccable, her classroom orderly, her diction flawless. Children learned early on: "Don't mess with Miss Mabel R.(ubenstine) Jenkins." Her voice had song in it, so that her perfect speech was musical, not stilted. When you heard her, you didn't hear a crow, you heard a nightingale.

She was quick in her thoughts and her movements. Her brain traveled faster than anyone's I can remember. What I find remarkable about her was her ability to encourage weak as well as strong students. She used a technique that I later adopted when I taught; she used the quicker students to help the slower ones. If you finished your assignment, fine. Now look around to see whom you can help.

When the school added high school classes, she was a natural to take over the English language and literature. She was in her element with such works as Whittier's "Snow-Bound," Poe's "Raven," and Longfellow's "Song of Hiawatha" and "Evangeline." I found out later a possible reason for her sympathy for unhappy heroines. Her fiancé had been killed before they could be married. She had adored her young man. The blow to her nature was such that she never fully recovered. She never was able to find anyone to replace him.

While I liked the rhythmical qualities of Poe and Longfellow, I was also engaged by thought-provoking pieces like Bryant's "To a Waterfowl" and "Thanatopsis," and Holmes' "The Wonderful One-Horse Shay." Years later I heard university lecturers explain who these authors were and their place in U.S. literature. Later still, when I taught my own classes, I was able to have students set "To a Waterfowl" against Alicia Ostriker's "Move." This assignment always resulted in a constructive discussion of origins, destinations, and more. In the Bryant poem the narrator appealed to a male Higher Power to direct him as He guided the waterfowl. In "Move" the instinct of attraction is within the order of nature.

I was able to take the foundation started in high school, enlarge it when I got to college, then later use it in my teaching. Miss Mabel Rubenstine Jenkins would have been proud.

Miss Jenkins was also a natural for advisor to *The Wolverine,* our school newspaper. I was editor in chief, with Doris Isaacs, school valedictorian, as associate editor. A Negro high school newspaper was a novel idea. Knowing of no other Negro high school models, we followed the paper at South Carolina State, which was more a journal than a newspaper. Like it, we did not cover events; instead we took pieces by various students. I learned later that the white high school had a journalism class and a regular newspaper.

Keeping us on track and getting pieces from students must have provided many a headache for Miss Jenkins, but she stood with us while we struggled. We printed our paper at South Carolina State. The printer there said our paper was better than the one put out by the college students. We didn't believe him, until we saw their paper. Our paper *was* better. We had trouble fitting our hats on after that, we were that proud.

Proud Miss Jenkins was part Seminole. Her mother was related to those who had joined those of the slave community already in the swamps rather than take part in the Trail of Tears. She wore her hair long, like the photos she kept of her mother. Both women had high foreheads and prominent cheekbones. She liked shawls and had many richly colored ones. Her aunt, also a teacher, lived next door to her. I liked to see the two of them, tall Miss Jenkins with her long strides, and the shorter Miss Addie Winningham with her bird-walking steps, in shawls, as they made their way to school each morning.

For their survival native peoples have always proved adaptable. To escape white bounty hunters who received fifty dollars for each of their scalps, Native Californians in the early twentieth century were to take Spanish names and meld into the Mexican population.

I never had to be urged to go to school. Fortunately, I was not a sickly child. Rarely missed a day of school because of illness. Played hooky only once. One of my buddies and I decided one sunny day to go to the white country club and see if any golfers might be taking in a morning round. A neighbor lady saw me and told Mama. That night I got talked to. She held both of my hands as she talked to me, her voice soft.

"A. D., I work twelve hours a day so you and John Lee can go to school. You a big boy and I know you need a little change now and then. You like money, like everybody else. Don't you like school no more?"

I was feeling worse, much worse than if she had taken a switch to me. I couldn't look at her.

"Yes'm, I still like school."

"Well, you better act like it." She let go of my hands.

"I don't want to hear from nobody you out there in the street, now."

Though her voice was sharp I could feel the pain in it.

"I won't do it no more, Mama."

And I didn't. Ever. Even with classes I didn't like, or teachers who were bores, I might doodle from a back seat, or do work for other classes, but I showed up. No teacher ever again dunned me for missing class.

• • •

My working after school was double-edged. I earned money we needed. But I missed out on much of what other boys my age experienced—the team sports, the boy/girl companionship, the give-and-take of teasing. I played none of the organized boys' games, track, football, baseball, basketball. During my time at Wilkinson High I worked afternoons when these games were played, so I couldn't go out for any of them. We had no tennis or golf teams. While I eventually picked up the languages of these sports enough to follow them, I never got the feel of what it was like to be part of a team competing against another team. I knew what it was to pull for a team member in a spelling bee, and to practice with a team to prepare for the bee, but these were coed events. I never developed the closeness, the camaraderie of team sports with other boys.

The dictum of Mr. J. C. Parler, our principal, "If the school interferes with the job, cut out the school," allowed me to miss fifth period so I could work. This philosophy sounds more like plantation philosophy (black children's schooling was delayed until they finished picking white farmers' cotton) than that of John Dewey, the guru at the university where Mr. Parler had received his education degree.

My emotional growth was skewed by too much time in my solitary head, in the world of popular song. I missed out on what it meant to be a boy among boys and girls, the walking home after school, standing at the gate or front steps until a mother or some other adult called the girl in. I saw these things from a distance, with a certain longing. So while I happily showed off my new clothes bought with the money I earned, the hole in my emotional life was not being filled.

• • •

I spent much of my childhood and adolescence hungry. During the Great Depression and after, food—the lack of it—accompanied me, waking and sleeping. There were times I dreamed of huge meals only to wake up with my brother grumbling about my tossing in my sleep. Go to bed hungry, wake up hungry.

Like countless many during those years, I scrounged for food wherever I could find it. The waste bin behind Maxwell's was a good source, where the clerks threw fruit and bread after it had passed Maxwell's high standards for sale. The fruit warehouses at the Atlantic Coast Lines yards were another good source. We boys, some men, would go to help unload the fruit up from Florida. An Atlantic Coast Line spur ran directly to the warehouse. I saw my first refrigerated cars; cars with ice in spaces at each end that kept the fruit from spoiling. We helped unload the cars, and were given fruit for our efforts.

Then, there were the cooks at select houses who were willing to give a sweet potato or piece of bread, if I caught them right. Timing was everything, since mistresses, both white and colored, kept eagle eyes on their tight food budgets. Cooks were enjoined not to feed hungry boys. So I learned to eat, don't tell. I can hear now, "You jes set right there behind that stove and eat this tater." I did as I was told.

The year I finished high school we were given our first school-wide tuberculosis tests. When I showed a positive I was given the news that I was undernourished. Nurse said I needed a diet that included more meat, milk, and eggs. On my two-fifty a week for shoe delivery after school and my mother's seven dollars a week from county hospital, we had no money to improve my diet. With barely enough to keep a household of three surviving at all, no way could we think of special foods for me.

Prior to this, *that* I ate rather than *what* I ate had been my concern. With a heads-up on this tuberculosis thing, to the extent that I could, I began to watch what I ate. When we caddied on Sundays, I made a lunch of canned salmon, sweet raisin rolls, and a pint of milk. On Saturdays I was able to use tip money from shoes I polished to buy a giant hamburger from the kitchen of the white restaurant across the street from our shoe repair shop. The colored cook there made certain I got full value for my money. I combined this with an occasional lunch in the kitchen of the hotel that housed our shop, where the colored cooks did likewise.

But what stands out in my memory most was the gift of Mr. Blasingame, Blas' father. He held the third chair in Mr. Charlie Pendarvis' barber shop, across the street from our shoe repair shop. Mr. Blasingame never ate his whole lunch, and hated the thought of it being wasted. When he learned that I needed more food, he offered it to me. Gladly I collected it when I came in after school, ate what was left of it, and returned the dishes to his house when I made my afternoon deliveries.

I kept showing positives on tests but, like millions of others with similar test results, I never developed the disease. My malnourishment may have improved, but did not disappear. When I joined the navy in 1942, at 5'9", I weighed 142 pounds. After eight weeks of three big meals a day, my weight grew to 165 pounds, the weight I kept well into my fifties.

But I leap ahead of myself. Let's go back some and pick up our narrative at the Gibson Hill house. Some of my experiences there and later on Railroad Avenue were seminal. We were in the depths of the Great Depression.

CHAPTER FIVE

My Mother Washed Other People's Clothes

Sometimes I feel I handwash clothes
to be near my mother

I feel her blood pulsing
through mine, as I press down
and pull up, press and pull, scrubbing

Sometimes I work the board
but mostly I use my fingers
press and pull our arms and shoulders

She scrubbed that we could eat

How she stood it when the trapped blond
pushed her. We are both pushed. She
by the blond, I by my desire to excel

I could pay someone, or
take clothes to the laundromat but
I love the smell of sunshine wash

In some things I take the easy way
but when I want to feel my mother
I have to slip into her rhythm

The blond boss lady was expected not to work
but to direct folk like Mama, Southern and black
before the Civil Rights Revolution

It was not a job my mother loved
She was a people not a thing person
(who aspired to nursing)
and she had us four to feed

Through the gray weather the line of clothes
was never clean, never dry enough. She heated
the smoothing iron on coals never hot enough

Their ashes smudged some things. "That woman's
whine drive me crazy," my mother would tell us
"Husband this and husband that. 'Beats me for

nothing when he comes in from the mill.' Says
she gets back at him but don't say how."

Mama was a small woman
and the iron was heavy

She talked to my older sister, who was twelve,
of a juicy roundness, destined too soon to go
North, mind babies, cook hash, learn the word
schwartze.

Told her to hold on.

We pulled together with the quarter
from the lawn I mowed, my sister's seventy-five
cents for a week's work after school

That's what we had,
that and my mother's pride

I love the smell of sunshine wash
and I feel my mother
as I squeeze it out

Hoover took away my Bull Durham / He gave me Golden Grain
                    —blues lyric during the Great Depression

Surviving the Great Depression tested the ingenuity and stamina of
families, ours being no exception. Similar survivor tactics sprouted
throughout the various communities. The family garden was a key
tactic. Whenever we stayed in a place long enough, my mother
always put something into the ground. Butter beans, string beans,
black-eyed peas, tomatoes and potatoes, peanuts, beets, and collard
greens were favorites.

Fuel for cooking and heating was always a problem, especially
when there was no money for kerosene. This is where we children
pitched in. I remember dragging a sack along the Southern Railway
track, picking up lumps of coal that had fallen from the coal hoppers
as they passed through. Sometimes larger boys and men would
climb onto the cars as the train slowed to pass through town, and
pitch coal into the ditch alongside the roadbed. This practice had
two dangers: the train picking up speed before you were able to
jump off and the railroad police, who were a vicious lot in protecting
railroad property. None of our people was ever shot, but we heard
of people who had been.

White owners of the wood yards and lumberyards would allow
children and women to bring crocus sacks and pick up bark and chips,
loose ends and sawdust. Colored men were usually responsible for
checking the bags on exit. The nicer looking the woman or big girl,

the more lax was the inspection of her bag. As a boy I never qualified for such treatment, but the far back rows of the lumberyard offered sheltered spaces for occasional necking.

When the automobile delivery trains came to the Southern Railway siding near Livingston's warehouse on Amelia Street near Railroad Avenue, we hung around it to retrieve the broken slats that had been used to stabilize the autos in transit. Some of the slats were long enough to be made into shelving, the rest made excellent firewood.

Women made most of the clothes their families wore. Girls, taught sewing in home economics classes and by their mothers, pitched in. Women held quilting bees, where several would sit around a quilt frame, making a social occasion out of quilt making. They created ingenious and colorful patterns out of scraps.

There was one colored seamstress, wife of the owner of People's Barber Shop, who sewed for upper-class women. Such a service was of particular value in the pre–Civil Rights South because no colored woman was allowed to try on clothes before purchase. No white woman would wear clothes known to have been tried on by a black woman. However, Mrs. Davis and her fellow seamstresses did also make dresses for well-off white women. I saw them picking up clothes and smiling at the door with Mrs. Davis as they left.

Fruits and garden produce were canned for winter. With some money from picking cotton in the fall, a few dollars from doing white folk's laundry, a few dollars from selling boiled peanuts in summer, a dollar or two from shining shoes, an occasional day "in service"—work in some white woman's house—we got through the Great Depression.

Our stay on Gibson Hill was notable for many things: I extended my range of movement by going downtown to shop for the first time, increased my reading, tried to use writing to contact the outside world, met white peers for the first time and had complex relations with them. I was made to face direct race discrimination for the first time, saw the violent result of jealousy, saw a "house" run by a mulatto woman patronized by white men, including the police. I was taught a curious morality lesson, liked a girl whose parents were cool to me, was cured of a fever by my mother, hurt my brother in what may have been a defining incident in our lives.

My mother could send me shopping, saving her having to go downtown. This even after I had tried to hold out a nickel from her shopping change, saying I'd lost it. More and more, I was reading for a retreat as well as for revelation. I never knew there were so many different kinds of people and places. I was fascinated. I read everything that came my way, including magazines with coupons for free products in them. Excitedly, I filled out a dozen of these coupons, and put them in the post box on the corner of Summers Street and Ellis Avenue. On my way to school next day I passed the box and found all my coupons on the ground at its foot. I had omitted the detail of putting them in a stamped envelope, so the irate postman had dumped them out of the box!

One Saturday night my sleep was disturbed for a moment by sounds from a house a little way up the street. A good sleeper all my life, I immediately went back to sleep. Next morning I went with neighbor boy Bujay to see what had happened. What we saw was a trail of blood that extended from Mrs. Banks' house all the way between two houses out to Gibson Street. A man who had been visiting with Mrs. Banks had been surprised by her estranged husband. In the fight that followed, the visitor had been cut badly. It was his blood that we saw. If it was the man I had seen at Mrs. Banks', I was truly sorry. He seemed a pleasant man. He smiled a lot and gave us children candy, which was more than Mr. Banks ever did.

Violence came at us in lots of ways. There was the violence of our poverty, brutal and relentless. We children contributed our share of violence. I was a fringe participant, and after a fight that left one of our Gibson Hill boys injured, I found other things more to my liking to do. How the fight started that left our boy hurt is unclear. I think we resented the new white school on Ellis Street that we had to pass every day to walk nearly a mile to Dunton Memorial. From their side certain boys would taunt us as we walked the path along the Ditch below their school. One afternoon several white boys came across Summers Street and began throwing rocks at several black boys playing at the bottom of the hill. Black reinforcements came and the white boys were chased back across Summers Street. But one of them hurled a good-sized stone that hit one of our boys on the side of his head, drawing blood. That ended the fighting for that day, and the fighting permanently for me.

But not my contribution to violence. One day my brother and I were playing in the yard and he was doing something I didn't like and wouldn't quit when I told him to. There may have been taunting, the "You're not my mama, you can't make me," then running out of reach. This time he ran to the corner of the house and poked his head around the corner and stuck out his tongue. Enraged, I picked up a small piece of metal and threw it at him. It caught him on the forehead. Upset by what I'd done, I ran to help him. He wouldn't let me come near him, screaming, "No, no!" and pulling away when I tried to reach out to him.

His screams brought Mama from inside. Not asking what had happened, she picked John Lee up and rushed inside with him, with me following, pleading, "Mama, I didn't mean it, Mama, I didn't mean to. Mama, he…" Her look told me that I might as well have been talking to a stone. She showed not a jot of sympathy for me in it, not one iota.

When John Lee had been cleaned up and bandaged and soothed, she turned to me for the shellacking I knew I had coming. Fortunately for us all, John Lee's injury was a surface one. He had not been hit face on. He was snatching his face back as I threw, so the blow was a glancing one. Since he was a good distance away, the force of the blow had been diminished by the time it reached his face. And I had not thrown as hard as I could have, even for an eleven-year-old. His forehead was skinned but would heal. I'm not sure how much the direction of our friendship was altered by this incident. Though we shared the same bed until I left home, we never developed the brother-to-brother touch relationship. I don't remember ever hugging him or being hugged by him. Ever.

• • •

My mother had her hands full trying to raise two active boys, especially when something unexpected happened, like me hitting

John Lee or catching fever. As she did with Leola, Mama first went into the nearby woods to search for healing roots and herbs. With me she found the combination to make a foul-tasting thick tea I was forced in my delirium to drink. This after I had chipped a front tooth by falling off a kick-skates board. The uneven sidewalk made the board impossible to control.

"Now you drink this, every last drop," when I hesitated, screwing up my face.

I had been sick for several days. Nothing she had in the house would bring the fever down. Mama prayed. She sponged me off with cold water, even though it was blustery cold outside. Finally she went into the wood at the top of Summers Street and dug until she found what she wanted. I was never told which plants she used. I was too far out of it to care. What I cared about was that on the morning of the next day after taking the new medicine my fever was broken. My mother gave a prayer of thanks. Within a week I was out playing. She had learned about medicinal plants from various women. Her sister Lucy was a skilled practitioner of West African traditional medicine.

Just down the hill from us, on my path to school at the corner of Summers and Ellis, was a Smithson house. It said so on the wood sign at the front gate. Two-storied, large and white, facing away from us. Being next door did not make its well-off white occupants our neighbors. They lived in a world we of Gibson Hill could only imagine. In its back garden were three fig trees, one on the side of the house which I passed daily on my way to school and back. One had branches that hung over the fence. I had watched those figs ripen and drop to the ground. On my way from school one afternoon I picked five of them. Three I carried in my hands, two I put in my pockets. Boy happy, I hurried home to share my bounty. Was not to be.

Standing in the yard talking with my mother was Mr. Miles. Mr. Miles was a World War I veteran who had cooked for us children one rainy day at Peasley II when Mama was at work. He was one of several men I remember who sat around the fire telling ghost stories that frightened me so I couldn't sleep. When I came up to them, Mama wanted to know from where I had gotten the figs, since we didn't have a tree. When I explained that they were from the Smithson tree, she asked Mr. Miles for his service belt.

"I don't want you growing up to be no thief," she said, as she laid on the leather. When she had finished and I was sniffling, I thought at least I would be able to salve my sore bottom and fill my hungry stomach with juicy ripe figs. I had had my punishment. I had paid for them. It was not to be so.

"Here, give them to me," Mr. Miles said, reaching out his hand.

Hesitating, I looked to my mother. She nodded agreement. When I handed him the figs he took them to the edge of the yard and, before my horrified eyes, smashed every one of them on the ground.

"I never woulda thoughta that," my mother beamed, as though she had received a revelation. "I woulda let him keep 'em. Hmnph, hmnph, hmnph! Now you git on in that house and don't let me catch you stealin no mo. That ain't how I raised you." She said this last for a smug Mr. Miles' benefit, as I was headed into the house. My back was turned so they could not see the hatred I felt for them both. What they had done was incomprehensible to me. I felt wronged in a way I could not explain. They were not my figs. I had stolen them. It was wrong to steal. Why, then, did I feel I had been doubly wronged, not by the beating but by the destruction of the figs?

My beating didn't stop my roaming with neighborhood boys to knock down pecans and gather golden pears when ripe. Though there were no trees of any kind on Gibson Hill, there were many on the surrounding streets. Though I joined other boys on pecan forays, I preferred berry hunting in the wood alone. Which is how I met Ned Jones, a white boy who lived on the corner of Cemetery and Summers Streets, a short block distant from our house. Edward Carlyle, or "Ned," Jones was about my age and size.

The wood, where my mother had dug the roots that had reduced my fever, seemed extensive to me. It was dense, though there were paths if one looked hard enough for them. Ned was on one such path hunting huckleberries. He had with him his small collie that darted ahead on the path or into the underbrush, chasing sounds. The wood, beginning across the street from his house and running north and east, was like Ned's private park. He could go there any time he wanted. I too liked the wood. It reminded me of Grandma's farm, where I had been happy.

The collie, after the obligatory sniff of me and the jar I carried, licked my hand and ran around me. Ned called "Freddy!"

"He doesn't like many strangers," he said. "You got a dog?"

"Naw, had one though."

"What happened, got killed?"

"Naw, died."

"Oh. Well, you can play with Freddy. He likes you." Freddy took off running, with us after him. Then Ned tripped over a vine across our path and fell on a protruding root, skinning his right leg below the knee. He tried to say that he wasn't hurt but when the bruise began to show blood, we both knew it was time to call in the adults to get it taken care of.

At the screened-in back porch of his house, we found Mrs. Jamison, their cook, getting food ready for dinner, and in a don't-bother-me hurry. She called Mrs. Jones, who came out carrying a baby, trailed by a boy not yet school age. Mrs. Jones' hair was thick, black, and untidy. She herself was disheveled. When she saw her son's leg she looked like she was hardly up to dealing with another distraction. The little blood had dried by then. Ned was walking fine. She glanced at it, at me, told him to "Get right in the house," and told me to go home. Freddy followed them into the house, but not before Ned told me to come back after dinner to play. On my way by the kitchen, Mrs. Jamison asked my name and who my mama was. When I told her she said they were members of the same A. M. E. church, and sent me away with a large piece of freshly baked buttered corn bread.

I didn't go back to Ned's house right away. Instead, after dinner I went over on Gibson Street, a short walk away in the opposite direction, to the Gaffney house, where there was a family with a daughter my age. Velma, the darkest member of a mulatto family, had light brown skin and freckles. Mrs. Gaffney would only let Velma play where she could keep an eye on her, which meant the dirt road in front of their house. Their yard had no fence but there were flowers, roses and tall red lilies. While Velma and I played tag or shared a book on the front steps, I was always intrigued by the way one of her older brothers cleaned out the cast-iron pot they cooked their grits in. He made it a thing of art. The pot between his legs, humming, he took a long knife, set it between the wall of the pot and the layer of caked grits, and spun the pot like a top. Off came the grits. I marveled at this and wished I had that skill.

I also wished that I had a family like the Gaffneys. There was Mr. and Mrs. Gaffney. Mr. Gaffney went off every day but Sunday to his restaurant on West Russell Street, leaving Mrs. Gaffney home with the children. The children, four at home and one out of the house, always seemed to have something to do, like Earl with the pot cleaning. Velma helped her mother in the house, and there was no playing outside until her work inside was done. On Sunday the family, all six of them, scrubbed and polished and in Sunday-go-to-meeting clothes, marched themselves over to the unfinished Trinity Methodist Episcopal church (founded 1866) on Railroad Avenue. Trinity Methodist Church was once in the center of town. Whites decided they wanted to put a courthouse on that site. They condemned a perfectly sound elegant structure. Lacking money to start rebuilding, Trinity members worshipped in a tent for two years. We went to the A.M.E. church on Glover Street, on the opposite side of town.

I was an all-right playmate for Velma. After all, my mother was a good churchgoing woman. My face and clothes were clean. I was a smart boy. And Gibson Hill, with its broken families and its "house" at the juncture of Gibson Street and Sunnyside, had so few children Mrs. Gaffney found acceptable. But I was not ideal. My skin was brown and my mother had no husband. So while Velma was allowed to play with me in the street and read with me on the front steps, I was never asked inside. Velma would never be a girl I would date.

Ned and Freddy showed up at my house a few days later. I was in the backyard pushing sticks of wood under the washpot of boiling clothes. It was the last load, the first having been put in before the summer sun got hot. Our washpot was a fire-blacked cast-iron affair with a ragged v-shaped nick at its top. It doubled as a clothes boiler, lye soap maker, or holder of neck bones, cow's-head, lights, or tripe during the butchering season. It had three legs set on three stones or half bricks, which I later learned was a West African practice. My job was to see that the pot was kept boiling and punch the clothes with a paddle to work the dirt out of them. Mama was at the side of the yard, at two tubs, washtub on the left, rinse tub on the right. She was bent over, elbow deep in suds with a scrub board, scrubbing, wringing out the clothes, then putting them in the rinse tub. Mama's clothes were soaked with sweat that slid down her back from under the tie, made from an old apron, that covered her head. I had told her about Ned when I had returned from berry hunting. She had merely said a "hmnnpf!"

"No siree, he can't go play at your house. Can't you see he working?"

"I can help him. Then can he go?"

Ned picked up the paddle and started punching clothes. His first attempt was awkward.

Mama laughed. "Let A. D. show you. Then when they done, you can go." Thus began a friendship that lasted until we moved from Gibson Hill to Railroad Avenue.

Having Ned as playmate had its benefits. I was permitted a child's view of a world different from my own. I saw close up how well-off white people lived. I learned to give them individual personalities, to see distinctions between them. I eyeballed them, they eyeballed me. Ned's father took us into the wood to try out Ned's .410 rifle, a Christmas gift. I was allowed to try and, not having been warned, was kicked by its recoil. After their laughter—they had assumed I would know, didn't every boy?—I tried again. This time I rode with the recoil and held the barrel steady. But the rifle did not become one of my favorite toys. And I played Chinese checkers and filled in jigsaw puzzles, swung in a backyard swing, and sat under the grape arbor with their playmates swapping stories. I learned that the stories they heard their elders tell and which they repeated were not the ones elders told around the fire at my house. I liked our stories better. They did not put people down, as most of the white people's stories did. Stories that titillated but were not funny. Children trying to be grown-ups. I had trouble joining in the laughter. While my association with Ned had its benefits, it also had its costs. Peership, I learned, has its price.

Late one afternoon I came upon Ned's mother arguing with a black gardener over payment for cutting the hedge on the Cemetery Street side of the yard. He said that before he'd started she'd said that she would pay him a dollar. When he finished she offered him seventy-five cents. The job didn't take as long as she had figured. Being large, strong, and an efficient worker, he didn't feel he should be penalized for finishing early. He was working by the job, not by the hour.

He wouldn't take less than the dollar. He said that she hadn't found anything wrong with his work and he wanted the money she had promised him. I didn't understand why she didn't want to pay him. She told him to come back later for his money. He wouldn't leave without it. Finally, she gave in and paid him, but was not happy doing it.

Mrs. Jones had been a beauty before her marriage and even after four children was still a handsome woman. Marriage to the top cadet at The Citadel, Military College of South Carolina, was to have insured her a future of success and plenty. That was before the Great Depression. I saw a woman in an adequate but modest house (still grand when compared to ours), with a husband who had not made a lot of money, struggling to stretch her house allowance to cover three adults (one hostile mother-in-law), four children, and a cook. I learned about her husband from overhearing remarks by Mitt Jeffords, who played golf and was also a Citadel graduate, not a top student but who was doing well in business. Jeffords spoke scornfully and with a tinge of envy of Jones and T. Alec Brown, the other top cadet of that class, a man I would later see drunk in his car on Broughton Street weekends when I worked in the shoe repair shop.

Then there was the sunny Sunday afternoon when a drunken black woman fell out on a corner of the Jones' front lawn where Summers Street joined Cemetery. She had plopped on the slope nearest the hedge. Several of us children were playing croquet at the other end, near the house. The woman wore Sunday dress and was carrying a bag of boiled peanuts that she had been eating as she walked. Though her middle-brown skin was flushed from drink, her clothes were intact. She had not been in a fight, just had had too much party. A young woman, probably in her twenties, she was not someone I recognized. I could not imagine what she was doing so far off course if she was on her way to Gibson Hill. It would have been a simple matter for her to go down Sunnyside to Gibson, or any of the other streets of the hill. But there she was, and what was I to do? I was angry at the woman and sorry for her at the same time. Why did she have to make herself so vulnerable? She stank of alcohol and tobacco. I felt somehow vulnerable with her and I didn't like it or myself. Yet I knew I could not leave her on the lawn like that.

The other children stood back, they were not going to touch her. Daughter Annette ran into the house to get Mr. Jones. I knelt down and gathered the boiled peanuts that had spilled out of the bag onto the lawn. Then I tried to help her up but she was too heavy for me. She had gotten to one knee by the time Mr. Jones came out. Together we got her up and headed down Cemetery Street, where colored people lived. I had brushed some grass off her skirt that she had seemed oblivious to. She didn't fall anymore, but had trouble negotiating the dirt sidewalk, with its uneven surface and hollows. She had mumbled something as she staggered away, something that I couldn't make out.

I was glad that Mr. Jones did not speak of the incident, nor did any of the children. We went about our play as though nothing had happened between us. But something had. And that something defined us in a way I couldn't name. A difference not before noticed had been revealed. Though no one said it, I was on the side of the woman, my playmates were on another side.

Mr. Jones had always insisted that I share the toys, the skates, whatever we were playing with. Mrs. Jones had not. Though she never crossed Mr. Jones when he spoke, she did not share his feelings about me as a playmate for her children. One rainy day Ned, Freddy, and I were playing under the house when she called Ned in to clean up for dinner. Grime-caked, we three went up and proceeded to advance to the shower. I was called back.

"Not you," she said. "I didn't mean you."

By this time Ned and Freddy were in the shower, with water running. I don't know what Ned was thinking while I was waiting outside the shower, or what he had heard. I was stunned. Hurt and angry, I took a while for what she had said to register. When I realized that I was not to be allowed to shower but that Freddy the dog was, I wanted to shed tears of frustration. But I was not going to let her see me cry. I didn't know how to phrase the question that was screaming at me: "Why Freddy and not me?" Collecting myself as best I could, I proceeded towards the back porch and out. But not before I was intercepted by Mrs. Jamison, who had a large buttered sweet potato for me.

"You not going out there in this rain," she said, as she handed me the spud.

"Yes'm," I choked out, "I'm going home."

"Well, you jes set here and eat this."

After eating the sweet potato and thanking her, I felt better, but I wanted to go home, in the rain. I wanted the water to wash me off. Splashing along in the cooling rain, I was glad to see Doot and Bujay and two other children playing our rain game. We chased each other from one porch to another, trying to avoid the tag of the one doing the chasing. I joined them until I exhausted myself. Then I went home to the expected "You get in here and get out of them wet clothes." I did as I was told.

Though we played at playing together a couple more times, I never went back to Ned Jones' house. He and Freddy came down one day and helped me finish my clothes pounding chore. He never got the hang of it and I didn't try to show him. It was just as well. Ned didn't mention the shower incident, and I couldn't find a way to bring it up. Not long after, my stepfather found us a house on Railroad Avenue, near Railroad Corner, two doors from the Maxwells' house, next to the last of the Railroad Corner shops, Reverend Sheppard's Candy Factory. We didn't know it then, but this was the last time that our stepfather would live with us.

• • •

We were returning to the Railroad Corner area after living elsewhere for eight years. We had begun life in Orangeburg on the corner of East Russell Street and College Avenue, a scant block's distance on the other side of the Southern Railway station. This fact meant nothing to me, as it was buried in memory. What meant more was that we were much closer to school. Getting to school was a simple matter of crossing the tracks, walking through State College, and through Claflin University to Goff Avenue, where Dunton Memorial was located. But, as was my wont, I sometimes varied my route, walking along College Avenue to Goff, which connected to it just beyond Claflin. Or I might take still a third route, through State to take a path to enter our school grounds from the rear.

Living on Railroad Corner also meant again being nearer the colleges. I could roam their campuses, and use the library at State. While I couldn't take books out, not being a student, I could read books there. The stacks were open, so I could take down books at will and spend as much time as I liked with them. Books became my friends, but being forced to be so active, I didn't read nearly as much as I ordinarily would have.

I could also scavenge behind Maxwell's and the meat market next door that opened onto the alley where I had cut my foot on a broken Ball jar many years before, and where I would see a man shot. Maxwell's set a high standard for the freshness of its produce and bakery products, so it was not at all unusual to find perfectly good (by my family's standards) edible food in their waste.

I took it on myself to earn money, and to do this in a regular way meant finding a regular job. Depression-era pickings for an eleven-year-old going on twelve were not plentiful, but I didn't know that when I set out to look. My efforts ended mostly in failure. The second barber shop on the Corner (the other, Bill Davis' People's Barber Shop, already had a shoeshine boy) gave me a week's trial. I set up in a corner of the shop and waited. Few people came. At week's end we had a mutual parting.

Next, Mr. Maxwell was set to give me a try at working in the Maxwell store. After giving me an interview at his house, two doors down from ours, he was convinced that I was teachable and could successfully be brought into the Maxwell fold. That was not to be. Between the interview and time for me to begin at the store I got into a fistfight with his youngest son, Henry. Henry ended up with bruises and face scratches. That ended my chance to work at Maxwell's. My mother had been happy that Mr. Maxwell had noticed me and was not sympathetic to my claim that Henry had started the fight. Mr. Charlie Summers of Summers Café and Restaurant, between the barber shop and the candy factory, came to my rescue, after a fashion. He needed someone to clean the fish he sold, one of his restaurant's specialties. A penny a pound. Same amount folk earned for picking cotton. I could clean them in my backyard. Work at home. I could keep the heads, which my mother could make stew with. He found his boy in me.

Twenty-five to fifty pounds was the amount I usually cleaned. Mr. Charlie told me the amount. I never questioned his weight. I liked cleaning fish but for their smell and their scales, which got into everything. The problem was not the fish themselves so much as what their smell did to my hands and clothes. The fish odor never seemed to leave. I was embarrassed one night at a recital I attended at State College. To begin with, my clothes themselves marked me as an outsider, as their quality and fashion did not approach those of others in the audience. I had scrubbed and rinsed and more, in an effort to remove the fish stink. But though I had thought I had it down to what was a manageable level for me, to the noses of the spit-polished and well-dressed audience, I was immediately spotted as, well, as a fish cleaner. I sat in an end-row seat near the rear. I don't remember, but I feel certain that I left at the intermission.

My fish cleaning was done mostly on Fridays and Saturdays for the weekend rush, unless Mr. Charlie had a special party and needed more. Along with providing me with a regular source of spending money, my fish cleaning had an accidental side benefit. It allowed me to share with the stranded young man who was staying with us. The couple who lived with us had lured him down from Harlem. The Watsons had promised Lemuel they would give him his return fare if he would chauffeur them home in an old car they had bought but could not drive. Once safely home, they reneged on their promise, leaving him stranded in Orangeburg, penniless and knowing no one.

They hadn't told him straight out they weren't going to pay him. They had strung him along, putting him off with one dodge or another. My mother's resentment grew the longer the Watsons temporized, and she would have thrown them out were it not for my stepfather. He had introduced them to my mother. Too, he thought that Lemuel deserved what he got.

"He a fool to trust them Watsons. Fifty dollars! He think money grow outta they behinds? Nigguhs ain't got no fifty dollars. Hardly got a pot to pee in."

Lemuel's sleeping in the car—we gave him food—proved to be a plus for me. After school and while we were cleaning fish, he would tell me stories of his life in Harlem. I found them exciting, though I think they were embellished for my benefit. I figured they had to be. After all, if life in Harlem was so grand, why did the Watsons leave it? And why was he so gullible not to get at least some of his money from them down front? I didn't tell him any of this. I simply enjoyed the stories. Besides, he was good-natured, and had volunteered to help me with the fish. I was happy he did. His helping broke the back of the onerous job. If you tired, you could let your knife slip and ruin a fish, or you could stick your hand on a fin. Lemuel, being older, was a faster, better cleaner than I. And he seemed not to mind the work. So when I began to split my earnings with him, he was pleased. He had tobacco money (he rolled Golden Grain, never asked if I wanted to smoke) and an occasional Butterfinger. I missed him when, after entreaty and threats from my mother, the Watsons did give him his fare home. My mother also got them to get him some clothes from Silver's, "so at leas' he look decent."

I earned money one glorious week at the circus that set up on the county fairgrounds. Lots of boys and men were out the Sunday the show came in, hoping to get jobs helping with setup. We went from concession to concession. A couple with a games concession hired me. My job was to clean in and around the tent and fill a container of water for their two small dogs. When I was not at work, which was most of the time, I could read magazines they had or roam the circus grounds. On the day of the week set aside for colored folks, the last, they allowed me to go on the rides. I rode the Ferris wheel and the merry-go-round. Along with my pay, which was more generous than I could have imagined, I also found coins people had dropped along the front of the concession. And, since I always got to work before the concessions opened up, I found coins in front of other concessions. At the end of the week, I poured a pile of money into my mother's lap. "A. D.!" was all she could exclaim, so overjoyed was she. And my employers also sent her a present, one of the concession's prizes. It had been a successful week for them, they said. They had liked my work and I had liked being around them. I had especially liked the freedom they gave me to roam the grounds. They were warmly rich, somber, and funny by turns. I think from their intonations that they were of North African or Eastern Mediterranean origin, dark-haired, she of clear skin, he of slightly darker skin. Though my mother was overwhelmed by their kindness to me and their largesse, she balked when they asked if I could travel with them. Of course I was eager to go. After all, had I not announced to all who would hear, "Now that I am twelve, it is time I went about my Father's business"?

To this bit of nonsense, my mother had simply snorted and said I'd better eat my dinner before it got cold. My stepfather, who didn't know the quotation from Jesus, as my mother did, was ambivalent. He was not at all sure, now when I seemed to have the knack of bringing in money, that I might not just be foolhardy enough to head out to seek my fortune.

"You kiddin, ain't you, A. D.?"

When my mother explained to him where I had borrowed the quote from, he said, with a mixture of condemnation and awe, "You don't be messin wit the Lord, now, no you don't."

In addition to my experience with the circus, there were other magical things. Like the whale that had been brought to a railroad siding south of town. People lined up to see this creature. I wondered if it was like the whale that swallowed Jonah. I thought Jonah's must have been bigger, as this one didn't seem large enough to hold a grown man. And there was the man buried in a hole at the juncture of Highways 21 and 178. He is supposed to have stayed there for twenty-one days. I wondered if he didn't have a secret apartment down there, else how could he do his business? He seemed content enough, not suffering at all. I never solved the mystery.

CHAPTER SIX

Night Trip Downtown

When I am eleven
my mother despairs
of my staying put
anywhere, except behind
a ball and chain.

"Keep out of the streets
at night." I don't hear her.
"And don't let me catch you
downtown."

House is no place
for anyone on hot steamy night.
Downtown is where store
windows glitter.

Toy crane swings, its scoop
reaches out, closes over
gravel, lifts, swings
back to pile, empties
and returns.

Sunday-dressed white people
pause, look briefly,

pass on. As long as
I don't move, or speak,
they will not see me.

It grows late,
the crowds thin.

"Come over here, boy,
I got something for you."

He stands across the narrow street,
right hand on a crutch, his left
jingling coins in his pocket.

His voice has gravel in it.
I do not know him,
not a white man I have seen
on my shoeshine rounds.

"Come on over here, I'm not
going to hurt you." This when
I hesitate. He starts to cross
over, his crutch makes a klock,
klock, klock as he advances.

I edge away, he wheedles,
I move faster, start to run.
Turning the corner I hear,
"...little black bastards downtown."

Except to steal, which for some reason I can't explain I never did, I
would do almost anything to make money. *Almost* anything. When a
college student offered me a nickel to "suck me off" when I had been
scavenging the dorm after graduation, I agreed. Nickel in hand I knelt
as he told me. He was not clean, still showing a cheese-like matter

under his foreskin. I tried to take him in my mouth and promptly vomited. But for the noise it would have made in the men's shower room, I probably would have gotten smacked. As it was, all he said was, "Damn, and my good pants, too!" When he looked around, I was gone. I've already mentioned that I did not succumb to the siren call of a man one night when I was scurrying through the railroad station on my way home. He was a white man with a peg leg and a crutch that klock-klocked as he walked toward my angle of passage. He wore one of the WWI long coats. When I didn't stop he began to wheedle and jiggle coins in his pocket. "Aw, c'mon, I ain't gonna hurtcha. I got something fer ya." My fear overrode my money hunger. When I veered away and started to run, he started swearing, calling me all the little black bastards he could think of.

Not all of my sexual experiences of that time were so harrowing. A thirteen-year-old girl, thinking that we were alone in the house, lay down and asked me to get on top of her. Although I had wrestled with girls in play before, and was excited by the feel of their bodies, I had never thought about having sex with one of them. So I didn't know how to do it. She pulled up her dress, and I saw a lovely mound with hair sprouting from each side of an opening. *That was it?* Eager to join her, I kneeled down. "Here," she said. "I'll show you." She proceeded to open her legs wider and as my member stiffened, she helped me enter. We were not alone in the house. Someone moved something around. Hardly had we begun to enjoy ourselves before we had to quit. Timing is everything. We promised to do this again, but we never got another opportunity.

We had at the Railroad Avenue house what was to be our last Christmas together as a family. Sister Edith had not gone Up North yet. Stepfather John Walker was still with us. I remember the sharp cold, a tree that we decorated, presents that we swapped and some we got from a children's Christmas party just up the street from us at the still not completely built Trinity Methodist Episcopal church (begun in 1928, it was not to be completed until 1944), where I had been Jack in the play "Jack in the Pulpit." There were a crossword puzzle, Chinese checkers, an Erector Set, fruit and nuts. I remember especially Brazil nuts, the juicy white meat when you cracked them with a hammer gently. And paper-shell pecans that could be cracked by pressing two together with the fingers. And a Christmas dinner of ham and sweet potatoes and butter beans and hot buttered corn bread, and lots of people eating and talking. Everyone seemed to be happy together.

My most shocking experience on Railroad Corner was an episode of violence at the bar/café near the Corner. Pee Wee was the chauffeur of a rich old white widow woman. He was a neat light-brown-skinned jockey-sized man, always sharp, with highly polished boots, his uniform pressed and creased, hair neat, his cap fresh looking. He had been Mrs. Lawson's chauffeur for some time. It was a Sunday morning. We were in the bar/café where Pee Wee liked to go for a bit of 3.2 percent alcohol beer. He never drank anything heavier and never but one of those. So he was nursing his beer when Mr. Dash started in on him. Mr. Dash was one of the brothers of the taxi-owning Dash family. He, too, had been drinking, but stronger stuff.

I never found out why he started picking on Pee Wee. Pee Wee ignored the jibes Mr. Dash flung his way. Angered at being ignored, Mr. Dash sidled over to Pee Wee and tipped his chauffeur's cap off the counter onto the floor. Pee Wee held himself in, bent over and picked up his cap, dusted it off on his pants, and set it in its regular place on the counter. By this time several of the fellows were telling Mr. Dash not to mess with Pee Wee. I could see the cords in Pee Wee's throat tighten.

"Pee Wee ain't botherin nobody, man, you oughtta leave him alone."

"What you got ugins Pee Wee? He ain't doin you nuthin. Damn!"

"Ain't need nuthin. Lil nigguh think he so high and mighty, jes cause he drivin some Miz Shriveled-Up-Pussy."

"Man you don't be goin under no woman's dress, now. You don know what she got."

At that, Pee Wee picked up his cap, turned to Mr. Dash, and in a tight voice said, "You just wait here, I'll show you."

Mr. Dash shouted as Pee Wee walked out, "What you gon do, lil nigguh, you gon bring ol Miz Shrivel-Up wit you?"

A short while later Pee Wee came to the door and called Mr. Dash out. Some of the men warned Mr. Dash. Told him not to go. "You don't know what Pee Wee got."

"Lil nigguh don scare me none," said Mr. Dash, much the bigger man. Some of us, I in front, followed him as Pee Wee led the way into the alley beside the café. I ran over to a corner behind Pee Wee. Mr. Dash started towards him. Before he got within ten feet, Pee Wee whipped out a revolver and fired. The shot sounded like someone had stepped on a partly deflated balloon. Surprised, but not stopped, Mr. Dash took a step. Pee Wee fired again. Mr. Dash dropped to a knee, reaching towards Pee Wee. Pee Wee turned and walked away. No one tried to stop him. Men ran to Mr. Dash to see where he had been hit. Both shots seemed to have gone towards his stomach. Pee Wee had apparently wanted to stop, not kill him. I ran home. I could not tell anyone what I had witnessed. My mother would have been scandalized, and frightened for me. I might have gotten a hiding, so I was taking no chances.

Nothing happened to Pee Wee as the result of his shooting Mr. Dash. He never even appeared in court. Mrs. Lawson's family lawyer appeared for him and pled self-defense. The judge, a friend of both the lawyer and the Lawsons, accepted the plea and dismissed the case. After all, Mr. Dash didn't die, and it was just one Negro's fight with another. No one, I mean no one, messed with Pee Wee after that.

Railroad Corner provided me for a short while with an opportunity to play with boys who had intact families, who were in school and would continue so, the children of academics and professionals, a far cry from the children of Gibson Hill with none of the above. It was summer. Our play areas were Treadwell Street between Amelia and Russell, where they were building a Catholic church, and in Henry Maxwell's backyard. Except for the fact of language, I did not belong with those boys. My clothes didn't match theirs. In their parents' eyes I had no family name, no family history. They went to school on the university campus. I attended Dunton Memorial. Sometime during the summer their families would take them away on vacations. Their families got them eye exams, glasses when needed, braces to straighten their teeth. Not mine. I could play with them in the street but, as it had been with Velma Gaffney, I was not invited into their houses.

So it was from Henry Maxwell's backyard that someone threw a rock out towards Railroad Avenue that hit a white woman's passing car. The other boys were paralyzed, they had hit a *white* woman's car. No one wanted to go out to the car, which had stopped. For a reason I can't explain, they all looked to me. I had never told them I had had experience dealing with white people. I knew that white women didn't bite. "All right, I'll go." I did with reluctance, and apologized. The car had not been damaged. One of the two women in it admonished us, but did nothing more. When Henry's mother investigated the commotion and found out what had happened, she, a thin white-looking woman herself, sent us all home.

While playing with the boys on Treadwell Street was an on-and-off proposition, I did find a playmate who became my friend all through high school: Nathaniel Fridie. Nathaniel had come late to our sixth grade class. I sat near the front row, opposite O'Donald Sheppard, son of the candy maker. We both competed for the new boy to become our seatmate, O'Donald by whispering, "Come sit with me," I by sliding over and making a space. To my delight, he slid into the space I had made for him.

Nathaniel was the oldest son of six children, the third child of an evangelical minister who had a church somewhere in the county. Eartha and Julia B. were the older girls, James and Naomi were slightly younger than Nathaniel, and there was a toddler crawling about their house. They were, if anything, poorer than we were. Their house was literally made of tin and tar paper. It was set so close to the ground that there was barely enough space for water to drain during rain. Though Mrs. Fridie got some help from the older girls, who left home as early as they could, she had an impossible job keeping her house in any kind of order. She was carrying still another child at the time I first went to their house with Nathaniel. When it rained their yard was a muddy pond. I never went inside their house. Nathaniel always asked me to wait outside while he got whatever it was we were wanting.

Nathaniel and I soon became good friends. We were both studious non-athletes. We later had newspaper routes and tried to sell magazines. Nathaniel never caddied or shined shoes. His father would not allow it. We even went down to the district superintendent's office to protest after Nathaniel had been beaten by his agriculture teacher. Having a solid friend for his Number One Son seemed to matter little to his father. He showed this by refusing to recommend my mother for credit at Sears Roebuck, when a letter from him, a Sears account customer, would have allowed her children to have school clothes, among other necessities. She had a job at county hospital and a reputation for honesty. But her not having a husband put her beyond the pale in Reverend Fridie's evangelical eyes. My friendship with Nathaniel survived this slight. The Sears account was a matter between adults.

• • •

Aunt Maude was living on Broad Street, on the west side of town, taking care of a house for a woman who was somewhere Up North. Aunt Maude herself wanted to go north and take Edith with her. We could stay in the house, at reduced rent, until the owner came home. So that's how our stays on Broad Street began. I hadn't wanted to move. Railroad Corner was convenient to much of what I liked: school, the campuses, stores, boys to play with. But it was a better location for my mother, who had gotten a job as a nurse's aide at Orangeburg County Hospital on Glover Street. So, dutiful son that I was, when Mama said, "Pick up and move," I picked up and moved. Our move was without my sister, who did go Up North with Aunt Maude, or my stepfather, who had left us again.

Mama loved our Broad Street house, number 243, so much so that she would eventually buy it and live in it until her death. She liked that it was roomy enough for us, even though one locked back room was taken up with the furniture and belongings of the owner, away Up North. She had a living room, where she could entertain visitors, a room that could be set aside for just this use. John Lee and I would continue to share a bed, but our room was larger than in our previous houses and had a window. She also liked the hedge around the small front yard. The deep lot she prized most of all. First she put up a shed for storage and put in a garden. Years later, when she owned the house, after having it wired she added an inside bathroom. In turn, a telephone and the ubiquitous TV. Then she put up two small rental cottages, becoming herself a landlord!

Her neighbor on the right was Mrs. Bowman, a widow, and like Mama, a member of Williams Chapel A.M.E. church, founded 1873.

On her left was a couple who taught in one of the county schools. He had come down from Washington, D.C. She was an Orangeburg woman. They had met at the country school where they taught but Mama thought them an odd match.

Our block was quiet except during summer, when young whites drove through our street on their way to the city's whites-only swimming pool on the Edisto River. Though we were only a long three blocks from that pool, we never considered swimming there. There was a Sanctified church across the street near Shuler. Its few members sang with gusto, a fact that would affect my sleep when we moved next door to it.

I adapted to 243 Broad, as I had learned to adapt to our other moves. I looked around for other marble shooters. Though there were no colored boys my age on our immediate block, there were two around the corner on Shuler Street towards the river, Teets and my neighbor Bujay from Gibson Hill, who became buddies, and two boys on the block of Broad towards Broughton, who became antagonists. I quickly learned that there was a gathering of marble shooters every Saturday morning under a giant oak at the corner of Windsor and Russell. I was to spend a lot of Saturdays there, building a large stash of marbles, a shoebox full. Marbles contented me until I discovered comic books, which several of the white boys already had. I traded them marbles for books as they finished with them. Thus I was introduced to the exciting world of "Famous Funnies" and "Tip Top Comics," a world of monsters and superheroes. Mama was not sorry when I graduated from marbles. No more dirt-ingrained scuffed knees.

This was the period when I remember being most influenced by comic strips and by advertising. Every possible experience seemed to be covered by an advertisement, a comic strip, or a popular song. Some ads that stood out: Carter's Little Liver Pills, "They do the work of calomel without the danger of calomel, cause they're Carter's Little Liver Pills." "When better automobiles are built, Buick will build them." "I'd walk a mile for a Camel." Johnny the midget and the Phillip Morris ad, "Come in and caaalll for Phillip Morris!" The Planters Peanut man with his monocle and top hat. "His Master's Voice," a dog with its ear against a speaker, stood for RCA Victor's records.

There was Buck Rogers with his exploration of other worlds.
Popeye's "I fights to a finish, 'cause I eats me spinach..." helped me
to like spinach. The Buster Brown shoe cartoon taught me not to
"waddle like a duck," as all the villains in the strip did when they were
being chased down by Buster Brown, who always caught them.

I don't remember being aware of or bothered that the people in
ads and comic strips were all white.

Some of these strips were insidious and damaging, the worst for
me being "Tarzan and the Apes." The problem was not so much the
portrayals of people, which my friends and I could see through, but
the portrayals of African space, especially of the forest. So deeply had
I received those images of snakes and wild animals that when, with
a guide, I was climbing the heavily forested Mount Cameroun years
later, it took two hours for me to stop expecting a huge snake to drop
out of a tree and block our path. I *knew* that the likelihood of such
an event was practically nonexistent, yet somewhere in my body this
childhood impression persisted.

Broad Street also brought me closer to the river, which I had not
seen since that miserable fishing trip with my stepfather and his
friends many years before. This time the river provided summer
adventure. It was a black-water river. While no black person could
swim at the municipal pool, we boys and a few brave (their adults
would say brazen) girls did swim at a bend in the river south of
Edisto Drive, a short mile below where whites swam. I looked
forward to the first part of the walk to our swimming place. It led me
through Edisto Gardens, a well-tended stretch along the river filled
with weeping willows, moss-hung cypress, dogwoods, azaleas, asters,
crabapple, wisteria, close-cut lawns, and many kinds of flowers.
These, along with a wasp nest big enough for a Guinness world
record that hung under the eaves of the municipal power plant, made
my walk memorable.

Since we had no lifeguard or adult supervision, we taught and
policed ourselves, with those who knew how teaching those who
didn't know, and with the warnings of some parents in our ears. Some
children asked no one, they just came. We dressed behind bushes,
and also did our business there. Another of my recurring dreams, for
years, was of avoiding feces on swamp paths. I don't remember any

fights. We were much too happy splashing and running about, seeking relief from sweltering heat, to be concerned with petty differences. No one drowned, but we did have one near miss.

At the bend in the river where we swam, the river split briefly, with a swift straight channel and a meandering backwater that formed an island. We swam on the near shore, where we had created a makeshift beach. Those among us who were strong swimmers crossed over to the island on occasion. Most of us, and all the girls and younger children, stayed in the backwater. One day two girls joined a human chain we had extended out into the river. I was between the two girls, the second-to-last link in the chain. Somehow we got too near the channel, the girl at the end lost her footing, and the girl holding my hand panicked and let go.

Before I knew what was happening, I found myself being yanked into the channel, under a struggling girl who didn't know how to swim. I remember seeing a green-brown translucence and being straddled by a flailing girl, who snapped the strap of my bathing suit. As I pushed her to the surface, I heard her sister screaming on the shore, which at the moment seemed far away. Reacting, not thinking, I took a deep breath and, frog kicking, pushed us towards the island. Two of the bigger boys had reached the island and were running towards us, one of them holding out a branch that was long enough for me to grasp. All the while our ears were being pummeled with the lamentation of the girl's sister. "Oh, Lawd, what am I gon do? My sister done drowned. Mama gon fix me…My sister, oh, oh, oh." Once safely on shore, we discovered that, except for a little water, the girl would be fine. Satisfied that her sister was all right, the formerly lamenting sister made a complete about-face and lit into her. "What you mean by goin out there?" And more that I didn't wait to hear. With my bathing suit on its way downstream, I headed to the bushes for my trousers. No one but me seemed to notice my pristine state. At least no one said anything to me about it.

That night I had trouble getting to sleep, which was not my habit. I twisted and turned so much that John Lee grumbled. Usually I went to sleep as soon as I hit the bed and slept soundly. I found myself reliving the events of the day and realizing how close we had come to having one of us drown. I had liked our swimming place until then. But now something about it felt less glamorous. I didn't form the thought that was lurking beneath the surface: why did we have to swim there, with the treacherous channel and no lifeguard, when less than a mile upstream was a public pool with two lifeguards, a clubhouse, and a tennis court? I had accepted watching the laughing boys and girls in convertibles race through my street on their way to *their* pool, waving back at them when they sometimes waved. It never occurred to me to try to join them. Nor did it occur to me that night. But I was uncomfortable. There was something going on that I could not put my mind around. Once again, I needed someone to talk to when there was no one.

My brother was transferred to a new elementary school for colored children while we were on Broad Street. Riverside Elementary had been built in 1930. It took some of the pressure off overcrowded Dunton Memorial and gave colored children on the west side of town a shorter distance to walk. Welcome though Riverside was, its construction showed me an example of "separate but equal," the lying claim of white Southerners. Riverside cost half as much to build as its white counterpart, Ellis Avenue Elementary, and lacked many of its appointments..

While it meant that John Lee had a shorter distance to walk, it also meant splitting us up. I continued where I was at Dunton Memorial, which had begun to add high school classes. While the move made sense, logistical and pedagogical, it may have been one more thing that added to the division between my brother and me. He would begin to have different friends, people I wouldn't know. The emotional distance between us would only increase.

• • •

Our Broad Street neighbors, the teacher couple next door, did not get along. He taught math and English, she history and home economics. Mr. Paul was a sophisticated Caribbean-born District of Columbia resident. She was from our small town, solid in her way but far too slow for him. He was slender, handsome, and high brown. He laughed a lot. She was quiet, sturdy, and dark. He seemed not much interested in women, her or any other. I liked Mr. Paul, who would tell me stories about the District of Columbia. He appeared to be from one of the "good" families there. At the end of one school year, Mr. Paul simply took off and returned to D.C., with no intention of returning. His wife did not appear to be much affected by the loss. Not too long after his departure, there was a black Plymouth coupe that belonged to a municipal utility official parked in front of her house on some nights. The car was always gone by morning. He— pudgy, blond, slightly red-faced, and married—and she maintained their liaison for several years, until she moved away. I never heard anyone even mention what was happening before our eyes, let alone comment on it. And she went to church most Sundays.

• • •

I took a big step towards what I thought was manhood at Broad Street. One morning I awoke to find a translucent sticky substance in my boxer shorts. Since I had long since stopped wetting the bed, it wouldn't be urine. I was puzzled until I remembered a dream of the night before. A pleasurable dream whose outlines were vague. It had something to do with girls, but their forms were not solid. They surrounded me. One put her hand on me. I felt a soothing warmth, then release. I never quite woke up. The sticky substance and the dream were connected somehow. This I felt, but had no word that connected them. What I would have given at the time for a big brother, or someone to explain the changes that were taking place in my body: the growth of pubic hair, the alertness I began to feel when in the presence of girls. My noticing them, their shapes. How they moved. It would be a while before my interest in them would displace marbles and comic books, but I mark that night as a beginning point.

• • •

Our moving from 243 Broad Street to Broughton Street coincided with several events, which from this distance I find hard to separate into concomitant and cause. Mrs. Ruth Dent, owner of the Broad Street house, returned from Up North, and found that the back room where she had stored her things had been opened. She pitched a righteous fit about it. "Can't trust colored people with nothing."

This hadn't set well with Mama. True, the room had been opened, but nothing had been taken out of it. This was demonstrated by the owner's inspection. She and Mama must have settled their misunderstanding somehow, because after the woman lived in the house for a while, she went back Up North for good, and we moved back into it. Was there an understanding between them that the owner's stay was only going to be temporary? My sister Edith came home from Up North to finish high school about that time. We needed more room for her. A couple my mother knew would take a room in the Broughton Street house. Their presence would help us pay the rent. Also, Mr. Miles, Mama's World War I veteran friend, had gotten a woman pregnant, and Mama had agreed to let her stay with us until she had her baby. I think Mama had added midwifery to her nursing certificate from the Chicago School of Nursing. So these things coming together landed us in a larger house at the corner of Broughton and Bull Streets, two and a half blocks away.

Broughton was a north-south thoroughfare, US Highway 378, which meant more traffic than on Broad Street. US 378 ran through town, up the hill through a white middle- and upper-class district, and away into the big world. Fortunately, not many people owned cars, the idea of the two-car family being years away. So traffic was light.

On Broughton Street, I began to make money mowing lawns and tending yards for white families in Hillcrest, the area upper Broughton ran through. From one of my gardening jobs, I brought home some azalea clippings that I planted on both sides of our front steps. It pleased me that they grew into healthy, colorful plants.

Gardening, shoe shining, and selling boiled peanuts gave me enough money to buy a bicycle with balloon tires, which was a good purchase, and a .22 rifle, which was a bad one. My bicycle gave me mobility. I could ride across town to school, around town on errands, to my jobs, and later I could ride girls on its frame. Buying the rifle was a foolish act. To begin with, I had no need for a rifle. I did not hunt. What is even worse is that I bought it on impulse solely to prevent someone else from having it. I bought it because I could.

Several boys and I were visiting at my house. One of the boys wanted to sell his rifle. He had offered it to another boy. I was holding it at the time. Guns can have a magnetic attraction. Brightly polished wood, polished metal, efficient design. Without quite knowing why I did it, I offered the seller more than the other boy had offered. He took my offer. Immediately after the high of his acceptance of my offer wore off, I began to feel a hollow, a drop-off like coming down from a sugar high. The other boy was disappointed and showed it. He probably had more use for a rifle than I had. His people did hunt. And it was a fine rifle. I wanted to say, "Aw, man, if you want the rifle, you can have it." But I didn't.

My rifle purchase was not my only excursion into guns. My next flirtation almost turned deadly. One warm lazy afternoon I was visiting Willie Mae and Jumbo, the young couple who had rented one of the front rooms. On the end table near the chair I was sitting in was an automatic handgun. While we talked I picked it up. Being the smart boy that I thought I was, I could see that the bullets for the automatic were kept in a clip in its handle. Playing it safe, I took out the clip and set it on the table. That done, I examined the gun, a .32 caliber. It fit snugly into my hand. I looked into the barrel, dark, well oiled. What I did not know, and apparently the young couple didn't know either, as I turned the gun generally in the direction of Willie Mae and squeezed the trigger, was that one round still remained in the chamber. The bullet missed Willie Mae, but it lodged in the wall behind her head. We were stunned by the sound of the shot. She and I sat riveted to our seats. Jumbo, who had been standing, walked over and reached out for the gun. I gave it to him in a daze. We three sat there for what seemed like a long while.

What to do?

No one was hurt. Except for extreme fright, Willie Mae was all right. The hole in the wall could be covered over. What about shooting the gun? No one else was at home, so we were safe there. Mama would bust a cap if she found out they had it. She'd make them move. She hadn't wanted me to buy the rifle. "What you need a gun for?" When I couldn't give her a satisfactory answer, she wanted me to sell it or give it back to its owner. "You better not let me see you with no gun." We'd all be in big trouble if anyone found out. So we kept it quiet. But I did not go back to their room again, and they didn't ask me why.

• • •

Mama ordered coal from Rickenbaker Coal Company for our kitchen stove, and when it came, it wasn't the kind she wanted. The round, red-faced Mr. Rickenbaker had already dumped the coal in our side yard when she and I went out to see it.

"That ain't what I ordered," she said.

"You ordered five hundred pounds, and that's what you got," he insisted.

Then began the oddest kind of conversation. When she had ordered coal, apparently she didn't specify what kind. Mr. Rickenbaker brought what was easiest for him, coal more fitting for a steam engine boiler, not the kind suitable for a chimney grate or a stove. He wanted her to accept this coal. After all, she hadn't said what kind she wanted. He had brought the amount she had ordered and had already dumped it out. What else did she want? She wanted him to take it back. I stood by, powerless to speak. Was it possible that this was the kind of coal some people used in stoves? Or did he not care what he sold us? Mama wouldn't budge. There we all were, shivering in what had begun to be a slight mist and would later turn to rain. Mama and the man, neither looking at the other. His black helper, leaning on his shovel, looked at me, then at Mama. I couldn't read him but I'm sure he was not used to colored people telling his boss what they didn't want. After what seemed like the longest time, Mr. Rickenbaker told his black helper to shovel the coal back into the truck. Since Rickenbaker's was the only coal company Mama knew, we were to do without coal for that winter.

• • •

One afternoon, John Lee was late coming home from school. Being responsible for him, I went to see where he was. His route was through Red Line, where Mama had told him not to stop and play. Red Line people were even poorer than we were. John Lee had reached the "Don't you tell me what to do" age, when no one could tell him anything. "You're not my mama!" was what I expected to hear when I found him playing in an abandoned lot with a group of Red Line children. He knew he was not supposed to be playing anywhere in his school clothes. He was supposed to come directly home, change his school clothes, and play close to home, where I could know where he was and who he was playing with. There were about a dozen children, of mixed ages, the youngest about six, the oldest a girl they called Big Lu, about sixteen. A group that included John Lee was happily playing a ring game. Big Lu, who seemed to be leader of the others, was standing a little off to the side.

My arrival on the scene changed things. I introduced another alien element into the equation. To a degree they had absorbed my brother—some knew him from their school. He spoke their language, took part in their games. Me? They knew I was his brother, even though we didn't look alike. We both had clean clothes. We both wore shoes. When I opened my mouth to speak, their worst suspicions were verified. I was not one of them.

As I walked up, one little girl ran into the house nearest the empty lot. I could hear her speaking to someone inside.

"Watchu want?" Big Lu asked, her voice wary, bordering on hostile.

"I came to get my brother," I said, in Miss Jenkins' English. "John Lee," I called, "Time to go home now."

"I came to get my brother," Big Lu mimicked me, pretty closely except for the "r," which came out "ah."

I ignored her, which may have been my mistake.

"John Lee," I called out, when he balked.

"Aww shucks, can't you see me playin?"

"You've got to change your clothes before you play. You know that."

"You got to change your cloz," Big Lu mimicked again.

I still ignored her.

John Lee reluctantly began to disentangle himself from his friends, some of whom surrounded me. Big Lu, furious at what she saw as my slighting her, set herself between me and the way I'd come, sticking out her chest and rearing back her head. A girl of about thirteen, on my right, sneered, "Why you want to come an mess with us? Dang! We wuz playing good."

As I took a step and turned to attend to this girl, my wide-angle vision caught a movement on my left. Big Lu had picked up a rusty spring from a Model T Ford's shock absorber and was swinging it at my head. Instinctively, I threw up my left arm and moved right. Her blow caught my elbow and lower arm, setting up a stinging sensation.

"Git in here!" a voice shouted from the porch of the house where the little girl had gone. An imposing woman, black and stern, in a housedress with no apron, stood waiting. Immediately the lot cleared, all the children, including Big Lu, scattering to their various houses.

On our walk home, following a little behind me, John Lee seemed more interested in whether I "would tell Mama on me" than in the condition of my arm. "I can't clean your clothes," I told him, and didn't really want to talk about it. Except for the tingle in my elbow, which didn't go away for several days, my arm wasn't hurt. Some rust from the spring was imprinted where it had struck. For days after, I had pictures of my head with a knot on it or worse. John Lee did come home from school first before play after that but didn't stop playing with the kids from Red Line.

When we were walking across town to Dunton Memorial together, I had been John Lee's big brother, his protector against some of the bigger boys who often made life miserable for the smaller ones. While I wasn't particularly large, I was fierce, especially when defending John Lee. I usually turned away attempts to get me riled over something about myself: my large feet, which they called steamboats and I called battleships, and nicknames like Spittacansah, because I used to spit a lot, and Snaggletooth, because of a broken front tooth. I was quick-tongued, and gave as good as I got. But I didn't allow anyone to pick on John Lee. Mess with him and they had me to beat. And they knew it. So when John Lee transferred to Riverside, I lost my role as protector. As it turned out, John Lee seemed to do very well fending for himself at his new school and making friends there.

CHAPTER SEVEN

Shorty the Iceman

I was a summer idler, Friday,
watching the blocks of ice crash klunking
out of the metal chute
to the waiting grappling hooks,
as a man slid it along the floor,
with a cruump into a waiting wagon.

"Boy, you want to work for me?"
He was the one they called Shorty, walked
with a limp. A summer job!

"All you got to do is take the ice in,
put it in the ice box. I'll pick it."

"Yes, sir. But I'll have to ask my mama,
if I'm gonna be working all day."

"All right. You akx your mama. Give
you fifty cents week. You any good,
make it a dollar. Be here Monday mornin."

"I don't know anything about this Mister Shorty,"
my mother was her usual skeptical self when I showed
enthusiasm over any new venture (she was usually right).
"But I guess it'll be better than hanging around
that old ice house. Worse yet, out in the streets."

Monday morning early I was there
while Shorty was backing Evelyn
into her traces. She was brown, alert, benign.
Gave a nod in my direction. I went to pet her.
"Leave that mule alone. I need you t'hep me.
Come on, hep me wit this ice." He was
struggling to arrange the hundred-pound blocks
in the wagon. I was slightly built, underweight
for my age; he didn't get much help from me.
Besides, my job was to begin when the wagon
was loaded and ready to roll. All the other
helper boys were standing around,
waiting for their drivers to call them.

Shorty's route was through a mainly white section
of town, large, well-kept houses, colonial-styled
white columns, with long shaded driveways
to the screened-in back porches, where the ice boxes
were located. Evelyn knew the route, Shorty knew
each house's daily order. Once in a while
a cook would send me back to the wagon for
"another twenty-five pounds if you got it.
We be having a party tonight."

Schooled by my mother to be polite to my elders,
and to move quickly when I worked, "none of that
slouching off there," I quickly became a favorite
with the cooks and maids on our route.

"Sonny Boy, you want a piece of this pie?"
I never had to be asked twice. "Now don't
let Shorty see it. He'll want some, and
he ain't getting none."

Nickels, a rare dime, many slices of potato pie
and deep-fried chicken drumsticks were
my fringe benefits.

I wanted to share with Shorty, another part
of my mother's schooling, "Don't be greedy now,"
but something in the cooks' warning made me
hold back. I pocketed my tips and ate my
yum-yums on the long driveways back to the wagon.

Miss Bronson, my fifth grade teacher, was working
as a maid that summer, when she was supposed
to be in "New Yawk."* She answered the door
as I was delivering their ice. She didn't need to tip
the dime (twice what anyone on the street gave)
to insure my silence. Her face as she opened
the door did that.

Our days were hot. Though our route wound
through tree-lined streets, making it cooler
than some, we were sweating by ten o'clock.
By noon our backs were soaked. Shorty's
limp became more noticeable as the day
grew hotter. He became irritable with Evelyn,
hitting her with a long cane if she stopped,
when a simple shake of the reins would have moved her.
I remembered the difference between the way
my uncles Ben and Johnny handled their mules,
Ben being the short-tempered one, going
for the whip at the least sign of a balk.

------

*It was not unusual for colored teachers to spend their summers Up North, working
"in service" to supplement their meager pay. Finding one working so close to home
was a surprise.

Using a grappling hook, Shorty positioned
the large blocks, and used an ice pick
to separate them into the weights each house needed.
I put the ice into a canvas bag that I slung over
my shoulder. Most orders were for fifteen
or twenty-five pounds, weights I could handle.

As the days passed, I sensed that Shorty
was looking to find something wrong with
my work. If a driveway was particularly long,
he would sometimes move to our next stop
without waiting for me. "We ain't got all day
you know," when I ran panting to catch up.
Determined to give Shorty nothing to find fault
with, I tightened up the time I used
for each delivery. This way
the week passed quickly, with no
further reprimand from him.

Each day I took my tips
home. By week's end they totaled a dollar
seventy-five cents. With my pay, I could buy
a pair of new secondhand shoes for school.
Had seen just the pair I wanted in Silver's window.

Saturday afternoon the helper boys gathered
around their drivers to receive their pay.
There was a lot of good-natured banter
between them. "What I'm o pay you for? Jivin
all them cute cooks and maids on the route.
Don't lie, now, I seed you. You ought to be payin
me."

I didn't see Shorty among the other drivers.
"He over there," one of the men told me,
when I asked for him. He was standing near
the barn. "I'd like to get on home now, Mr.
Shorty. Appreciate that little change."
"Boy, I ain't got nothin for you. You know
they took a lot out of my pay envelope
this week. I come up a little short."

I was stunned.

No money? I couldn't buy my shoes.
They cost two-seventy five. I was counting
on a dollar because he hadn't found
anything wrong with my work.

I looked over at the crowd of other drivers
and their helpers. They had stopped their
banter to pay attention to us.

When I recovered sufficiently, I asked him,
"When you go pay me?"

The other drivers started laughing. "Shorty,
he don't pay nobody. Be a fool to work for Shorty."

"Naw, he'll pay you. He just want you to beg
him for it. Then he'll throw it on the ground."

I looked at Shorty, standing there, jingling
coins in his pocket. The others looked to see
what I would do.

At first I didn't believe them.
How could he, how could anyone,
not pay me till I had begged
for my money. They were joking,
had to be.

But, looking at Shorty standing there,
jingling coins, I knew they weren't.

My mother hadn't raised me to beg. I mean,
from nobody. The money, keep it. I started
to walk away.

"Boy, you ain't going to walk off and leave
your money like that." "I wouldn't let him…"
I kept walking. My mother said mark it up
to experience. "I didn't figure that little
cripple nigger was no good nohow."

It was not unusual for people other than immediate family to live
with us during my growing up. My mother rented rooms to people
to help with the rent. She also took in a pregnant woman and kept
her until her delivery time when we lived on Broughton Street, and
another woman in one of our Broad Street houses. These pregnant
women were kept as favors to the men who had impregnated them.
In the first case it was Mr. Miles, the World War I vet. I never knew
who fathered the second child.

This sharing of space with others that helped me to become
acquainted up close with a lot of different people was a plus, but it
cut into my private space. Looking back, I can see myself spending
a lot of time in the street after school. One reason is that our houses
were small, crowded, and dark. The other is that there was almost
always someone in them. My mother may have thought that some
of these people helped take care of John Lee and me, though I think

leaving us with strangers while she had to work must have given her pause. And with reason. Some of the people who lived with us did not have her standards of child rearing, eating habits, or ethics. But she needed the money to keep a modest roof over our heads. So she took the gamble. With what had almost happened on Broughton Street, she almost lost.

After a very short time, Mrs. Dent, the owner of 243 Broad, wanted to go back Up North. She was successful there, and didn't feel the South was her home anymore. "The Negroes here are just too backward," she complained. "They won't get up off their behinds to do nothing. They make me sick." Mama, of course, jumped at the opportunity to go back to the house she liked so much. Mrs. Dent was not ready to sell the house then. She thought that she might want to retire in it, "if these folks down here ever get their act together." I had never heard "get their act together." I figured it was something she picked up Up North. My mother could not have bought the house then. Though she had her hospital job, she was still living from paycheck to paycheck. Mrs. Dent gave her the same deal she had earlier, modest rent for our keeping up the house and property. So back to 243 Broad Street we went.

My need to make money drove me briefly to a newspaper route, to selling a weekly magazine, and eventually to caddying. The newspaper route was my friend Nathaniel Fridie's idea. The *Augusta Herald*. He had a route of customers on the eastern side of town, which he walked before school. "You got a bicycle," he said, when I wondered how I could do a route and get to school. "Won't take you more'n an hour to run the route." My bicycle up to that point had been used strictly to get me back and forth to school. I was picky about where I rode it. Most of my customers would be people who lived on rutted dirt streets. There would be the danger of flats from nails or broken bottles, and when I took shortcuts through certain areas, there were clotheslines to duck under.

Once I accepted the route, I learned that there was more to it than delivering papers—picking them up from the distributor and seeing that they got to the right households. There was collection. We route boys were expected to make weekly collections from each house. Our pay was based on the amount we collected. This gave us incentive to add customers, since the more customers we got, the more money we made. This worked well in theory. The joker was in the collecting. While most customers paid, enough didn't, so eventually I found myself spending study time knocking on doors, listening to excuses. So I quit. Nathaniel fared better on his side of town because his customers were mainly college-trained people. Where he fell down was his need to walk his route. To get to school on time, he had to get up increasingly earlier. He began sleeping in class. Finally, giving fear for Nathaniel's health as his reason, his reverend father made him give up his route.

Selling *Liberty* magazine turned out no better for me. Except for the ones I sold for cash, walking the streets downtown, the problem of collection kept me from making enough to make the venture worthwhile. Working downtown did have an unexpected bonus. It allowed me to meet Willie (William Warren Adams, as he liked to tell anyone who'd listen), who, as it turned out, lived in my neighborhood. But this was not before I spent a lost week working for Shorty on an ice delivery wagon.

Willie was selling boiled peanuts on the courthouse steps. I carried my shoeshine box. "Better git one now. They'll be gone in a minit!" He was right. Hardly had I bought my nickel bag than he was shaking his tray upside-down like a magician's tablecloth, "See, gone!" he laughed and spun around.

"Where you from? I haven't seen you 'round here."

"School's just out. First time out this summer. I live over on Broad Street, next to them holy rollers."

"Naw! You do? I live around the corner, down foot of Windsor. Right next to the Ditch. How come I ain't seen you before?"

"Haven't been there that long, I guess. And I've been going to school." I shared my peanuts with him, he having sold all of his, and we sat on the courthouse steps, at the edge where the sun hadn't reached yet.

I remembered seeing a small house on Windsor down near the Ditch, which was open at that point as it meandered its way to the river, a few blocks away. Willie was my age, going on sixteen, but had left school after the Christmas season. "I had to make me some money," he explained. He was living with a woman he called

Grandma, with whom his mother had left him as a baby when she went Up North. Grandma had also raised his mother, who had likewise been left with her. He had only seen his mother a few times, at Christmas, when she'd brought him new clothes and presents for everyone. "She say she gonna send for me or come get me," he said confidently. "Take me with her up to Harlem. Hot dog!" His eyes sparkled as he said "Harlem," and he danced a few steps with his tray as partner. What I knew of Harlem had come from Lemuel, the boy the Watsons had lured South when we lived on Railroad Avenue. Lemuel's Harlem didn't seem like a place I'd be dancing about. But that had been a while back, maybe Harlem had changed. I didn't say anything. We were walking and as we passed Doyle's drug store and ice cream parlor, Willie hit on the idea of ice cream cones. We had money, Willie from selling his boiled peanuts, I from selling my shoeshines. But we wouldn't be served ice cream at Doyle's Drugs. Coming up Russell was a white boy about our age, a boy we hadn't seen before. He didn't walk like the white boys we knew. I couldn't figure out why until he came abreast. He smiled. Willie, ever the opportunist, smiled back and asked him if he'd do us a favor. "What's it gonna cost me?" he asked, with a non-Southern accent, still smiling. Willie walked into the cave made by the front of Betty's Dress Shop, next door to Doyle's. "What we'd 'preciate is if you would get us two ice cream cones from Doyle's. We got the money." He held out a quarter. "Wait here," the boy said, picking up on our dilemma, and not missing a beat.

When he came back with our cones, vanilla for Willie, buttered pecan for me, and chocolate for himself, the boy told us his name was Lloyd Castile. His father was one of the new administrators or something at the Hawthorne air training school, he said. Home from school for the summer, Lloyd hadn't yet made many friends. He was on his way, he said, from Charlie Suggs' house. "You know Charlie?" he asked, as though we might be acquainted, buddies with people he might know. Willie shook his head no. It just so happened that I did know Charlie Suggs. He was one of the few white boys who had come down to the great oak on Russell and Windsor for Saturday morning marble shooting. "I know Charlie," I said. "Least, I used to see him down on Russell where we shot marbles." "Neat

O!" Lloyd said. He liked "Neat O!" and used it every chance he got. I didn't tell him that Charlie never won any marbles. That we saw him as a shy runt who had a paper and pencil stuck in his back pocket, forever making cartoon figures. We wondered why he had come to play. "Charlie has a neat backyard," Lloyd said, "I was just by there."

"We have to be getting on," Willie said, as our conversation began to attract the attention of passersby. "You gotta come by sometime," Lloyd continued, walking back a way with us. He seemed oblivious to anything but what he was engaged in at the moment, talking to us. I found later that this being able to block out everything but what was in front of him was part of his character. I learned to admire this ability, especially as it was one I lacked, being constantly alert to every passerby.

"You going?" Willie asked, when we were walking down Windsor towards our houses. Lloyd had said he lived someplace up on Ellis Avenue, a well-off white neighborhood. "I don't know," I said, which was not quite true. I had liked the cartoons Charlie was always drawing, and wondered how he did it. I probably would go.

I did go.

Charlie Suggs lived a long block down from the shoe repair shop, so after I started working there, we got better acquainted. His house was the first one past the end of the stores on the west side of Broughton.

He lived with his mother and an older sister, Veronica. His family lived modestly, being supported mainly by a father who had been separated from them before we met. I learned this from Mrs. Suggs on cold evenings as we sat by the fire, Charlie at his table, drawing. I occasionally dropped by on my way after work. They kept a warm house, with books and lots of comic books around. Mrs. Suggs, as a woman of modest looks with no husband, had little chance at much of a social life in Orangeburg. In a culture where a woman's social worth was defined by the position of her husband, she had little or none. So she was lonely. Were I not there, she would have talked to Charlie, when she could pry him away from his drawings. Charlie could be cranky once in a while, but he was not mean, so I got along with him by ignoring him when he was cranky. This he didn't seem to mind. He had developed his comic book art to where I thought some of his work was just as readable as some of the comic books we bought from the newsstand. I expected him to go on and become a comic book writer. We lost contact after I left, so I never knew what happened to him. I wish I did.

• • •

Willie took me by his house to meet his Grandma Anderson. We found her sweeping the front yard. Before she even asked who I was, she offered us each a slice of watermelon. "You set down heah'n eat this. Hits bilin out heah," she said, as she handed us generous slices from a large melon she had just picked that morning and had cooling in a tub of water. *I am going to like this lady,* I told myself, as I dug into the deep red meat, spitting out the black seeds.

"'n who is this young genulmun we got heah?" she asked Willie, when we were comfortably settled around the small kitchen table. The kitchen itself was small, like the house was small, a box shape of three small rooms and the kitchen. Her garden was large. It seemed to stretch a hundred feet along the Ditch, in fertile bottomland. I could see rows and rows of beans, peas, corn, squash, and melons, and some stalks of sugar cane. And there was more that I couldn't see. There were chickens picking-picking up and down the rows. Occasionally one would be airborne to snatch some winged insect.

Willie told her who I was and how we had met. She asked about my family, and was pleased to hear that my mother was a God-fearing woman. "'n she keeps you in school. That's good. I wish this'n woulda gone on. But he heps me a lot, sellin and like that. I can't get around like I useta, with my rumatiz and that. An the garden. Somethin all the time hurtin." Willie's being able to read also helped, as Mrs. Anderson was unlettered.

She did not get to church much herself lately, "'smuch as I'd like to." And she wasn't picky about her church. Said she was always like that. "Don't they all pray to the same God?" I had no answer for her. I did notice that she had a hand-painted picture of a black Jesus over the fireplace mantelpiece, something I had never seen. Since I only went to church when I couldn't avoid it, it did not bother me that she only went to church once in a while. With a garden that large, I didn't see how she would have time to do much of anything but rest. She was short, compact, like Geechie and Gullah women, of a lovely blackness. Life radiated from her dancing eyes, though her movements were slower than they must have been when she was younger. Her garden produce was what she lived on, plus money from Willie's mother. Whatever money Willie got from selling, he brought home to her. He made his spending money caddying at the city-funded white country club, where he said that he would take me.

Soon after, I went with Willie to caddy. A wood separated the country club from the houses of well-to-do whites. Beyond it stretched farmlands. To its west were a swampy wooded stretch and the Edisto River. Orangeburg Country Club had a nine-hole course, mostly flat, with hard fairways, untended rough, and a water hazard on the fourth hole. The clubhouse was at the highest point, with the holes sloping down and winding around it.

Ozzie Slater, a black man in his thirties, was the caddy master. He lived on the club grounds with his father, the greenskeeper. Mr. Slater kept the greens in excellent shape and kept the fairways trimmed, but had only water enough to keep the approaches to the greens soft. The roughs were another matter. Once a ball left the fairway, a golfer was in big trouble.

As caddies we had to position ourselves to be able to follow the flight of the ball, and to mark in the rough where it landed. Some caddies could do this, some couldn't. Helping the golfer with club selection, especially a golfer unfamiliar with the course, and helping judge the direction the ball would break on the green, and finding the ball in the rough were the skills that separated good caddies from mediocre ones. Willie taught me well. "Always mark it with a bush or tree, a rock or something," he would say as we had a practice round. "And don't take your eye off it. Go straight where you see it land."

I learned. It always pleased me to do something well enough to be praised for it.

Especially when the praise was accompanied by money. Tips were an essential supplement to the pittance we received for our work, twenty-five cents for nine holes. If our golfer played eighteen holes we made a half-dollar. Golfers paid the club twice what we were paid.

The difference between the money the golfer paid and the money we received was supposed to go to our maintenance, the caddy pen. Fiction. There was no maintenance. Our caddy pen was kept worse than a pigsty.

On Sundays we were sometimes lucky enough to catch a bag both in the morning and afternoon. That was a boon—but a boon acquired by ten miles of walking, carrying a heavy bag of clubs and balls under a scorching sun. There was no water fountain on the course, and no bottled water. The fourth hole wound back near to the clubhouse. We caddies were made to run to the caddy master's shack and bring Cokes back for our golfers. On rare occasions a golfer would offer a Coke to his caddy. We couldn't afford Cokes. Where would our wages go? We would run to the shed where the machines for working the grounds were kept, and drink from a hose, ever alert in order to be back at our posts before our golfers reached the fifth tee.

Caddies cultivated "regulars," golfers who looked for them each time they played. The better tippers were sought after, and usually were taken by caddies who came every day and depended on this work for their livelihood. They were older, usually larger, and were not above using their size to intimidate smaller caddies. Over time I acquired several regulars, one by default.

No one wanted to caddy for Harry Wannamaker Jr., because he had a large heavy bag and was a stingy tipper. This despite his being a well-off insurance broker, real estate agent, and secretary to the country club. A tall slender man, he was always nattily dressed. I took him because he was an accurate driver, with a roundhouse slice that usually landed him in the fairway. He was an excellent putter. This was good for me since I often worked barefoot. On bare feet the rough could be brutal. And a tip from no golfer was assured. My loyalty to Mr. Wannamaker was to cost me.

One year, '40 or '41, Orangeburg was host to the state amateur championship. Golfers from all over the state would be coming to play, golfers from wealthy clubs where larger tips were the rule. I was counting on Mr. Harry to be eliminated early, so that I might have a chance at one of the out-of-towners. No such luck. My man, familiar with the course, hung in until he was a finalist. I consoled myself with the thought that in a tournament, and him winning, he might loosen up a little. Willie's golfer, Mr. Horne of Horne Motors, had given him five dollars after he had won his first round match. So I had hope.

The final match was played on a cold rainy day. My golfer wore a waterproof slicker and rubbers with cleats in them. I had no such gear. Fortunately, the match was closed out, at four and three I think, with my man four holes up with three to play. We were able to go to the clubhouse early. The losing golfer gave Sugar, one of the older caddies, three dollars. After having me dry his bag and clean his clubs and shoes, while he showered and had a bourbon and soda, Mr. Harry Wannamaker Jr. came out, inspected his clubs. Satisfied with his inspection, he thanked me. Buoyed by his thanks, I didn't move. Realizing that I wasn't moving until he did something more, he reached into his pocket and handed me a dime. He lost a caddy with that action. I felt an utter fool.

Fortunately, caddying was an occupation neither Willie nor I considered seriously. I needed some kind of work to add to my income. Caddying, even with its many shortcomings, filled that bill. As I found other jobs, lawns, gardens, I caddied less. Willie said it was something to do until his mother sent for him to join her in Harlem. Meanwhile, he made the most of it. Because he was pleasant and outgoing, he received many perks. His golfer, Mr. Horne, took him for a ride in his private plane.

Willie was also a caddy for Miss Jane Crum, daughter of the Crum/Livingston family, wealthy, generous, highly respected townspeople. Tall, tomboyish, her father's favorite, people said, she was Orangeburg's hope for a major female golfer. At first, she played well in practice but wilted under competition. Willie had to be cheered up after Miss Jane was eliminated in the second round of the ladies' state tournament. "Man, two holes, just two holes, and we coulda done it!" he lamented. I suffered with him because Miss Jane Crum was always nice to us caddies. She remembered our names and tipped us well. She even gave us rides to town when she practiced late. I remember only one other white woman who would be so kind, Mrs. Dick Horne. Maybe, as a woman in what had long been an all-male sport, Miss Crum understood what it was like to be discriminated against. We had been pulling for her. She did go on to become a highly successful golfer, winning numerous statewide tournaments and awards.

My caddying ended on a sour note, one that led me to question the nature of Willie's friendship. It was on a warm moonlit night when several of us were hanging out on the fifth tee. We either hung out there or under one of the few corner street lamps in our neighborhood. I always liked this kind of night, when dew had fallen, there was a slight haze from the swamp, and there were sounds of insects and night birds, and an occasional screech owl. I lay back on a rise at the back of the tee as the others talked the interminable boy talk, of their golfers, of the women they had or wanted, of their scores the last time they played, and why they hadn't played better. The "if only." I had drifted off when Donnie G, one of my hostile neighbors from lower Broad Street, noticed that I had not been taking part. Donnie G and his brother had stolen my marbles during my marble shooting days. We never locked our house—few people did—so a person could come in and walk off with almost anything they wanted. Within limits. There was always someone home on the street in one or other of the houses, so a body would be stopped and questioned if a large item was taken. Marbles could be carried in pockets and go undetected. They denied they had taken my marbles, even after I'd found Donnie G's brother using one of my taws in a game. "It got yo name on it?" Donnie G had sneered.

I don't remember what triggered Donnie G's assault. I remember grappling with him and trapping his arms, finally throwing him to the ground and holding him there as he struggled.

"Nigger, let me up from heah!" he shouted, as he tried to wiggle out from under me. He was crying with rage. The other boys, including Willie, said nothing and did nothing to stop us.

"I'll let you up if you'll leave me alone," I said, still holding him down but looking to Willie and the others for help. They still did nothing. Finally, I said, "All right, get up." As I moved so he could wriggle out from under me, he got up, ran over to the edge of the tee, and grabbed one of the markers for teeing off. It had a four-inch spike in it to hold it in the ground. Donnie G started towards me with this marker. I looked to the others to help. There was no one. They seemed to be enjoying our predicament. I was furious. I was stronger than Donnie G. I had proved that. I could take the chance of dodging the spike and taking it away from him. Or, if he happened to gash me with that spike, I would be hurt seriously. I was less angry at Donnie G, even as he was being foolish and potentially dangerous, than I was at the other boys, especially my friend Willie, who could have easily pulled us apart and stopped the fight; and who even at this point could call to Donnie G to put the marker back.

Seeing no help in them, and not wanting to take further part in something that could result in serious injury—I had enough of a temper that if I had taken away the spike from Donnie G I don't know what I would have done to him—I ran away. Down off the tee, across the fairways, into a path though the woods, eventually to a path that led out to Broughton Street and home. I wanted to be away, away from Donnie G and the fight, from Willie and the others. How could I tell them that I left the fight scene because I did not want to hurt someone, or to be hurt, over nothing. I had seen too many people injured over some triviality. I had nearly blinded my own brother in a burst of anger.

I didn't stop being friends with Willie, even though I didn't accept his explanation for not intervening. "Man, you were doing all right. You had him down. You shoulda beat the hell outta him. That's what I woulda done." I still went to movies with him, still called him friend, but not a friend I could count on to watch my back.

•   •   •

That summer, several of us boys pulled what we could call our boat caper. Willie and I joined Teets from around the corner on Shuler Street, and with Lloyd Castile and a redhead named Rod, met in Charlie Suggs' backyard. Charlie's yard was deep. It had several trees and a shed we could use as a kind of clubhouse. Mrs. Suggs was glad to have us play in the yard, since she would know where her son was. Occasionally she made lemonade for us. We played cards and checkers, Charlie drew cartoons for us. Charlie was a sore loser, and would sometimes take up his cards and stomp into his house. It was at one of those times that the rest of us ended up at Slater's Landing.

Slater's Landing was a worn dock located on a bend in the river on a line just below the golf course. The landing harked back to the days when stretches of the river had some commercial use, when cotton could be loaded there and floated downriver. But what we found were a couple of old rowboats, one on each side of the dock.

"Let's take one out." This from Lloyd Castile.

"Who knows how to row?" asked Rod.

"I don't know about taking out this boat. We don't know who it b'longs to." Teets introduced caution.

"Aw, nobody's gonna care about this old boat. I can row," Willie said.

"And I can row." Lloyd had been on the rowing team at his school, he said.

It was only an old boat, we reasoned. Who would care? It was tied up with a rope. Not even locked. There was nobody in sight up and down the river as far as we could see. We were in a wooded area at the end of a dirt road. Teets, Willie, and I had planned to go to caddy after wandering through the woods. Lloyd and Rod had said they were going back to town.

The boat sat four easily, five could be squeezed in. Lloyd and Willie would row, the rest of us would sit. All went well as we went upstream. But as we turned to come back downstream, we became unbalanced and spun around in the water. Teets, in the bow, stood up. Lloyd tried to halt the spin with his paddle but couldn't.

"Sit down!" he shouted to Teets. Teets, shocked, plopped on the gunwale, tipping the boat. I, in the stern, tried to tip the boat the other way. Before anyone knew quite what happened, the boat had capsized, and we were standing around in the shallow water. The others waded to shore, leaving me with the boat. As they reached shore, we heard a motor struggling up the road. Someone had come.

My friends all took to the woods, leaving me alone with the upside-down boat. Though I was frightened by what whoever came might do, I decided to keep trying to right the boat and get it to shore. The white men who got out of the car with their fishing tackle were the boat's owners. With one of the miscreants in hand, they didn't give chase to the others. I must have made a picture both pitiful and comical, trying to right the boat while keeping it from pulling me downriver. It must have been mostly comical, because although they weren't pleased that we'd taken their boat, their only punishment for me was to make me right the boat and bring it to shore, and extract a promise, backed by threat of dire consequences next time, to leave their boat alone. That was an easy promise. I kept it. Wet as a doused puppy, I was mostly dry by the time I reached the golf course, where a contrite Willie and Teets awaited me. I wasn't buying it.

• • •

Willie's mother did come for him. She brought an air of "city" with her. Her clothes, which set off her features well, were of a fashion not seen in Orangeburg. She was tall like Willie. Their resemblance was strong. Willie adored her. Her coloring was such that her father most likely had been white. Since she'd had Willie in her mid-teens, she was still a young woman, and striking—as was also the man who drove her down from Harlem. They made an elegant couple, either sitting in their new-looking Buick or walking the streets.

The man had relatives in town and went to stay with them until she was ready to leave. He was introduced as a friend, not a husband, so could not have stayed with them even if there had been room in the tiny house.

For a woman of such looks, Willie's mother was surprisingly modest. And so helpful. She immediately set about buying new things for the house, such as new curtains for the living room, a new rocking chair and throw rug. She worked the garden with Mrs. Anderson as though she had never left home. And she took Willie into town and brought back a large bag of fruit, nuts, and candy. She flattered me by saying she was glad that Willie had such a nice smart boy for a friend. She insisted that I had to live with them "when you come up to Harlem." "South's got nothing for you. Young Negro men don't stand a chance down here. That's why I'm taking Willie with me." Infatuated, I was ready to pack up my things and follow them. "Miz Esther, I'll be there," I promised.

When they left, I missed Willie. Despite the knowledge that our friendship was conditional, he had been the most fun of all the boys I knew. As such, he was irreplaceable.

His leaving also affected Mrs. Anderson, who did not live long after. Willie seems to have been her life, her reason for existence. She was inordinately proud of him. What bothered me at the time of her death was that neither Willie nor his mother came down for her funeral. On reflection, I have tempered my criticism of them. With communication being as tenuous as it was, it is possible they didn't know she had died. Who knew their address to tell them? I didn't know she was dead until her funeral was announced. She had no relatives that I knew of. Her funeral was attended by friends and fellow churchgoers. I forced myself to look at her when her casket was opened for viewing. She looked peaceful in death, relaxed in the eternal sleep of the dead.

• • •

The Great Depression ground on, slouching through our communities, leaving devastation like a war. Throughout the thirties, our people were stretched to their limits just to hold on. Subsistence was a prize and came at a price. Mama, herself too proud, would send John Lee and me to seek out my stepfather when she heard from her sources that he was working at some lumberyard or other. She sought to shame him into at least providing for his son. Rarely did he give us anything. We seldom found him, and when we did, he usually brushed us off with promises he never kept. When I went alone, I learned to ignore him, and take my crocus bag into the back of the yard and collect wood chips and bark for our stove.

My stepfather finally played out his string. He had not been around for years when he decided he wanted to come back to live with us. Mama, having been on her own for so many years, with a job now that allowed us to move up from destitution to poverty, felt that she didn't need him. She told him that he could not come back. He refused to accept her decision. Apparently, since he had always been able to sweet-talk his way back into our lives, he thought he could do it one more time. He didn't recognize or appreciate how much things had changed. When she refused him, he insisted on his right as a husband. If he wanted to come back, she had to take him in. She balked. I supported her. John Lee was not asked what he felt. We developed a plan.

One night we three were in the kitchen, sitting around the table, when he opened the front door and came into the front room. I shut the kitchen door, got the rifle from its wall rack and called out to see who was there.

"It's me."

"What do you want?"

"Open the door, I want to talk to your mama."

"She say she don't want to talk to you."

"Open the door and let her tell me that herself."

I looked at Mama. She shook her head several times.

"If you don't open that door, I'm comin in."

"I got a gun. If you come in this door, I'll shoot."

There was a silence on the other side. A long pause. Then a voice that didn't want to believe but seemed afraid of the consequence of not believing.

"You wouldn't shoot me, would you, boy?" I didn't say anything.

"I always knowed you wuz a little crazy. No, I b'lieve you would."

Nothing from our side of the door.

After a short wait, a shuffling, then steps to the front door and out of our lives.

What John Walker didn't know was that the rifle was empty. Always had been. Mama had refused to allow me to buy bullets for it. "What fuh? Who you gon shoot?" I didn't take a lot of convincing. The rifle was a kind of albatross for me. It had followed me to Broad Street from Broughton, the scene of that nearly disastrous shooting with the "unloaded" automatic. It was irony that allowed us to use it as a bluff. It was a gamble we had to win. And we had won. That was the last time Mama was to have direct contact with him. I wish I could say the same.

Several years later, Mama got word that John Walker was injured and in Tri-County Hospital. A sawmill accident somewhere down near Augusta. She wanted to know how he was but didn't want to go herself. So I went. I was of mixed mind. One part of me didn't want to go. He had been out of our lives for so long. He had not come up in conversation. Until then. Why did he have to come back now? Another part of me was curious, to see what he looked like, to see the new hospital, built on a rise beyond the wood where Ned

Jones and I used to play. So I went during afternoon visiting hours. It was a sunny day and the hospital spaces were bright and airy, a far cry from the dinginess and grime Mama had suffered through at the old hospital on Glover Street. Mama had given me a bag of Florida oranges to take to him. "He ain't got no peoples," she said. He seemed glad to see me, did not appear surprised. He took one of the oranges from the bag I had set on his nightstand and ate it.

What surprised me was how much he had changed in the few years since I had last seen him. Never a large man, he had shrunk considerably. I hardly recognized this pinched black face surrounded by all those white covers. He had been thrown off a cat skinner. Not one to talk much, he didn't elaborate. I didn't pursue. His injuries were internal. After the perfunctory greeting and news of the family, I sat awkwardly. Neither of us mentioned our last encounter. I don't know what I would have said if he had brought it up. Then I asked if there was anything I could do for him. There was. He wondered if I might rub his feet. His feet in my hands were like those of a big child. I stretched his feet and pulled on each of his toes. That pleased him. He was on an open male ward, so he did have people around. Though I didn't ask his ward nurse, I suspect I might have been one of few visitors. After sitting for a while, I left, promising to return, knowing I wouldn't. Mama was satisfied with my one visit. And so was I. We heard later that he had been discharged from the hospital. We assumed that he went back to Augusta.

CHAPTER EIGHT

While I Thought God, My Mother Saw

While I thought God, my mother saw
She worked, watched and prayed
"Living humble," knowing the bell
Had rung.

"Rock" to my mother was a place to hide
While I, ignorant though not innocent of sin
Played "can't ketch me"
Around the huge stone in the lower yard.

My mother's hell was a fiery furnace,
Rock-melting hot,
A vision she wanted me to share.

God knows I tried. But at twelve I found
Her longing for my salvation
A burden too great to bear.

When she cried, "Jesus, Jesus," I fell outside
Her pain and ecstasy, as she walked
And talked with One who gathered her
In His arms and saw her home.

Mrs. Dent came down for what would be her last visit to her house at 243 Broad Street. Mama found some roomers who would cover more than the rent, and we moved across the street to a larger house, one next door to the one-room Sanctified church, whose members were called "holy rollers" by outsiders because of their practice of throwing themselves about the church and falling down in the aisles in their religious ecstasy. Their congregation also "spoke in tongues," an experience that caused my skin to crawl the one time I witnessed it. The minister, Reverend Louis Shipper, and his wife, Janice, lived in a corner house behind a wire fence next to the church. I thought them a narrow-minded couple. They held themselves apart from their neighbors who did not practice their brand of religion. We were included in their censure, especially since my mother had no husband and allowed all kinds of people into our house. They were later to cause Mama trouble, and earn my undying enmity. John Lee and I drew a back room next to the church, about even with the pulpit. We eventually accustomed ourselves to the drums and tambourines, but for a while they cut into our sleep. Asking them to tone down their services would have been out of the question. These were "people of God." In their view, our duty was not to complain but to join them. During my time at home, I never saw a single neighbor ever set foot in Reverend Shipper's church.

Our roomers made up an interesting lot. I especially liked one couple, a tall woman with a short husband. They were much in love. When the woman was teased about having such a short husband, she would reply, "He little but he heavy." That usually shut up their nosey friends.

The other family got itself into trouble with Mama for two reasons. They were a young grandmother, her daughter and granddaughter. Mama said that the woman told her that she had a daughter, but conveniently forgot to mention that her daughter also had a daughter. Adding to the woman's debits were her personal habits. Mama was especially offended by her lax personal hygiene. This Mama could not tolerate, so they were not with us long. Their place was taken by our second pregnant woman, who was also to stay with us only until her child was born.

It was more the rule than the exception for us to have people in the house who weren't relatives. The Great Depression was especially hard on family unity, forcing people out of their homes in search of livelihood and breaking up families through desertion, the poor people's substitute for divorce. Or forcing families to take in strangers to help with the rent. Which made Sanctified Reverend Shipper's put-down of us all the more off-base.

• • •

Mrs. Bowman, our widowed neighbor and a member of Mama's church, boarded Eartha Mae, a girl from the country. Mrs. Bowman was a friend of the girl's parents. It was common practice for those who wanted their children to have a high school education not available to them in the country to board their children with friends who lived in town. Eartha Mae's parents would let her stay in town as long as she did well in school. She loved school and wanted desperately to succeed in it. Sometimes when I did not take my bicycle, we walked to school together. As it was a long walk, we had much time to talk. She was going to be a nurse, she said. Her grandfather had some kind of illness the doctor didn't cure, and she wanted to learn about it. She had been talking to the folk at the college about how to get to a nursing school.

We had some good talks, about her people in the country, how much she wanted to succeed for them, so they could say they had someone finish high school, at least. She would be the first in her family. I didn't know what I wanted. Some of everything, I guessed. I was working at the shoe repair shop afternoons after school at that point. I might do that when I graduated. I didn't know. Everything I thought of took money, money I did not have, money I had no idea how to get.

As Eartha Mae and I enjoyed talking with one another, we became friends. With her heavy study schedule, and my work and study and no money, we never considered dating. We were just good friends.

She was allowed no boyfriends. Not that she wanted any, but Mrs. Bowman didn't want "any of these little raggedy-ass boys smelling around. First thing you know, you bigger than a cow." I was the boy across the street. She knew my mother. They went to the same church. I didn't count.

Then as spring approached, I noticed a change in Eartha Mae. She was quieter, often with long silences between topics. This when she usually could match me word for word, idea for idea. She could out-talk and out-think me seven days of the week. Her silences bothered me, so one day I asked her why she was so quiet.

"I might not be keeping on in school."

Her grades were excellent, I knew. That was the condition for her parents to let her stay. Her parents were well-off farmers, so it couldn't be money. When I didn't say anything, she continued, "Me and Miz Bowman don't get along too well."

She said that Mrs. Bowman had been pressuring her to do more around the house. She had resisted.

"My people paying her for my room and board. Nobody didn't say nothing about me being no servant. Now she want me…" She stopped. We had reached her front yard. "Come by if you can after work tonight. Just knock on the window like always. We can talk then."

It was fully dark when I had put my bicycle away and walked around to the back of the house where her bed/work room was located. The shade was pulled, which was unusual. As I got close enough I could see two struggling shadows, swaying across the plane of the window. A space had been left at the bottom of the shade. The room was lighted by a kerosene lamp on a chest of drawers that gave off little light, so at first I had trouble making out the writhing figures. As my eyes got more accustomed to the light, I could see Eartha Mae twisting and turning, trying to keep a man from pulling down her panties. He was hampered by his own trousers, which he had opened and which kept slipping, so that he had to keep one hand on them. He had got her panties almost to her knees.

I could hear a muffled "Naww, naww," from her, and a "Aw, come on, I ain't gonna hurt you, girl," from the man.

Shocked and excited, my thoughts were falling all over one another. Who was this man? What to do? Then he turned towards the window. More shock. The man was attorney Jones, our town's one colored lawyer, and first deacon in our church.

Before I knew what I was doing, I rapped sharply on the window. Startled, he let her go. She pulled up her panties and put down her dress in a single motion. I bolted just as she was smoothing her dress. Watching from behind our front hedge, I saw his car speed away soon after.

"Miz Bowman said it was you," Eartha Mae told me on our way to school next day. "I told her I couldn't see who it was, and I didn't care. She said she'd whip me if I talked like that to her. I told her that my mama didn't whip me and she sure as hell wasn't gonna. She said we'd see about that, but she let me alone."

Suddenly she began to cry, a little at first, then with body-shaking sobs. "A. D., what am I to do? I can't afford no being sent home." This between sobs.

"She can't send you home. You haven't done anything."

"Oh, but yes she can. My daddy thinks she the Lord almighty. That's why he trust me with her."

"But what she did, and Deacon Jones..."

"Oh ho-o." She stopped crying. "You think I'm the first seventeen-year-old cherry the deacon tried to pick?"

"But, I mean, she..."

"Yeah, she? So what? And I think he gave her money, too. I heard him say something about ten dollars, and she promised him it'd be easy." Her eyes flashed. "It's my word against hers, and your word against Deacon Jones. Who's gonna believe a seventeen-year-old girl and a hot-pants boy in something like this? You got to know better than that."

We had reached school. She said she had to go to the girl's bathroom. I told her I would ask my mother. She said all right, if I wanted to waste my time.

"A. D., why you want to get in the middle of something like this?" Mama complained, before I had time to tell her everything. How did I know the girl wasn't lying? I had witnessed. "Witnessed what, A. D.? Now, you know you wrong getting mixed up in other people's business. That's not the way I raised you. Stay out of other people's business. Mind your own."

"But she's my friend."

" A. D., I didn't know you had a girlfriend."

"Not like that. Aw, Mama, you don't understand."

"I understand enough to know that when you come in here telling me the deacon in our church smelling around some little stinking-behind girl, you talking dog doo-doo. Now you just mind your own business."

Eartha Mae had only two months to graduation. She decided to tough it out.

"I won't bother her if she don't bother me. I'll try to stay out of her way. But I'm going to get my diploma, if I have to walk over her body to do it. And she better believe it."

She got her diploma with honors and left the state.

• • •

My soul's salvation had long been of concern for my mother, herself a God-fearing member of the venerable Williams Chapel African Methodist Episcopal Church. Even as a small boy I had needed clearer explanations of the mysteries of faith and belief than those offered to me. They were not forthcoming.

Mama and I tiptoed around the questions of faith and belief during my early teen years. She assumed we were hearing the same things as we sat together in church on the Sundays I went with her. Since it was easier for me, I did nothing to dispel her assumption. My mother's religious beliefs had been established in the Saint Paul's African Methodist Episcopal community of Pregnall, South Carolina, during the early years of the twentieth century. She had been born in 1894. She grew up accepting Bible stories as fact, as did the people around her. They interpreted them literally. Their religious services, with Bible-thumping, shouting preachers who pranced up and down the church aisles, chanting, singing, even screaming at congregations, with "sisters" who fainted after heaving their bodies in ecstasy, were closer to those of the Sanctified churches than most of them would care to admit. People went to church to be "moved by the spirit," and it was the minister's job to call the spirit in.

My mother believed in the efficacy of prayer. She kneeled at her bed every morning after she got up and every night before she went to bed. Without fail. Most of her prayers were brief, except when she was troubled, at which times they were extended until she felt satisfied that her burden, the one that she brought to her Jesus as she had been taught to do, was lifted. "The Lord will provide," when times were especially tough. "Didn't He deliver Daniel?" (from the lion's den) "If Our Lord delivered Daniel, He'll sholly deliver us. Now, ain't that right?! Let me hear 'amen'!" A chorus of shouted "amens," accompanied by fervid clapping and stamping of feet. She heard these things as she prayed, and was sustained by them. "Work, watch, and pray," were the three legs of her moral stool. These three tenets were thoroughly ingrained in the songs and lore that are still constantly revived. "He taught me how to watch, watch and pray" are words from a contemporary best-selling gospel, "Oh Happy Day." "Work" is the leg my mother added to the "watch and pray." I don't know where she got this addition from, but she practiced it as faithfully as she did the other two. Work was her breath.

Not that there ever would have been a good time, but Mama picked the very worst time to try to make me get myself "right with God." Getting right with God in the A.M.E. church meant giving up one's sinful ways, giving oneself up to Jesus, and being sprinkled with holy water before the entire congregation. I was having as little truck with God as I could manage. When, during our senior year, Eartha Mae and I had talked about our church elders, we agreed that we were not eager to serve any God they represented. "I can't see what their God ever done for me," she said. I couldn't find anything He had done for me either. Yet, in a moment of temporary insanity at a weeknight revival, I succumbed to my mother's pleading and joined some others at the altar.

It was a warm spring evening after a long day. The visiting minister had aroused the congregation to a high pitch. Several other people had gone up and kneeled at the altar. My mother looked at me. At home she had been lamenting that she had not done her Christian duty. She had been unable to bring her own son into the House of the Lord. She counted herself a failure. I didn't much care one way or another. I was mainly concerned with the begging look in my mother's eyes. All the things I hadn't done for her, all the times I'd come up short in some way suddenly presented themselves, came flooding in on me.

"Why not now?" the plea from the pulpit, echoed by the congregation. If my joining would make Mama happy, why not? So I gave myself up. Walking to the pulpit, I had to look at the deacon who had tried to force himself on Eartha Mae. He sat to the minister's left hand. I immediately regretted my decision. I could not with clear conscience join this man in church, or anywhere else.

So it was with misgiving that I went up, with the others who also had been converted during the revival, to be formally brought into the fold. It was on a Sunday when our regular minister and this deacon were having one of their tiffs. He and the minister were on opposite sides of a long-running church split. About half of the congregation sided with the minister, the other with the deacon. It did not appear to matter who the minister was, he would have to deal with a divided congregation. The revival had been an attempt to heal the split. It had not worked, if the squabble between the deacon and the minister was any indication. I wanted to go back home. Anywhere. I certainly didn't want to go up there to that pulpit. My mother wasn't hearing it. She would be disgraced if I did not go up when my name was called. So I went up. At least my body went up. I mumbled my way through the ritual, hardly hearing the congregation as it greeted us new Lambs of God.

Mama got a good cry out of it. She had done her Christian duty by me. "The Lord be praised!" I had been saved. Instead of feeling saved and elated, I felt violated. I slunk along home with her, feeling bad, as bad as I had ever felt within memory.

CHAPTER NINE

Graduation

There was a space in the front of my mouth
where a new tooth should have been. Dr. D
would have replaced it had school closed
when they said it would.
But the polio epidemic pushed everything up.
We let school out three weeks early.

I don't remember what I said,
after their laughter, so spontaneous
as to seem planned. Welcome is what
the salutatorian gives. That was me,
and welcome was what I attempted.

"I greet you all…""Hahaha! Hahaha…"
The front rows began it and the other rows
joined in. I heard my voice but I could not hear
what I was saying. Something about
joy in friendship.

These were my classmates? These were they
whom I'd sat next to in rooms, played
with in yards, one of whom I thought
I was in love with? Was she
there among the laughers? Then one

reared back in her seat and swung up
her heels. I remember a scarlet slip
and yellow shoes. Yellow patent leather
shoes moving up and down, up and down.

Summer over, my senior year opened with a rush and passed in a
blur. There was the excitement of having a new high school in its
own building with its own name: Wilkinson. Students were no longer
cramped into ancient Dunton Memorial, under the smothering rule
of Professor H. D. Sharperson. Our new school next door would
have its own principal, Mr. James C. Parler, fresh out of a Northern
university's school of education, young, enthusiastic, neatly dressed
at all times, with a lovely smile. My three favorite teachers were
moving over there. The year was 1938. I was in school heaven.

Even when our teachers had to put their own books in the empty
library since the district didn't provide money for any. We students
went from door to door collecting books. Some of mine made it
into the mix. And even though we had no laboratory for sciences,
had no French or Latin or business classes or class in journalism
or gymnasium or vocal and instrumental music, all of which were
provided at the white high school, we still were glad to be in our
new building. This despite the fact that students, including myself,
with the help and supervision of men from the neighborhood,
spent several Saturdays digging in the yellow clay to put in modest
plantings in front of the building. There was no lawn.

Wilkinson's founding coincided with Claflin University's parent
Methodist Church closing its high school. With no Claflin to send
them to, well-off parents sent their children to other schools, some
in South Carolina, such as Mather Academy in Camden and Robert
Smalls in Beaufort. Some sent them out of state, to Atlanta. The
population of Wilkinson was lightened by a sprinkling of mulatto
children whose parents had been taking advantage of Claflin's
church-subsidized education, but who couldn't afford to send their
children out of town to school.

I raced through that last year in high school as though I were going
somewhere, with people and events creating a kind of bittersweet

chaos. I laughed a lot, cried some, was learning that things and circumstances were constantly changing and that I had to change with them. Over my short life, because I was people-curious, I had met many people. Because I had been able to see many different kinds of people close up, I had individualized them. I refused to accept group labels because I had not experienced people as groups but as single persons.

I was willing to try almost anything. I was eager to learn. I embraced History Club, co-edited the paper we students got out at the end of the school year. I wanted new clothes for graduation. The shoe repair shop job would help me get them. I got my first eye examination and discovered that I needed glasses. For how long had I needed them, who knows? I got glasses, thin gold-wire nosepiece, scholarly looking, I thought. They were promptly broken when, visiting a friend, I stepped on a rake, throwing the handle into my left eye, smashing the left lens, and embedding tiny glass pieces in my left eyebrow. Fortunately the sight in the eye was not damaged, and the white optometrist took pity on me and replaced the lens at no cost to me.

My first TB test had returned positive. Better diet had been recommended. Though I scored well on a statewide academic test, I don't remember ever having its significance explained. There was no one at home to talk about it with. I think our principal, Mr. Parler, was trying his best to make us a good school, even though colored education was not a priority for the school district. We were not an accredited school and would not be for many years. Except for industrial arts classes, like carpentry, masonry, and, for girls, sewing, our schooling was only preparing us for more schooling. We had a tough row to hoe and a long way to go. But few of us felt any of this. We ran blithely around as though we were going somewhere. Somewhere fine.

• • •

"Somewhere fine" was not where I went after graduation. Commencement over, I went to church with my mother on Sunday. Monday morning I reported as usual to my job at the shoe repair shop, where I would now be employed full-time.

"Goodyear Shoe Shop."

That's what people heard when they asked the Southern Bell operator for 4903, the number of our shoe repair shop. We were a few doors down from the main business artery, next door to a state-licensed liquor store. Next door to the bottle shop was Sanders feed and farm supplies. Sanders was a white man who sold primarily to black farmers. I never saw a single white person ever buy anything from that store.

The black farmers liked Mr. Sanders because he gave them credit (the job the U.S. Farm Bureau failed to do, though it gave credit to white farmers), and would sit with them, over Cokes he furnished, to settle their accounts. They paid dearly for this credit and false camaraderie, and some knew it. But they had nowhere else to go.

Mr. Sanders had a Negro man who did his heavy lifting. He was a quiet man who kept to himself. In his grandness, Mr. Sanders rarely ever dirtied his hands. His son, an ugly blond boy who was not bright, was groomed to take over, and did. He did not go to university, as his father's money would have allowed him. Instead, he took over the business and married a stringy-haired blonde with country written all over her. She, like he, tried to look important, but despite a new car and money spent on expensive clothes, they failed. They made a plain, not a handsome couple. They had a baby boy, a spitting image of his parents. We laughed at their pretensions.

While Mr. Sanders, a white man, made his living selling to Negroes, Charlie Pendarvis, a Negro in name only, owner of the barber shop across the street, made his living attending to the tonsorial needs of whites: he ran a "white only" barber shop. These men lived on the same street, Sanders in a colonial-style house. Mr. Charlie was never allowed to remodel or even paint his house, modest on the outside but luxuriously furnished inside, for fear it might show up white houses in the neighborhood. The Pendarvises were as "white" as any of their neighbors, whiter than some of them. They lived there on tolerance, a fact of history. From their looks both Mr. and Mrs. both had white ancestors. They had a golden-haired daughter that they sent away to college. She married and moved away.

A tailor shop run by Mr. Patterson, a slender gentle mulatto man, completed the stores on our side of the street. Mr. Patterson, whose customers were mostly white, was pleasant but not very social. We liked and respected him. Though he dropped by to say hello once in a while, always with his tape measure around his shoulder, and always spoke when he passed, he was not part of the shop's gossip circle. As he was not a young man, we assumed he'd end his days a bachelor. But he surprised and delighted us when he found a slender gentle mulatto college student to court and to marry.

A job. A regular one for pay. I had started when I was still in high school. It meant dropping out of my last-period social studies class, but I thought that would be all right. I was carrying a sure A in social studies, my scores all being in the high 90's. When I approached Principal Parler with the idea, he said it was fine with him. I can see him now, slender, bespectacled, chocolate brown. I can hear his tenor voice as he intoned his blessing. I had his permission to miss my last class for the remainder of the term. No, it would not adversely affect my grade or my graduation. I was glad.

My main job at the black-owned shoe repair shop was that of delivery boy. We delivered all over town, rain or shine, to stores, offices, homes. My slicker covered the basket so shoes were kept dry. I wish I could say the same for myself. Shoes were delivered to the front door, unlike groceries, which were delivered to the back. Most of the time the person receiving them was a woman, more often than not in the home alone. That never presented a problem to anyone. Occasionally a regular customer came to the door in a robe or housedress, some when they could easily have sent their maid to receive the shoes. I don't remember that any ever did.

I also shined shoes, those that had been repaired and those brought solely to be shined or dyed. When I was in the shop between deliveries, I answered the telephone that hung on a wall at the right front window. I kept the shop clean, sweeping, dusting, and washing the windows. It was my duty to see that the liquid wax pots were filled so that wax could be applied to finished soles and heels. I wrapped and ticketed shoes once they were repaired. I ran personal errands for boss Fes and Charles, carried the bank deposit around the corner to First National Bank, and got change there as needed. Waiting on customers, taking in work and returning it to customers when it was completed, While U Wait or home delivery. Thus I was allowed to be a part of most shop transactions.

Our shop was sunny, welcoming. People dropped in. A white man with a false leg, WWI veteran, came to use our phone to arrange dates with a woman with whom he had to plead to let him visit. One or both of them were married. While continuing our work, we listened eagerly to the progress of his suit. He always got over, but only after struggle. While Fes didn't like the man coming in, his using our phone without our consent (he just walked in and went over to the phone), there was nothing he could do. The man was white. One day he surprised us all. After he had triumphantly hung up the phone, he handed me a fifty-cent piece. "Get everybody a Coke," he said, as he limped out, "And keep the change."

Though I was hired as delivery boy, I served other functions as well. As message carrier I was the one who told Fes's wife, Miz Bertha, that he was going to work late or go out with T. K. Bythewood or Bob Knight to play cards. T. K. and Bob were a tall and short Mutt and Jeff-like pair; the one lanky and lean, high yellow, always dressed in a black well-fitting suit, white shirt, and black tie, no matter the weather; the other short, barely 5'7", high brown, usually wearing a dress shirt rolled to the elbow, depending on the weather. The one was sharp-faced, clean shaven; the other round-faced with a small moustache. It is hard to picture two men more different in their persons or their personal or professional lives. T. K., the town's one black undertaker until the Newton family decided that the town could support two, and its most eligible black bachelor, placed a strain on the waiting ladies by expressing not the least interest in marriage. He had taken over the business from his father, A. E., and ran it with the clean efficiency and courtesy for which the Bythewood Funeral Services were known. Bob was married, the father of two mid-teens, lived on the colored "Gold Coast." He ran his dry cleaning business in the most haphazard manner imaginable. Though your clothes were well cleaned when you finally got them, you were well warned to never trust Bob Knight's Dry Cleaning to deliver them when promised. These two men were Fes's best friends and the most frequent visitors to our shop. Both were Fes's whist partners for their Thursday afternoon sessions in T. K.'s back office. Bob was Fes's running buddy on his nights out.

I was interested in conversations that covered everything from the latest headlines to what was going on in town. I was not allowed to join in. Nor was Charles. No one ever told us, "We're talking now, you can't join in." We knew. These were Fes's friends.

Though Fes would often have me tell Miz Bertha that he was staying late or playing cards, in fact he might be doing neither of these. I am not now nor was I ever good at lying, so she must have seen through me when I came by in late afternoon, on my way back to the shop, to tell her that her husband would not be coming home to supper. She never let on, or questioned why he hadn't told her when he was there at dinner, but I could see disappointment in her face. Lying to Miz Bertha was a burden I was never comfortable bearing. Though I never told him so, I was happier when he had Blas take his messages home.

There were four of us in the shop: two shoe repairers with lasts, Fes and Charles; Blas; and me. Blas (Alfred) Blasingame was a college student who did not intend to become a shoe repairer. He finished and shined shoes and made an occasional delivery, dropping things off at Fes's house as it was convenient to his way home.

Slender, handsome, and dark, Blas was more interested in women than either college or shoe repair. And women he had. One was a well-off young widow in Columbia, the state capital, who commanded him to spend weekends with her at her pleasure. She gave him gifts: clothes, a watch, money. Fes and Charles warned him that if she ever caught him fooling with the college girls, which he did, that he'd be off her gravy train and that she'd probably put a hurting on him. Their caution was lost on Blas.

When he had a hot date he was likely to let his work in the shop slide, and Fes called him on it. I liked Blas. He was close to my age and in college. He knew lots of girls and seemed to have an easy way with them. He was bright-faced and personable, so different from his older brother Otis, who was serious and studious. Little seemed to bother him, even when he was skating close to not graduating with his class. Fes said it was the good grace of his teachers that got him through, rather than the quality of his work. With his degree in hand, he followed a lot of colored graduates to D.C., into one of the entry-level clerks' jobs the war-fattened District had created.

The college administration was scrupulous in its relations with whites in town. To avoid trouble with them, it tried to make its students as inconspicuous as possible. This meant keeping them out of town except on certain days of the week for movies and Sundays for church. Blas knew what those days were and would meet girls in the colored section of the movie house. But they could not stop by Doyle's soda fountain for ice cream floats as white teens did, no matter how hot it was. That was white territory.

From Fes's standpoint, I was an ideal employee. My attributes were stellar: I was trustworthy, honest, industrious, punctual, loyal, courteous, healthy. I did not miss days at work. I took instructions and was curious, eager to learn, a quick study; a self-starter. He did not have to tell me to do work: if I saw something needed to be done, I would do it. I was responsible, clean, noncombative, and friendly, laughed easily. I could take a joke, minded my own business, and kept my own counsel. I liked what I did and I did it well. Or so it must have seemed to Fes.

I already knew how to shine shoes, and occasionally took my box out on Sunday mornings before I went up to caddy. Tips from shoe shining were a source of extra money.

I think I was being groomed to take over the shop one day, to let Fes pursue other interests. He had fallen into the possession of that shoe repair shop by chance. When he'd graduated from Claflin University with highest honors, he had been expected to become a professional, a doctor, lawyer, or undertaker, the professions open to blacks at the time. He could become a minister for one of the better churches. It was well known in the North that it was easier for a colored man to become a professional than to become a plumber or another skilled tradesman, because of the white ethnics' lock on Northern craft unions. South Carolina's white college graduates went into the military as officers, or left the state to seek their fortunes elsewhere.

I do not know how Fes squared it with Charles, who was my senior and a journeyman repairer, and who had been with Fes much longer. It may have been because Charles had not finished high school. Showed no intellectual curiosity. He had a wife and two children but had women on the side. He was a steady, careful worker and generally dependable. But unless Charles got further education or some kind of business management training—either one highly unlikely—Fes was not going to put him in charge of the shop. As it was, Fes did all the ordering of stock and keeping of records. Though Charles was nominally in charge when Fes was out of the shop, it was I who was put in charge when he went for a two weeks' vacation to New York City.

I was being brought along gradually, as I expressed interest in learning new skills. On the sewing machine I could change needles, sew on buckles and straps, and mend seams. I could finish heels and soles, cut away the sole from the welt without damaging it, remove stitches, put cement on soles before they were stitched. While not yet ready to be responsible for the whole shoe, I was fast approaching that level of competence. Within months, I would be a journeyman repairer.

Shoe repair as we did it was hard, exacting manual labor. Hammering the soles on the last, placing the nails at just the right distance between the stitching on the welts and the inner soles. Grinding the edges of the soles on the big sanders to just the right evenness, smoothing the edges without cutting into the welt. The noise, the dust, the vapors of dyes and cleaners. No ventilation to take the dust outside. Why Fes chose this line of work over one of the professions is beyond me. Perhaps because he had to support a family, and getting a good deal on the shop allowed him to do that.

My identification with the shop led me to be zealous in looking out for its interests. Fortunately, most of our customers paid for their shoes when I delivered them. A few did not. When customers were not home, I took their shoes back to the shop. Some who asked for credit paid quickly. I took it as my job to keep after those who did not. Fes encouraged me. One man, who lived alone in a large house in a wooded area, managed never to be at home when I dropped by. I knew he was there. Once I saw him peek from behind an upstairs curtain. So, frustrated, I threw rocks on his roof. That didn't shake him out. He didn't call the police but he never paid. I didn't tell Fes how foolish I had been.

CHAPTER TEN

When You're Foolish, Forty Miles Isn't Far

Polio epidemic
had forced school
out early.

Fat with knowledge,
feeling the urge to travel,
brief independence before
fall and the nothing job,
what better time for a visit
to Grandma's farm
in the Low Country?

Balloon-tired excitement
on heat-softened tar.
Sweet isolation
of pine-jammed roads,
broken by shoulder-high corn
bright-tasseled against
broad-leaf tobacco green.

Shirtless black workers
offer water, shade
and surprise.

Everyone offered surprise.

Malindy Barnes, girl friend
from school,
that I found the way
through the backcountry,
at the newness
of my bicycle,
that I came by
at all.

"I thought after school
you would forget me,
you being
salutatorian
and all that."

"'The Barnes place
be up the road
'round the bend
cross the branch
back in there,'
they told me. How
could I miss that?"

My mother said
what my mother
always said
when I did
something different:
"You think you grown now,
I trust you know
what you doing."

Malindy's father
was surprised
the most: "You
better sleep
over here. Those
drunk boys run
over that man,
you know. Said
he was too dark
to see at night."

I didn't want
a bike ride
in the country
to be something
special. Being
special was nothing
I craved. I wanted
most of all to be
like everyone else.

So I stayed
and heard him say,
"You don't think
if white folks
go to war, we won't be
dragged in, do you?
They go off and leave
us here?"

Biscuits, grits and eggs
as sun breaks
cocks crow
hens scratch,
dew on fields,
tiny frogs
crowd cool highway.

Low Country cypress.

From tarred road
onto white sand
crossed by black
snake tracks.

My first summer after graduation was broken up by two events, a
bicycle ride to Grandma's farm and the production of a play. Neither
event was in itself unusual; what was unusual about both was that I
would be directing them. Thirty-five miles was not a long distance
for a bicycle trip. My bicycle was relatively new and had been kept up
by Cummings Bicycle Sales and Repair, the colored-owned bicycle
shop, around the corner from our shoe repair shop. Earl Cummings,
the shop's rotund red-faced jovial owner, insisted on putting oil in
the rear-wheel brake drum with his own hands. He wanted a report
on how well the bicycle held up. Colored boys did not, as a rule, own
bicycles. Those few who did, did not take them for trips on the road.
(The road belonged to white people.) And they did not produce plays.

My mother did not like my making that trip. She liked the idea of
my wanting to visit Aunt Cather Lee and them on the farm. None of
us had been there for a while, and she wanted to know how everyone
was. But couldn't I take the train? Or find someone with a car? Surely
somebody must be going down that way. When I insisted on riding
the bicycle and going alone, she simply shook her head, "I hope you
know what you doin."

As it turned out, I did. Sometimes fools get lucky. But a lot of
people were surprised. Colored workers along the highway waved as
I passed. They gave me directions to a girl's house. Malindy Barnes.
As graduating seniors, many of us exchanged addresses, swore
undying friendship, and promised to visit. I was keeping one of mine.

Malindy's family home was off the highway, "Cross the branch, go
on pass the next woods, then wind your way 'round to the right. You
see the house settin in a grove a oaks." The sun was setting, taking
with it some of the heat of the day. I was received like visiting royalty.

You would think we hadn't seen one another for months, the way she greeted me. My bicycle was admired. Balloon-tired. "You came all the way from Orangeburg?" one of her little brothers asked. She must have told them about my being salutatorian, because I was treated with deference.

Her mother sat me on the front porch with a tall glass of lemonade, "Rich (her husband, Richard) 'n them be in ina spell. They in the field."

Malindy and I visited a bit before she had to help with supper. She thought she might be going to D.C., where some of her people were. She'd heard the government was adding a lot of jobs, and her cousin thought she could get her one. She was expecting the applications any day. "I'll see what they look like. Maybe I'll try for two or three of them," she said with a laugh. "I'd hire you," I said, snapping my fingers, "Just like that." She threw a wicked look at me as she closed the screen door.

After an early supper, with me helping feed the livestock, we all settled down at various spots on the deep porch.

"You stayin over, ain't you?" her father asked, as though it was a given. I had planned on pushing on, since there were still several hours of daylight. When he noticed my hesitation, he said, "We got plenty a room. Two uh the boys done left."

After I had agreed to sleep over, he told me his real reason for wanting me to stay.

"I don't want you out there on them roads at night. You know that man them boys done run over up there 'round Ninety-six?"

I did know, and he didn't have to say any more. An older black man had been walking at night along a highway. A group of white boys who had been drinking ran over him. They said it was dark and they didn't see him, "black as he was." Whites accepted this explanation. Colored people thought the boys ran over him for sport.

We talked about the coming war and the chance we coloreds would be called up again. Mr. Barnes had served in France during World War I. I told them I would join the navy but not as a mess attendant. Both Barnes boys said they'd rather stay on the farm.

"Them white folks kin keep they war," they said, almost in unison.

"They ain't no war yet," Mr. Barnes said, "But if they is one, and

they got to go, think they leave *us* here? Be jus like it was before.
When they need us to help them with they killin, Ol' Sam he be
come a knockin." He chuckled, but there was sadness in his voice.

After a breakfast of grits, eggs, and buttered biscuits, Malindy
walked me out to the road. I thanked her for her hospitality. We
promised to keep in touch, but we never did. I lost touch with people
after my exile. I didn't know what to write to them.

• • •

My play production was notable only for the fact that I did it. I had
pulled together a group of friends about my age, found a play, and
rehearsed it. We performed it. People worked with me. I had not
disappointed them. What I remember most about the experience was
the "betrayal" of my leading lady. I thought I had her for my own.
As it turned out she had eyes for the leading man. At the cast party,
she went off with him. Losing out with two women in less than six
months, my would-be prom date and my leading lady, should have
taught me something. Not so. Self-reflection was a trait I had not
developed yet, so these examples were lost on me. There would be
more such bumps ahead.

What I find unsettling about my play production experience is how
little of it I remember. It was the summer after I graduated. There
was the long bicycle trip, a lot of uncertainty about what I was going
to do with my life. There was the business of my infatuation with
my leading lady. Heavy emotional stuff that leaves me with only
splotches of images of anything else that happened that summer. I've
pleaded and fought with my memory, but no dice. I cannot raise that
production.

• • •

The first term I was out of school, when he may have thought I
would be joining him at college, Blas took me with him to meet the
incoming freshman women. He even tried to coach me on how to
talk to them, how to lay down a jive. Though I was not an apt pupil—
I could not think up flowery phrases on the spur of the moment,

inflating my affection and my desires—I did meet one young woman. She was from one of the rural high schools, so my broken and halting spiel was effective enough that she sat with me on Sunday afternoons for a month. She was a basketball player, tall and lithe. I listened to her tell how she was the first in her family to come to college. Much rode on her success. Making the varsity was her first goal.

When she did not show up for two straight weeks, one of her classmates told me that she was dating a football player. I was disappointed but not crushed. We were just getting acquainted. She did not return to school after Thanksgiving vacation. On one of my shoe deliveries to the campus, this same classmate told me, with some scorn, that she had "got herself bigged," and would not be back. I felt terrible. Selfishly, because I liked her. She was lively and funny. And I knew that it would mean the end of any ambition she might have. "Don't you be bringing me home no baby now," was the last thing a girl's mother told her before sending her out into the world. This was devastating news.

When I told Blas about my loss, he neither offered sympathy nor showed surprise.

"Man, it happens." Then he countered with, "You got a rubber?"

"A rubber?" I didn't know what he was talking about. A rubber?

"Yeah, you know, a condom? She got knocked up 'cause that fool didn't use nothing."

Since I did not know about condoms, he proceeded to enlighten me. He pulled a Trojan out of his wallet, demonstrated its use, cautioned me to be sure to put it on right, and not to use it a second time. He gave me one and said I could get more at the drugstore. Better to carry two, just in case. I thanked him and put it in my wallet, where it stayed until the cover became grimy and I replaced it with another. I never added a second one. I retreated to caddying on my Sundays off.

• • •

As I have since understood, but did not understand at the time, Fes, though black himself, exploited our labor like any white boss. It was the Southern way; get your labor as cheaply as possible, but do it with a smile: gentle servitude. The foundations of this system were established by white-imposed apartheid-like racial discrimination and a rigid caste system: inequality by design.

From the summer of 1939, when I began to work full-time, until the spring of 1942, when I was forced to leave town, my wages were four dollars a week. I worked from seven to seven on weekdays and seven to ten on Saturdays. Saturdays could be shortened by an hour if Fes had somewhere to go and I had no work to keep me. Christmas was our only paid holiday. I made a few extra dollars most weeks from tips on deliveries and from shining shoes.

Fes and his wife, just as white employers would, kept Sara, Miz Bertha's woman of all work, in what amounted to a kind of servitude. Sara, a short black Gullah woman, had been brought into Miz Bertha's family, the Frasers, as an orphan. The practice of making perpetual servants of young girls is an old one; brought over from Africa, it is currently prevalent in Haiti. Poor girls, as young as ten years old, are promised an education, a promise rarely kept. Poorly housed, often bedding down in a corner of the kitchen, overworked, underfed, and abused, many run away as soon as they are able. This did not happen with Sara, who stayed with the Williamses until her death. Each case is unique, with its own special social dynamic.

When the Fraser daughter, Bertha, married John Calvin, our Fes, Sara was brought to Orangeburg to do housekeeping and childcare. She was given an upstairs room across from the master bedroom, some modest clothing. No salary but occasional spending money. She cooked, cleaned, did laundry, and cared for the children, Johnny and Fraser, as they came. She had no official day off. She was a "member of the family."

Because she was unlettered, her life was severely circumscribed. She restricted her movement to the neighborhood of Treadwell Street. She could not bring the few friends she made to the house where she lived and worked. One Sunday night she was in a car just below the house with a male friend when Fes came home from drinking with his friends. He beat on the roof of the car, frightening its occupants. In weeks that followed, Miz Bertha told the story in her Geechie lilt as a joke on Sara.

"The idea, Sara, with a *man!*"

I liked Sara. I found her warm and kind. I liked the song in her Gullah intonation. It was deeper than Miz Bertha's Geechie, more substantial. When I heard them I thought of two songbirds, the one twittering, the other with more solid notes. Though like all cooks she was told not to, Sara gave me food, partly, I think, as an assertion of independence. An act of defiance. She did not like being Miz Bertha's perpetual servant and said so whenever Miz Bertha got on her for something she did. But being unlettered and having no disposable income, she was powerless to do anything about it.

And I protected her. Once she left baby Fraser unattended in his carriage at the side of the house while she was in the kitchen making supper. He had been asleep. He got himself entangled in his covering. The more he struggled, the more entangled he became. I was attracted by his muffled cries as I passed the carriage. He was red. I snatched off his covering and pushed the carriage back to the kitchen door, calling for Sara. We both knew how close Fraser had come to either strangulation or suffocation. Neither of us said a word to the other. Sara moaned as she untangled Fraser's covers. When Fraser was again comfortable, I was recipient of a dish of the peach cobbler she had made. Unless Sara told someone, and I can't imagine why she would, the incident died there.

Southern labor in general was exploited, black labor egregiously so. My mother earned seven dollars for a seven-day week as a certified but unlicensed nurse in the colored ward at the county hospital. More than she had earned at a private hospital clinic run by a doctor and his nurse wife.

Seven dollars for a six-day week was what the men earned who delivered groceries for the store on Russell Street at the corner of our hotel building. These were men with families. Charles, in our shop, earned about the same. I guess at his pay because we never discussed salaries between ourselves. I think Charles was given a small raise when Fes got the contract from the military when they began training pilots at Hawthorne Aeronautical School at our local airport after the war began in Europe. I heard them talking about it one evening near closing time. Though Charles was given a raise, I was not.

Because of such poor pay, I think almost everybody stole. Charles and Blas did. Charles took small sums from the cash register, Blas

took such things as shoe laces or cans of shoe polish. But mainly
Blas stole time. Many evenings he and I were left to close the shop.
Knowing I wouldn't peep his hand, he simply took off when he
felt Fes and Charles were safely gone. The young white clerk at the
jewelry store on Russell Street stole. I bought my first watch from
him. The men who delivered groceries added items to bags they
would drop off along their route. Women workers at the hospital, my
mother included, and I suspect in some ladies' kitchens, brought pans
of leftover food home to their families. The colored chefs may have
occasionally cooked too much.

Why I did not steal like the others is beyond me, unless it was
because I identified with the shop and felt that I would be stealing
from myself. It was important to feel trusted. Another reason could
be the belief the fairy tales I had read ingrained in me that thieves
were awful people. Besides, they always got caught in the end and
received horrible punishments, like losing a hand. And there was the
talking-to I got from my mother when, as a ten-year-old, I "lost" a
nickel from the change I returned from a shopping errand. She had
not whipped me, nor accused me of stealing, though I am sure she
knew I was guilty. She talked to me about the seriousness of being
careless with money, as tight as it was. Holding both my hands in
hers, her practice when she wanted my undivided attention: "Now,
A. D., you old enough to know how hard I got to work for the little
change I get. You don't want to be playing in the street with it. Now,
you won't do that no mo, will you?"

"No'm. I won't, Mama."

• • •

Not being in school when fall came around that first year after
graduation was at first disconcerting. It seemed that I had been in
school as long as I could remember. School was what I knew best. I
had been successful there. It had been my refuge. It was not so much
the people as the place itself. Our new building. When I gave most of
my books to help start a library, since the district provided no money
for one, I did so gladly because it would mean we would have a
library, a place where students could go and read books, as I had done

at the state college library as a child. School was the kind of place I liked to be around. School affected the way people thought and behaved in good ways. I had been safe there.

In truth, while there were a lot of students I could work with in various school activities, my only friend at school was Nathaniel Fridie, whom I would lose when the college term began. Our moving apart would please Nathaniel's father, who had long thought my influence on his son unhealthy.

At my insistence and with my support, his son had learned to stand up for himself and to question unfair authority. Together we had gone to the white superintendent's office to protest after our agriculture teacher had struck Nathaniel for a reason we were never given, except: "I'll show you who's boss around here!" The superintendent received us with politeness, listened to our story, and promised to "look into it." We never heard any more about the incident, but the teacher did not beat any more students. Nor was there any retaliation against us.

We had broken two unwritten codes: "Going to the white man with our colored folk's business," and going over our principal's head. We knew our Mr. Sharperson would take the teacher's side. He always did in disputes between teachers and students, no matter what were the merits of the case. And I don't think we thought of Superintendent Thackston as white as much as of someone with the power to help us.

Fes didn't think much of what I'd done, though he was guarded in his comments. We had broken precedent and protocol. Who did we think we were? I think he saw me as someone he didn't know as well as he had thought. Someone whose judgment he was less sure of.

Reverend Fridie was furious with Nathaniel. He made no attempt to understand his son's side. Who *did* we think we were? He didn't beat his son but railed on and on. You'd think Nathaniel had pulled down a saint's statue. Being suppressed at home by such a tyrannical evangelical father, it was no wonder that Nathaniel found my company a relief.

There was no one to replace Nathaniel, since my West Side friend Willie had gone up to New York to live with his birth mother. He had left in the spring of '39. Except for Willie, I had no friends among my fellow caddies. My continuing in school threw up an unbridgeable barrier between them and me. Most of them had spent only intermittent time in school. Many could barely read and write. Although we lived in the same neighborhood, most of the caddies coming from the western side of town, we inhabited different worlds. We all lived in abject poverty. The difference in our lives was that theirs were lives of poverty further degraded by ignorance. It was because of this ignorance, which showed itself in so many hurtful ways, that with rare exceptions I could find no true buddy or friend among them.

Since I had escaped being crippled or maimed, barely, I knew that it could happen, and did happen to others. Sugar's bully brother Marshall, who had tried to humiliate me by bragging that he had slept with my aunt, bullied one boy too many. Jessie O was quiet, very dark. Though he talked with a stutter when excited, he got along well with everyone. One day in the caddy pen, Marshall aped Jessie O's stutter before the other caddies. A couple of them tried to warn him.

"Jessie O, he don't bother nobody. Marsh, man, why you be messing with him?"

"Mess with anybody I want. Black as he is. Nigguh, *you* want some?" He struck a boxer's pose and strutted.

We caddies took a shortcut through the woods to go home in the evening. One evening Jessie O hid behind an oak. When Marshall came by, he smashed his face with a Ball jar. This crime, for it was a premeditated crime that resulted in grievous bodily harm, was never reported. Marshall did not return to caddying.

• • •

Although the shop absorbed most of my hours and most of my life revolved around it, more and more my nights and Sundays— especially my Sundays—competed with it. What I was doing off the job enlarged my life, and extended it in ways the shop didn't.

While caddying provided little money and no friends, it did provide a rich source of "information." White golfers treated their colored caddies like white people in general treated their colored servants, as if they had no ears. And the servants never disabused them of this misconception. They played deaf, better to learn what master had in mind. So with my big ears I picked up tidbits of gossip and rumor about various people and events.

Our most elegant white town drunk and the father of my friend Ned had been top cadets at The Citadel, Charleston's top military academy. The Dibble twin that ran naked through the street and later committed suicide had done so over money lost in the stock market. The white girl who ran away with the Maxwells' oldest son was sister to an accountant at Livingston's warehouse on Railroad Avenue. This accountant sometimes played golf. Someone was marrying someone who was a Catholic! A cocksman who hung out at Doyle's Drugs was sleeping with the new insurance man's wife when he was out on the road. I happened to like that lady. I did their garden one hot summer day, and she made me a lunch of the fattest hamburger, a slice of tomato so red and delicious that I can see its color now, whipped cream, lettuce on a bun, and a tall glass of cold milk, served on a plate with napkin. Of course I ate it on the back steps. All I cared was that it was the most luxurious hamburger I had ever had. And I ignored the talk of her having a lover. And on and on. Fact or falsehood, I ate up all the gossip. It broke the tedium of caddying rounds of duffer golf.

On my way home from the shoe repair shop I would occasionally swing all the way down Broughton to Broad, on the corner of which was an auto salvage company that had all sorts of wrecks piled up on its lot. Once in a while I hung around it, intrigued by the distortions of the different wrecks. Some of the cars had been pancaked. No way, I thought, could there have been any survivors. One Sunday after church I was allowed by Big Tom, the weekend manager, to go with the wrecking truck to bring in a car that had been in a two-car accident north of town. When we got to the scene of the crash, we saw that one car had been flung into a cornfield. The other, on the opposite side of the road, hung nose down in a ditch.

People from nearby farms, on hearing the noise, had come out and were standing around. Still in their Sunday-go-to-meeting clothes, blacks and whites, all ages milled around, even after the dead and injured had been removed. A state highway patrol car was there, and two patrolmen were taking statements from white people. Ambulances had carried the injured away by the time we arrived. Our tow truck pulled out the car that was in the ditch.

"Drivin drunk," was the verdict Big Tom gave on our way back to the garage with our load. "Them fools jus' won't learn, alcohol and gasoline don't mix." He pointed out a poster on the wall behind the counter that showed thirty-three thousand people had been killed the last year in road accidents. The figures were inside a whiskey bottle. Damn, I thought, that's more people than in all of Orangeburg County. I piously made a solemn promise to myself never to drink and drive. Which I did not keep.

On another nice sunny Sunday afternoon, Mr. Burton, who lived on the corner of Broad and Windsor, asked me to take a ride with him and Mr. Fred, his running buddy, across the Edisto River. Always game, and itching to go, I accepted.

"You kin put your box in the back there," he told me. I had been on my way home from one of my shoeshine rounds.

Mr. Burton, whose wife taught school, was a mechanic at Blank Motors. His job was a good one for colored men; he made ten dollars a week, more than some schoolteachers. But he was unhappy because the white mechanic in the bay next to his was making sixteen.

"Now A. D., is that right? I got more 'sperience'n he got. I do better work, but he get the most pay. Say he ain't go work in no place nigger make more'n him. No, it ain't right. But what you gon do? Ain't nothin you can do, you want a job."

True, everything he said. But he had said it. I only nodded my head and took a handful from the bag of roasted peanuts he handed me.

He owned a comfortable Dodge sedan that he kept clean and in good running order. He was proud of that car. I was proud to ride in it. He bragged that his car "know the way home" on nights that he had been out and had had one too many. As long as I knew him, he was never involved in an accident or pulled over for drinking and driving, so he must have had his mojo working. He would park his Dodge in his driveway after a late night out, turn off the engine, and fall asleep. Before she left for school, Mrs. Burton would roust him. He never forgot to turn off the engine.

"This the place?" Mr. Fred asked.

We had arrived at a modest bungalow. The house was partly enclosed by a stand of pine trees, thus was not visible from the road. There was another car parked in the front yard. The curtains to the front windows were closed. I thought I heard the sound of music from inside.

"Sho nuff," Mr Burton laughed. "The very same."

"I guess it was dark when we was out here last time. Didn't look like the same place. I don't remember them trees over there."

I didn't know if I should wait in the car.

"No," Mr. Burton said, "You can come on in. You just wait out in the living room while we mens do our little business." A Wurlitzer played the Ink Spots' "My Prayer."

They did their business in the rear rooms while I read newspapers and magazines that were spread out on a coffee table. After a while, an older, well-dressed woman came out to sit with me. She was wearing makeup and smelled of strong cologne. Much too strong for the small room and my nose. I was tempted to go outside but some instinct told me not to. I was thrown back into the Gibson Street "house" of an earlier time. Once inside you went outside only to leave.

"Let me get you a RC Cola," she said, going to the red cooler in the corner before she sat. "Fred an them ain't got no manners." She laughed, shaking her body in a pleasing way. She got herself a Nehi orange.

As we drank from our perspiring bottles, she wanted to know about my school life. Slightly built and younger looking than my age, I could still be a schoolboy. She was surprised to hear that I had been out of high school for more than a year. I realized as I answered her that I was ashamed, not only that I was no longer in school but that I could see no sure way to return. I told her I was working in the shoe repair shop. That pleased her, but as I heard myself saying it, a thought flashed through my mind: You're saying this but you really want to tell her the fib that you told Ned Jones' mother, that you were going to be in college. This thought arrested me for a moment. My inner and outer life were in conflict. The moment passed and my body and thoughts were absorbed by the Ink Spots' "If I Didn't Care."

• • •

My visit to the "house" was a one-time thing, as were most of my experiences. Except for the shop, which was my anchor, and just a few people, I seemed to flit mothlike from person to person, minor event to minor event, restlessly, sampling here and there, nothing for long.

Miss Jenkins and Miss Beatrice Thompson were disappointed when I did not accept the partial scholarship and go on with my education. They had spoken strongly for me. Because she lived on the eastern side of town across from the high school, I lost close contact with Miss Thompson. Because she lived on Windsor Street, on my way to town and work, I grew closer to Miss Jenkins. I dropped off items she might need from stores in town, entertained her twelve-year-old niece one summer when she was sent down from New York. I listened to Miss Jenkins talk about her family: how proud she was of her brothers, professionals Up North; her annoyance at her father for marrying after her mother's death. She also spoke proudly of her mother, whose Native American forebears had sheltered runaway slaves. She refused to accept her stepmother, though she would accept help from her father when something needed to be done on her house. I witnessed with sadness her increasing bitterness as she aged into spinsterhood.

One day there was a house fire in Red Line, the poorest section of town. Three children had been locked inside their house while their parents worked. This was a common practice. A neighbor woman had been asked to look in on them from time to time. As there was no effective means to fight the fire, it destroyed the house completely. The children, trapped inside, were charred like the ruins of the house. I had not seen the fire, but I did see the blackened lump covered with lime, in a back room of Newton's Funeral Parlor. The children, one of whom I knew, as she had played with my little brother, had huddled together for comfort or safety as the flames ate up their home.

Newton's Funeral Parlor's back door opened on Miss Jenkins' side yard. She expressed horror when I told her what I had seen. She had a way of bringing her hands to her face when she was upset over something.

"How could you stand to see those children?"

"I didn't know they were going to be like that."

"Then why did you go? What did you expect?"

"I expected...Ester was John Lee's friend. He was going to ask me. I had to tell him something."

"You could have told him anything. He didn't have to know. Oh, what a terrible thing."

It was a terrible thing amidst a lot of other terrible things. For a long time I had bad dreams about what I had seen that afternoon in Newton's mortuary. Throughout my life one of my dreaded dreams is that my house is on fire and I have no effective means of saving it.

• • •

On warm evenings I listened to Ruth Amaker, just around the corner, tell endless stories about her loves. Having no love of my own, I went home singing the Mills Brothers, Ink Spots, Cab Calloway, Count Basie, Duke Ellington, Earl "Fatha" Hines—some of my favorites.

When the Hines band had come to the State College gymnasium, it was impossible to keep their posters up for the event. Soloists Billy Eckstine and Madeline Greene had their glossies stolen as soon as they appeared. I didn't pull down a poster but got as close to the bandstand as I could, to gaze at what to me were two miraculous beings. "Turn out all the lights / Call the Law / Play it 'til nineteen fifty-one!" now seems quaint, but in 1941, when the Hines band played "Boogie Woogie on the St. Louis Blues," it "set the joint a-jumpin'" and brought down the house.

• • •

My caddy buddy Sugar and Lynette from our block had been sweethearts since grammar school, which was as far as Sugar got. They made a lovely couple, both sugar-crystal brown. I thought them very much in love. Of the regular caddies, Sugar was the kindest to Willie and me. He taught me how to get out of a sand trap, on some of the mornings we caddies played. Sugar was master of this most difficult shot in golf. He was also one of the few caddies who called our two deaf-mute caddies by their names instead of Big and Little Dummy. I never saw him drunk and he didn't run around.

So it was with surprise and sadness that I discovered that Lynette had succumbed to the blandishments, including money, of the new undertaker.

Miss Jenkins and I, sitting on Miss Jenkins' screened front porch, would see Lynette enter the back door of Newton's Funeral Parlor, where the undertaker kept a room with a couch. Miss Jenkins "tutt-tutted" when we saw her. She didn't know Lynette except as "some girl from down the street there," but she knew that the undertaker was married, and she had seen other women go into that back room. I didn't tell Miss Jenkins who Lynette was, nor did I tell Sugar that his Lady Love was chippying out on him. I did wonder how much he knew, how either one of them accounted for Lynette's improved material state—the new dress, shoes, and silk stockings, for starters. She only worked sporadically, in service, so she earned little.

The undertaker was suave, college-trained, and had money. While Sugar was attractive and a good man, his prospects, as a caddy, were zilch. His pretty woman must have felt that she deserved some of the nicer things of life, which Sugar certainly could not provide. The adultery itself was not a problem for me at that stage of my life. I had seen and heard about enough adulteries so as not to think of one as exceptional. What hurt me so much was that it was happening to my friend boy Sugar, and that neither he nor I could do anything about it.

• • •

I've mentioned my aborted attempt to join the army after high school. I'll elaborate. In the build-up for our eventual entry into World War II, two army recruiters came and set up a station in front of the First National Bank. A table covered with pamphlets and forms, two chairs, U.S. and Confederate flags in stands behind them. One day, out of curiosity, I stopped by and presented myself. I told the sergeant in charge that I wanted to serve my country and started to reach for the nearest pamphlet. I thought I detected a slight snicker in the men. The sergeant clutched the enlistment information and pulled it beyond my reach.

"We not takin yawl," he said, straightening up. His partner, a private with one chevron, moved closer to him. They both seemed to be waiting for me to accept what they said and walk away. Wrong person.

"How can I serve?" I asked. "I want to do something for my country."

"Yo country." There was a question in his voice, as though the idea puzzled him.

"Yawl kin join the navy," his partner cut in. "Navy's takin yawl. Kin go right down to Chawstun navy yard."

"Yeah, that's right. Navy's place fo you. 'Join the navy, see the world.' Ha! Ha!"

When I got back to the shop, Fes and Charles had an "I told you so" laugh at my expense.

"You ain't thinkin bout joinin no navy now, is you?" Charles asked, after he'd finished laughing. Hanging onto his shoe last he explained. "You kin be a mess attendant, or a steward, clean up behind them white officers. Clean up thuh vomit after they parties."

"Dorrie Miller…" I started to offer, thinking of the black sailor who had shot down Japanese Zero fighters, after coming out of the scullery to take over from a gunner who had been shot out of his gunnery post.

"A mess attendant," Fes cut in, "That's all he was, and that's all he'll ever be, in This Man's Navy."

I compared my experience to that of Charlie Suggs, my white childhood friend. Charlie Suggs could join the army, I could not. Charlie could also, and did, go to the CCC (Civilian Conservation Corps) summer camp for six weeks, restoring creeks and preserving forests. He came back tanned and displaying newfound confidence. He almost seemed to swagger with his short self. He was my Charlie and then again he wasn't. He told a story of how his troupe celebrated the end of their tour by bringing a prostitute into camp and "running a train" on her. I would have loved to have been able to work in the woods, but I did not congratulate him on his "train." To begin with, I wasn't quite sure what it meant. If it meant what I thought it might, I wanted no part of it. But I was curious.

"You say you all ran a train on her?"

"Yeah, you know. She lays down, all the fellows line up. You put your money on the ground next to her, and then you do it."

"Oh."

We didn't stay talking much longer after that. I don't remember ever visiting him again. Our friendship may have run its course.

CHAPTER ELEVEN

Kilroy Was Here

6000 years of art draws you?
You want to save these
meager markings whacked in stone?

When with one slip you drown,
what drives your body
inch by inch against
the sloping rock,
lugging your case of cloths,
crayon and pestle, not
daring a look at icy
fjord dancing below?

From what center urge
the hands that chipped,
braved sun, ceaseless wind,
to create record of their presence?

Children make spirals, meanders, curves,
bankers in meetings scribble on pads.
Those who record on high rocks, in caves,
on fences, city walls, figure on figure
figure into ground, what moves them?

What is your tie to the hands that drew
what you now save? Name the urge to push
beyond the usefulness of things,
decorate bark, cloth, a door,
ladle or a cup, to toy with chaos,
to key life.

Only a fool would answer, "fame."

In our shoe repair shop I heard more than Fes's conversations with
his friends, from which Charles and I were excluded. While at
Claflin Fes had specialized in the work and life of Bert Williams, star
vaudevillian of the early part of the twentieth century. He could and
did recite many of Bert's songs for us. He also talked about Bert and
his partner Walker's lives. This had an immeasurable influence on
my later life in art, though it passed at the time as practice for Fes and
entertainment for us.

Fes was a "natural" for Bert. He was lanky tall, with a strong but
pleasing voice that could growl when needed, a thin face, and sleepy
sad eyes. He had been disappointed in love and had suffered in his
life. He had had to make do under conditions similar to those Bert
faced, suffering under racial prejudice and walking the tightrope of
discrimination. Fes was gifted as a performer but would never be
given a chance to do more than entertain people at Claflin University,
friends at parties, and us in the shop. That he did. And *how* he did.

I can even now hear the Bert Williams lines beginning, "I'd rather
hear them people say, 'How that man did run' than 'Here he lie' /
I'd rather be a coward walking 'round on earth than a hero up on
high…" or "Cruel Judge Grimes got his name because / for the
simplest crimes he charged ten laws / Now you take the case of
Andrew Jackson Boles / He slipped on a banana peel and fell into a
hole / When the case was brought before Judge Grimes / Mr. Boles
was charged with the following crimes…" Charles would be hanging

onto his shoe last, laughing so hard, and I, with my shoeshine brush
suspended, would be in performance heaven.

This droll humor, with its sly wisdom, the subversion; the fact that
Bert Williams could bring down a house by merely sticking his foot
out from behind the curtain and withdrawing it; that he could thrill
audiences in hotels he could not sleep in; that Bert could put up with
this but his partner, Walker, could not; that Bert said once, "I like
being colored but sometime it is awfully inconvenient": all this stuck
with me. The long narrative poems my mother had recited before
I started to school were joined by Fes's recitations. Unconsciously, I
was developing an esthetic and an ethic that were more influential
than I knew.

I boldly tried writing verse. On my sturdy Underwood, I patiently
pecked out two rhyming quatrains. Proud of what I'd done, I showed
them to a young professor at the college who had come for a shine
and to chat with Fes. Fes had suggested him, thinking that since he
was in the arts, he might be helpful. I watched as the sun produced a
bright film on his smooth high-brown brow. He took a handkerchief
out of his back pocket and neatly mopped his face and brow. Then,
after a cursory glance at my verse, he handed it to me, along with a
dime tip for his shine.

"This don't cut it," he said, with a laugh, "But you shine shoes
damned good."

I was damned by his judgment. As a professor, he must know
what he was talking about, I figured. I bit my lip, took my verse,
and put it away. It was a long time before I again tried writing
poetry. My impulse to express myself in verse was too strong to be
suppressed forever, but it would take my reaction to war before it
would surface again.

This downer was not my only contact with State College
professors. One was especially uplifting. A warm and generous
couple named Danforth from New Jersey worked at the college for
a year. They left when Mr. Danforth took a job as an administrator
in a port authority in their home state. When they learned that I
was interested in books, they invited me to come to their house on
campus to read from their Book of the Month Club selections. I could
understand fiction and biographies but was stumped by *New England*

Indian Summer, a book of literary criticism. I lacked the background reading that would allow me to make sense of the books and authors being discussed.

I had to read books in their house because there was no suitable place in mine. I bought a lamp with a mantle that when lit gave off good light, but it was impossible to adjust. In summer it gave off much too much heat. I had to abandon it. I didn't think that the college library, welcoming to me as a child, would be open to me as an adult who had no connection to the college.

The couple's departure left a void not only in my life but also that of Fes. Mrs. Danforth was a frequent visitor to our shop for her shoe repair needs, but also for conversations with Fes, with whom she found a lot of common interests. Fes was delighted because he was starved for intellectual stimulation. They kidded one another a lot.

One day Professor of Mathematics Joshua Williams, Fes's older brother Josh, parked a new cream-yellow 1940 Buick Century coupe in front of the shop. All big-eyed, we emptied the shop, workers and a colored customer who was not going to be left out of the show. To appreciate how much of a show we thought it was, you need to know that Josh was modest bordering on shy. A bachelor, he needed Blas to act as go-between in his amorous pursuits. That he should buy a sporty yellow coupe was something that would never have entered our minds. But there it was, and there was Josh, smiling and taking our compliments with grace.

We in the shop learned later that money for the car had come from a textbook publisher. Professor Williams had apparently found an error in one of their mathematics texts and been rewarded for his discovery. Though the car gave us a glimpse at another side of him, Josh seemed unaffected by his new purchase. To us all he was still the same kind, smiling, unassuming Josh. But I don't think that he was unaware of the looks he got as he tooled his new coupe through the streets and around the campus. He must have lifted his head just a little higher. After all, it was the only car of its kind in town; its only rival for being sporty and having class was the new Packard convertible owned by one of the town's white stockbrokers.

• • •

Something was pushing me, resulting in gross dissatisfaction, even with my job. So one day I quit. Not in anger or protest, more in confusion. I quit, having no other job than caddying, which was not really a job. I couldn't get a job at the Orangeburg Shoe Shop, our competitor on Town Square, even if there were an opening. Fes and Mr. Bailey, the proprietor, were friends, members of the same Methodist Episcopal church. I was dissatisfied, but my dissatisfaction was so vague I could not put it into words. There was the low pay. I did need more money. I would need clothes and other things if I were to join other young men in visiting and taking out young women. But more than money I needed some intangible something "out there." Opening and closing the shop. Clean out shop, sweep off street. Steadying but also deadening rhythm, dead ending.

After a live performance at our local movie theatre, I had visited backstage with some out-of-town white musicians. No one else had come back. They were friendly, called me a "cat." I wondered if that was their way of saying "hep cat," which the Harlem boys used when they wanted to say someone was groovy. I liked it.

Truth was, I needed to be doing something else in a town where there was nothing else for me to do. I needed a ticket out. But there was none. And no place to go if I had one. After a few days in the country club's stinking caddy pen and in the bleak streets, I was more than ready to go back to the shop.

When my mother found me at home and learned the reason for my being there, she was most unhappy.

"A. D., you quit your *job?*"

"Yes, Mama, I…"

"Don't you 'Yes, Mama' me. You done gone and lost your senses? What you plan to do, A. D.? In this town, where you gonna get another job? Tell me that. You plannin on moving?" This last when I didn't say anything.

There was nothing I could say.

"Answer me, boy. Or are you a man, now?" This last with a sneer.

"No, Mama, I'm not going nowhere."

"Then you better get on back and tell John Williams to take you back."

"Mama, I can't just walk up to no man and say, 'Here I am, I want my job back,' like that. Man ain't no fool."

"Then what you plan on doing?"

"I don't know. Let me alone. I'll think of something."

"Well, it'd better be quick. I ain't feedin no grown man. John Lee's enough."

I couldn't go to Fes and ask for my job back, as much as I wanted to. I felt I had let Fes down. He had given me more than a job. He had given me an opportunity for a meaningful occupation, a trade, given me a chance to develop a craft. Though he did pay us little, he was one of the first employers to sign his employees up for the new Social Security. And he encouraged me to keep up a small twenty-year paid life insurance policy with colored North Carolina Mutual that my mother had taken out for me. And I did enjoy the camaraderie of the shop. We would make up games, one of guessing the home regions of our flight trainees by their accents. We got to be pretty good with our guesses, to the surprise and delight of the young men. "How do you do that?" they wanted to know. We didn't tell them that we had asked the early arrivals where they were from and had simply memorized what they told us.

All that I had walked away from. And I wanted it back. While I didn't feel I could go back to Fes directly, I could go to Miz Bertha. She might act as go-between. After all, she knew me as a competent respectful worker. Fes needed me as well as I needed him. She would see that. And she did. I don't remember how I approached her or what we said, but the result of it was that she interceded between Fes and me and I was given my job back.

Except for a brief sense of freedom, I don't remember any particular satisfaction in quitting. Fes and I never talked about it, so I never learned how he felt. He hadn't hired anyone to replace me. He may have realized that I was acting from a pique that would wear off. He may also have known that if I did not return to the shop I had nowhere else to go. That is, unless I left town, which at the time had not occurred to me and which in any event would have been a frightening prospect.

The only person I knew out of town who might help was my sister Edith, who worked in service in some place called Rockville Centre, Long Island, in New York. Though Edith did not like Fes, for a reason

I could never get her to divulge ("A. D., he is not your friend," she'd said), and she would have liked to see me leave his employ, she had not suggested that I come North with her. She had no place of her own. So I was back in the shop, but not as a contented worker, as the incidents that followed my return began increasingly to show.

The Carter's Tea Room job, coming as it did, was a boon. It provided me with one of the keys to eventual freedom, money. Considerably more than I could make in the shoe repair shop, even if I was paid as much as our journeyman, Charles.

• • •

I got my job as a carhop at Jack Carter's Tea Room because I was a regular daytime customer at a time when he needed someone. I would like to think that I got the job because I was neat and well-spoken. Not so. The boy I worked with was not well-spoken. So it was chance. Mr. Carter had noticed Willie and me over the past couple of years sitting on the Roman pillars at the entrance to the city's country club where we caddied.

Willie and I bought our lunch at the Tea Room, sweet rolls, canned salmon, and a pint of pasteurized milk. As we ate, we chose cars that passed on the highway. Willie picked Chevrolets, I picked Fords. Next time, we switched brands. For some reason, we never chose Chrysler cars, though the town had a large Chrysler dealership. We wanted to stop some of the cars as they turned into the club driveway so we could carry the driver's bag. This was a delicate business. Some of the drivers had their regular caddies. To cut in on someone's regular was a no-no. Regular caddies depended on these jobs for their livelihood and could be brutal to anyone who cut them out of one. Among the unspoken-for golfers were some known to be poor sports or thoughtless. These we tried to avoid. Often we ended up not getting anyone to stop and having to walk up the long winding lane to the caddy pen and take our chances that someone might select us over the other waving hands and mouths clamoring for their attention.

While my being neat and well-spoken didn't get me the job at the Tea Room, it helped me to keep it. Customers spoke well of me to Mr. Carter. One couple wondered if I was born in this country; I was not like the local product they were accustomed to. My demeanor did add to my tips, which turned out to be many times my salary. I worked Saturday nights, an occasional Friday night after my work in the shoe repair shop was done, and all day Sundays. I was delighted at how much more I made than at the shoe repair shop. On one weekend alone I made seventeen dollars, four times as much as I was paid for working seventy-plus hours in our shop.

Were it only money I sought, the Tea Room job should have replaced my other one. But money was a means, not a goal. In the shop I was being allowed to learn a craft, acquiring a skill I could carry anywhere. I liked Fes and Charles. Mr. Carter was all right. He was a nice enough man, in a smug self-satisfied sort of way. He talked a lot but I could never remember what he said. The Tea Room job was part-time. It never occurred to me, even after my most lucrative weekend, to leave the shop to work full-time for Mr. Carter. Being a carhop as a lifetime occupation did not excite me in the least. Take the money, yes. But take myself out of there as soon as I had the money I needed. I was readying myself for something, a something I didn't know.

• • •

Pearl Harbor attacked was the announcement on the Tea Room radio, where the usual Sunday contingent of Evangeline Carter's suitors was lounging. Four or five of them usually hung around until she had to set up the dining room. December 7, 1941, was no exception, except for the announcement. *The Japanese attacked Pearl Harbor,* our Pearl Harbor. A "sneak attack." U.S. ships had been sunk, white lives had been lost.

Those who gathered around the radio and several who had come in later were traumatized. Their first reaction was disbelief. Some of them had heard Orson Wells' *War of the Worlds* on the radio and thought that this might be another spoof. As more confirmed reports came in, their mood shifted to outrage. *How dare they attack us! Those slant-eyed yellow-bellied so-and-so's. We'll show 'em. Attack the United States Navy!*

It was a cold, cold afternoon. I had been sitting in Mr. Carter's blue Ford sedan, trying to keep warm, and only partially succeeding, as the occasional car required me to get out and serve its occupants. I did not have gloves or a winter coat. The afternoon, thankfully, from my standpoint, had been slow. I didn't want to expose myself more than was absolutely necessary.

What could I make of the announcement and the consternation it was obviously causing Mr. Carter and all the other white men? What did I know about Japan and things Japanese? Because I liked geography and maps, I could place Japan off the coast of Asia. From my tenth year, that would be 1932, I remembered a lot of paper and straw and fabric toys at Christmastime from a place called Jaypan. While I was still in high school, I had seen the picture of the baby on the railroad tracks after the Japanese air force had bombed Nanking. They were the people who had colonized Korea, attacked China, and were trying to create something they called a Greater East Asia Co-Prosperity Sphere or something like that. And I remembered that recently we in the U.S. had put a boycott on scrap metal to Japan. The Japanese were part of the Berlin-Rome-Tokyo axis, a union that sounded pretty ominous to me. They were going to do to Asia what Hitler and Mussolini were doing to Europe. This information had been absorbed and filed as background chatter along with the rest of my increasing body of information about world affairs. The attack brought it to the forefront of my consciousness. But nothing I had read about Japan helped me to understand why they would attack the U.S. What had we done to them?

Most of the young men at the Tea Room pledged to join the navy, for a chance to avenge this affront to white men's honor. "We'll be home by Christmas," they swore. To them, it was merely a matter of joining up, showing up in the Pacific, and poof! The ugly dragon would be dispatched. There was a rush of feeling in them that made me apprehensive, as though they were glad it had happened, glad for a chance to go and kill the fiendish Japanese enemy. Pity the Japanese they encountered.

Young white men had paraded through the streets, giving rebel yells and shooting firecrackers, after the first Joe Louis/Max Schmeling fight. After the return fight between the two, when the *schwartze* had destroyed the Aryan, the streets were deserted. The streets were deserted except for three wary black boys, reduced from four, who snuck up Middleton Street to Town Square and took turns urinating on the statue of the Confederate soldier there. This was after a gathering of a dozen boys under the light at the corner of Broad and Shuler Streets, a common hangout on warm nights. Following Louis's victory, every boy wanted to do *something* to return the favor of the white breakout from the first fight, when our hero had been vanquished. After much wrangling, and warning to keep our voices down, we selected four boys to go up and christen the statue of the soldier. I was one of the four chosen. One boy dropped out when we reached Middleton Street. He was afraid the police might see us. I knew better. I had been out many nights and had never seen a policeman. Soldiering on, we three reached the statue. Then we got cold feet. Did we really want to pee on the soldier? One boy rallied us: "We got to do it, lest we can't go back." That did it. We each took turns firing away. One boy seemed to take forever. "Dang, hurry up. You gon drown the soldier." The deed accomplished, we returned to the corner only to find it deserted. They had said they would wait for us. And next day none of those at the corner would admit knowledge of what we had done. We felt let down. What had been the use of putting our butts on the line if we got no backing and no recognition? We had nothing we could brag about.

Now the young whites would have a chance at a real live, flesh and blood enemy. I was careful, riding home, to go a roundabout way, off the main thoroughfare.

Next day at the shoe repair shop the talk, all the talk, was about the coming war with Japan. The U.S. would win, of course. We had never lost a war. That was the consensus. None of us thought the white boys, who had fled the town in droves to sign up for the navy, would be home by Christmas. "Yaa, come Christmas, but I wouldn't betcha which one." "Maybe them Japanese know something we don't know." While no one wanted the Japanese to win—we were much too patriotic for that—no one minded that a "colored" people had smacked the white folks a good one. "Bring 'em down a peg."

We had all seen the pictures of Mussolini's pilots strafing fleeing Ethiopian civilians and warriors, many of whom carried old muskets and spears. What the Italian invaders were doing was shameful, attempting to destroy what was one of the world's oldest Christian civilizations. We were not allowed to understand this. Instead, we were told that the people being attacked were "savages" and would benefit from this odious contact. Though some of us colored folk thought this picture strange and did not swallow the hype, others did and were confused and ashamed.

• • •

I continued to work at the Tea Room, saving up the money to buy that lot across town for my mother. I was happy watching the sums add up each time I made a Monday deposit at the First National Bank, with its great clock out front. By the time I was run out of town, I had saved enough.

When I did leave, saying good-bye to the Carter family was out of the question. First, they were white and would probably share hostile white feelings about my act. Too, even if they understood, they would be risking utter ostracism in showing that they did. We were partners in crime, but only in some crime, like selling bootleg bourbon. White suburban development eventually took over the area occupied by Carter's Tea Room.

PART III

I'd rather hear them people say,
"How that man did run" than "Here he lie"
I'd rather be a coward walking 'round on earth
than a hero up on high.

—Bert Williams, vaudevillian

Staying in jail was easier after seeing my mother, even though her visit was all too short. My spirits shot up for a while. Fes was doing something, though I didn't know what he could do. I had seen what they did to that man who had made that girl pregnant up on Sheriff's farm. Ten years for that. They had said it was rape he committed. The golfers had said it was no rape, that he had been living and working on the farm. My spirits dropped again. What was going on out there?

I have mentioned how my mother had been put in jail for sitting in her bedroom fully clothed because she had a man with her, who was also fully clothed. He was given thirty days on the chain gang, as he had no money for bail. How much time would my mother have served, and where? They called it adultery, what they were doing. Entertaining a man who was not her husband. My mother was a woman of impeccable reputation, a church-going Christian. She would never go against the tenets of her religion, one of which was "Thou shalt not commit adultery." The police had walked into her house on a wintry Sunday morning, and despite her telling them that she and her friend were simply visiting, they took them both to jail.

Attempted rape. That was the charge being hung on me. I couldn't keep it in focus, it kept slipping in and out of my mind. I tried sleeping, like the boy across from me. Didn't work. All my contacts with whites kept being played back to me. Not only my contacts but also those of every black person I had ever heard about. I could hear conversations, discussions, argument; warnings. Clear then jumbled.

There were those young women on their way to work, they who had given me nickels to hear me say "thank you." And my mother putting a stop to it. My fight with Ned's sister Annette over who should push baby brother Bernie home from the Ellis Avenue playground. Teets' mother telling my mother to warn me about waving at those children. And Dambee's "You bettah watch yo step." My fights with two poor white boys, Coley and Basil Milhouse. I would beat the younger one only to be chased by the older one. My contacts with numerous boys on my marble shooting rounds. The "house" down at the juncture of Gibson and Sunnyside run by a mulatto woman for white men—the chief of police was reported to be her lover. Fes telling of grabbing and threatening a young white punk when two of them had insulted Miz Bertha one Sunday when they were out walking. The policeman who shot his wife, a fellow officer, and himself when he caught them in bed. The Dibble twin who ran through the streets naked before killing himself over losses in the stock market. Mrs. Jones, the shower, and Freddy the dog. My running over the two white men who were beating that man that Saturday night. And on and on and around and around, rumor, gossip, hearsay mingled with fact and what I had witnessed.

None of what ran through my head added up to me. I was simply being made crazy by it. Or had I been crazy before? What I had done or not done would not matter, only what white law said I did. And nothing I could do or say could change that. The capriciousness surrounding my situation continued to weigh heavily on me. I felt like something being dangled from a dirty string.

Next morning after breakfast, which I again did not eat, Sheriff came to my cage. His step was light, he was almost smiling. After asking how I was feeling and getting the lie, "All right, sir," he followed with, "That's good, 'cause you gittin out today. Git your things together and be ready." Without waiting for my stammered response, he turned around and left, his light step pausing only a moment before he clanged the door to the cell block.

Hardly had the sound of the door subsided when the boy across from me called over, "You gittin out!" He had not been asleep. In my concern for my own situation I had forgotten about him. *I was getting out, he was staying in.* I wanted to tell him I ought to be getting out, as I hadn't done anything to be in jail for. But something stopped me. I'd be saying he had. I didn't know what he was in for and wouldn't ask; he might be just as innocent as I. So I said simply, "Yeah, I guess so." And put my things into the bag my mother had brought my clean clothes in.

He wouldn't let me get away so easily.

"Boy, you lucky."

Yes, I was lucky. I had people on the outside. Who did he have? He looked younger than I, was of slighter build. No one had come to see him. I would not strike up a conversation with him. When I left he would be completely alone. Even though I didn't talk to him, at least we shared the huge space. Yet I couldn't talk to him. I couldn't talk to anyone about what I had done. So, using the bag for a pillow, I lay on my bunk and looked at the ceiling. Inside my heart was racing. *I was getting out.*

They came for me a little before noon. I was hoping for Fes. Instead, it was Cassandra Maxwell, the lawyer, and a man, one of the deans at the college, the same one who had been with her that night at Carter's Tea Room. Cassandra had recently graduated from an eastern law school. Fes had spoken of how brilliant she was. The pair—she could easily pass for white, and he for any of a dozen nationalities, having a suave complexion, soft hair, sharp face, thin nose, lips covered with a neatly trimmed moustache, and a composed manner—were all business. Having only seen her sitting in a car on a darkened parking lot, I'd had no idea of her size, hence was impressed by it: she was easily 5'10", solid, no fat, and movie star handsome.

No one recognized anyone. I had never seen them; they had never seen me. They were cool to Sheriff and his deputy, and not warm to me. After some talk between them, Sheriff handed her some papers, which she read and signed. "Got your things?" was the only question she asked me. I showed them the bag. "Good. Let's go." They seemed not to want to waste time. I was taken quickly through a side door, the Meeting Street exit, out of sight of casual passersby. Once in the backseat of their car, I was made to lie down and they covered me with a blanket. I couldn't see why I needed to be covered with a blanket to be driven home.

"You're not going back home," she told me. "We're taking you to your grandmother's. We had to tell them you'll be joining the navy."

All the more reason. I wanted to swing by the shop, say good-bye to Fes and Charles, pick up some things at my house, my bicycle…

"You're not going anywhere. We'll let you sit up when we're far enough out of town." Cassandra's voice was brusque but not unkind.

"You lucky to be getting out," the man said, in his first words spoken. "Lucky to be alive." This last was said with bitterness. I didn't know if his bitterness was directed at me, or against those who had put me in jail. Perhaps a combination of the two? After all, he'd had to expose himself to the hazard and ignominy of discovery at a Tea Room that sold illegal liquor. And as for her, her passing sometimes for white must extract its psychic toll. We were in the same wretched boat, only they were riding cabin class while I rode steerage. And I was rocking the boat. Big time.

My relief at being released quickly vanished. I was not being taken out to go home. I could not go home. *Too dangerous.* What was dangerous about it? I saw myself walking the streets, riding my bicycle, working in the shop, doing pretty much as I had always done. But that could not be. All the way to Grandma's farm, my mind fought against accepting the extremity of my predicament. My situation was dire but there was no place in my mind to receive it. It simply would not register. *I could not go home and had no idea when I could.* I was being taken to Grandma's farm. I could stay there until it was safe to come back. That thought gave me a modicum of comfort. Meanwhile, my lawyer and her friend talked between themselves as though I were not in the car. "I hope they'll all be this easy," she said. "I think they wanted him off their hands. You know, he wouldn't eat. They didn't know what to do about it." I couldn't hear his wind-muffled response. "…wanted to stay in the background…protect the shop…" The wind allowed me only snatches of what they were saying. Some of it seemed to be about Fes. They did need me to confirm the road from Pregnall to the rural route on which Grandma's farm was located. "After St. George, she said watch out for

Pregnall. Take a left there. You remember it?" This was thrown over a shoulder.

Giving a surprised Grandma a letter from my mother, they left me, not staying for the customary cooling water and a short rest before starting back. "The letter from Mrs. Walker explains everything. You'll be getting one from your sister Edith any day now," Cassandra looked at me. She answered the query in my grandmother's face. "Thank you, but we have to get on back" was her answer to Grandma's request that they "rest awhile." Hardly had Aunt Cather Lee time to change aprons and get to the front before they were gone. I never saw either of them again. While Cassandra was handing Grandma a large envelope, the man had set a cardboard suitcase on the porch. In it were some of my clothes and an envelope with two crisp five-dollar bills. Mama's accompanying note asked the Lord to place my feet on a path of righteousness and to keep me safe. In the large envelope was a note to Grandma telling her that I had gotten into some trouble in Orangeburg and would need to go to stay with Edith in New York. Also enclosed was a long bus ticket. One way.

• • •

Grandma's farm! Waking up in a clean bed with the sun on my face. The chinaberry tree outside the window. The sounds of birds. I could see the woods beyond the hog pens. I could hear Aunt Cather Lee in the kitchen and smell bacon. What a difference a day had made.

It had been more than two years since I had ridden my bicycle down to see everyone. Little had changed except that Grandma seemed to move more slowly. Her energy seemed lower than I remembered from my last visit. Aunt Cather Lee still had her sharp tongue and eyes that twinkled as she sliced bits off people here and there. Uncle Johnny had married and gone Up North. Uncle Ben was restless. He had more on the farm than he could manage, and was thinking of ways to leave. The war had taken men from the countryside, had drawn them into the military services or to the cities where jobs in war factories awaited them. Or so they were told. When I walked the rows with him later in the day—I never left their farm—he told me he envied my going to New York.

"I'm not going because I wanta go," I told him.

"I don't give a daggone why you goin, you goin. That's the main thing."

Any curiosity anyone might have over why I was in trouble was not communicated to me. They knew that what I had done was serious. Because I had to leave the area as a result of it, they knew it involved someone white. That I had been transported down by white-looking people did not faze them. Though there were none in the area where they lived, they had seen white Negroes before. I was one of theirs and I was in trouble. That was all they needed to know. If I told them, fine; if I didn't, it was my business. I could no more talk to them than I could talk to anyone. I was grateful for their help. It all seemed so familiar. The farm, after all, was where I began.

Out of jail. Grandma's farm to wait for my sister Edith's letter. She would tell me how to join her in Rockville Centre, would provide me with the details of how to get there. That was the plan they had worked out for me. "They" would have been Fes, my lawyer, and my mother. What was Cassandra Maxwell thinking, whose brother had run off with a white woman? Sheriff was apparently happy for me to be out from under his care. I suppose they told Sheriff that I would join the navy, thus putting me out of reach of anyone who might want to do me harm. Also a long distance from Orangeburg. What if news of my jailing had become widespread? Cassandra and the dean from the college had said that folk at the county jail didn't know what to make of my not eating. I suppose they didn't know how long I would keep it up. I didn't know either. It had been impromptu, not a planned act on my part. I don't know what got into me. I don't remember reading of anyone else ever having done such a thing.

All of my savings were withdrawn to pay for my legal expenses and travel. There would be no lot on the "good" side of town for my mother. My writing a note to the wrong girl had blown that idea.

"They" had decided for me. From the time I had written that infernal note I had not made a single decision, I had been consulted about nothing. I had been told do this, go here, take this, eat this…My only decision—my decision not to eat—was negative. Everything else had been decided without me. It was as though by one act I had been

transformed into a being without volition, a being incapable of even discussing what should happen to him.

Edith's letter came. Uncle Ben was to take me over to Florence, South Carolina, to meet the bus coming up from Jacksonville, Florida. That bus would take me overnight to Richmond, Virginia. In Washington, D.C., I would change buses, and take a different one to New York City. For a boy who usually jumped at the chance to travel, I was less than eager to make this trip. Grandma's farm had provided relief, temporary as it turned out, from the kind of paralysis that was creeping into one part of my being. Part of me was smelling the fresh plowed field, the musk of the farm animals, seeing the dogwood and azalea, hearing birds calling—in short, feeling alive. Part of me was still locked in trauma, with images tumbling over each other, battling for my attention.

In Florence we stood around waiting for the bus, colored people in one group, white people in another. We were standing outside a drugstore. Some white people were sitting inside at a soda fountain. Some colored people were squatting near their belongings. The sun was setting, the bus was late. Uncle Ben had asked Elder Duncan, one of the men he recognized, about it. "Ain't never on time," he was told. Uncle Ben had not wanted to be driving home after dark. "We'll take kearaum," a woman who seemed to be with the elder said. "You go 'head on home." So Uncle Ben left me in their care. They said they were going as far as Richmond.

Neither Uncle Ben nor I knew what to say on parting. So he said what was easiest for both of us, "A. D., now you mind what Elder Duncan tell you, now, 'n tell Edith hello from us down here. We be up there befo she know it." He laughed, and gave me a squeeze on the arm.

"I'll tell her, Uncle Ben," I said. Then he was gone. That was the last time I would see him.

When Uncle Ben left, I missed him. I missed the farm, Grandma, and Aunt Kat. I missed Orangeburg, the shoe repair shop, Fes and Charles, my mother and John Lee. I missed them all. The missing descended on me with a crushing weight, which the Duncans' smiles and pleasant talk did nothing to lift. I'm sure I smiled back, but I was glad when we were settled into the back of the bus, where I curled up and promptly went to sleep, waking only when the bus pulled into the Richmond terminal.

I awoke to find my seat partner was a woman who had not been there when I had gone to sleep the night before. The Duncans were not on the bus; apparently they hadn't wanted to wake me from what had been a sound sleep. The woman, a more seasoned traveler than I, said that if I watched her place while she went to wash up, she'd watch mine. She had apparently been talking with the Duncans. They were all church people. I had been with them, so I could be trusted.

At the men's urinal I pulled my first social gaff. Wanting to be friendly, I did what I would do Down Home, spoke to an army private my age in the next slot.

"Hi, kid," I beamed, with what was to pass for a right-hand salute.

"I ain't your kid," he spat out at me, pulling himself up and striding away. "Well, excuse me, Mr. Pistol," I said silently to his back. "I didn't know you wuz loaded." Lesson Number One: Don't speak to strangers as familiars just because they happen to be black like you.

Back on the bus, the woman and I shared the food we each had packed for the trip. About my mother's age, she was going to D.C. to visit her children for Easter. As we rolled through Richmond's streets, we saw groups of colored children on their way to school, laughing and cutting up, boys chasing girls, girls swatting boys with their book bags. Their play threw me back to Orangeburg, and as my seatmate chatted on about her children, I saw myself on the playground at Dunton Memorial. A group of girls were doing an English round to an African rhythm. I could hear, "How you caper 'round / How you caper 'round / How you love caper 'round / How you love caper 'round..." They were dancing a tricky rhythm, clapping to a beat I never could duplicate, no matter how I tried.

In the Washington bus terminal, there was the great changeover, the North/South shift. I could now move from the back of the bus if I wished, but passengers going south from D.C., colored passengers who had been free to select their seats, now had to go to the back. I happened to like it at the back of the bus. From there I could see everyone without turning around, though I did wonder what it would be like to sit on the seat behind the driver. So that was the seat I aimed for, and through a stroke of luck got it.

Somehow the reshuffling of people from the Chicago and New York and Philadelphia buses to those of Richmond and Atlanta and Birmingham awoke an awareness in me of something I had been living with but had not allowed myself to think about: the pernicious nature of Jim Crow discrimination. My school. The public library that I never entered. The public golf course and swimming pool likewise. Public meant white. And white I was not. Something in the illogic of the changeover almost made me laugh. It was crazy. Some of the same passengers who had sat together from Chicago to D.C., now going to Birmingham or wherever, would find themselves in a forced rearrangement. Some might be in the middle of a conversation they would have to break off.

These thoughts and others like them rolled around in my mind as the bus rolled north and east through graying and sooty towns and cities. As the bus often went through back streets, we passed factories with tall smokestacks and huge pyramids of coal next to them. The air was hazy in some towns. Mostly faded red brick buildings, many covered with ivy. More people than I had ever seen. Towns closer together, and more and more people. Everything, the looks on people's faces, the way people dressed, the haste with which they moved, their variety, the very air they breathed, all was so different from Orangeburg, where there was unclouded sun, where people moved in a leisurely way and often had smiles on their faces. I saw not a single bicycle, though I'm sure there must have been some. What would it be like dodging autos, buses, and streetcars? Not for me. I finished my last drumstick as we pulled up to the toll plaza for the Holland Tunnel. A large slice of pound cake was all that remained of the feast Aunt Cather Lee had prepared for my journey. "You got uh long trip uheadaya," she had said, as she gave me one of her infrequent hugs.

I had seen magazine photos of the New York City skyline and of the toll plaza of the Holland Tunnel. The photos had not prepared me for entering the tunnel, the move from bright sunlight into what at first seemed stygian. Once my eyes adjusted and my heart rate slowed, I could see an endless row of overhead lights and the lights of oncoming traffic. My heartbeat picked up again. How long *was* this thing? What would I find at its end? I could feel a wave

coming from all the other cars and a constant drone punctuated
now and then by acceleration and the pop of an exhaust. I kept my
eyes glued ahead. Except for the steady drone of its engine, the bus
was quiet. I wondered if other passengers had my thoughts about
being so far underground and under so much water. I don't think
I was so much afraid as apprehensive. Were something to happen,
a breakdown, a wreck, and nightmare forbid, a leak or break, what
plans did the transit authority have for us? From their apparent
contentment, I imagined the other passengers had made this trip
so often that they did not share my apprehension. The drone and
gentle rocking began to lull me. As the other riders seemed to be
doing, I gave myself up to the tunnel. I began to feel safe. Then,
after what seemed like the longest ride, we burst into the light of
the Canal Street area downtown. Though no one left their seat,
there seemed to be a collective stirring, an awakening. I breathed
easier again.

• • •

Penn Station was where Edith's letter said I should take the train to
Rockville Centre. Getting there. I was happy to be on a bus rather
than in the melee that passed for traffic, shouting, horn blowing,
screaming drivers swearing unspeakable oaths that made some of our
knock-down-drag-outs Down Home seem tame. Traffic was jammed
at one corner—we hadn't the words "bottleneck" and "gridlock"
yet—and was being untangled by two policemen, hefty men who
brooked no nonsense from drivers. "Git along now, Ahm a tellinya,
ur yull git this upside ya hed." There was no arguing with a billy
club, which the officer waved with menace. At one intersection, a
policeman stood like a signalman, doing semaphore with his arms
twirling and his whistle shrieking, halting one stream of traffic
with his white-gloved hand and waving another through. I was
overwhelmed by the sheer noise of the city and hungered for a way
to shut it all off. I found it. In the cavernous Penn Station, the outside
sounds diminished, became undistinguishable, being replaced by
sounds from below of iron on steel, the occasional squeal.

"Lungylun's rait ovuh theah," the lady at Information said, all the sounds running together at a rate that made my already confused head spin. I had asked for "the Long Island Railroad, ma'am," marking myself as an auslander. Fortunately, she waved her arm in the direction she wanted me to go. Her visuals saved me. After a "Thank you, ma'am" I'm sure she didn't hear as she turned to serve another traveler, I headed in the direction she waved.

If I'd thought there were a lot of people in the Richmond and D.C. bus terminals, I had another think coming. If I'd thought people in those two terminals were fast-moving, I quickly learned that nobody, I mean nobody, moved as quickly as those people in Penn Station. I found myself sidestepping as folk bore down on me, men mostly, with leather briefcases in their right hands which they slung like battering rams, and newspapers folded and tucked under their left elbows. They all wore dark gray or black suits with white shirts and highly polished black shoes. There were more military people than in the earlier terminals, many soldiers, some sailors, fewer marines, and a sprinkle of WACS and WAVES. I hadn't known that there were women in our military. A few colored people whirled by me as though they too were in a hurry. I bought a newspaper from a stand where the vendor had thick wavy black hair and spoke with a lilting accent, folded it, and tucked it under my left elbow. "Yammio leweegy," I thought I heard him say to a man who answered, "Say vah." I guess I wanted to be considered one of the locals, despite my hesitant walk, and the dead giveaway of setting down my suitcase to look around me.

At each point of my departure—getting into the auto outside the jail in Orangeburg, leaving the bus stop in Florence and the bus terminals in Richmond and D.C., and now, boarding the Long Island train, I'd had a growing feeling of being propelled away from home, of being hustled out into an increasingly alien world, into a world that I had only the vaguest inkling existed, into a world that I had seen in picture books and magazines and RKO-Pathe News. A world of Shirley Temple and Clark Gable and Tom Mix, a world of popular song. What I was witnessing was a world of brusque, hurrying people, people who had no time for anything or anybody that stood in their way to where they were headed. This world clashed with the world of my imagining. I found this world discomfiting. I didn't like it. Yet there was something about the new spaces I found exhilarating, a beginning feel of freedom.

Ask the conductor to call your stop, Edith's letter had read. The train, destination Patchogue, was made up in Penn Station, so we had a few minutes to wait before the doors would close. This was my second train ride, in a vastly different car from that packed, steamy, soot-filled car of the segregated Southern Railways train of my childhood. I found a window seat in the middle of the car. Passengers, who had been waiting for the doors to open, poured in, jostling each other, filling the seats in front, behind, and across from me. Then they started hanging onto the overhead straps, swaying as the train wheels screeched around curves.

No one sat next to me.

I started to open my newspaper, then noticed how the men in the seats ahead and across from me folded theirs, into column-wide strips. I followed their example, and had got mine just about right, when a young woman, short and round, with glowing skin and wavy black hair, sat down next to me. After a cursory glance in my direction, she took a fat book out of her book bag and began to read.

Walk right down the street when you get off the train, Edith's letter had continued. *The Wilson house at the top of the street. Mrs. Wilson or the children will be there, if they home from school. They'll take care of you. See you Sunday on my day off. Be good. Love, Your Sis."* I would see my sister on Sunday. I was to stay with her until I could join the navy.

The navy. The *navy.* I had never told anyone, except for talk in the shop, that I wanted to join the navy. There I'd said I'd rather join the navy than the army, but that I would not join the navy and be a mess attendant. Now I was being put into the navy, just like that. There was no "Would you like to join the navy?" I was being banished from home to join the navy. It was too much to think about then, with everything else. But I would have to. And soon.

Edith. We were never close. She was four years older than I and away from home during most of my teen years. I was the brat of a brother who wouldn't leave her alone with her boyfriend until he paid me off. Her letters home were always to Mama, never to me.

What would I say to her when we met? How could I tell her what I had done? What would she understand? Mama had simply told her that I had got into some trouble with white folks and had to leave town. And could I stay with her until I could join the navy. That was all. I would have to fill in the rest: "I wrote a girl a note." "A. D., you wrote a *white* girl a note?" "Why, yes I did, but I…" "A white girl?" There is the hint of scorn. "What did you say to this, this, *girl?*" "I just said, 'I would like to know you better.'"

"With all the colored girls in Orangeburg—beautiful, nice, sexy girls—you, *my* brother, you had to pick a white one to write to. Hmnh! Hmnh! Hmnh! So *we* weren't good enough for you? *You*, you had to go looking for a *white* girl." There it was, the *curse*, the tribal curse. The withering look in Aunt Maude's eyes. The look of failure in my mother's eyes. Black women could take my leaving. Men had left and had come back. They could take on another black woman. That was fair competition. But a *white* woman. In their minds, that was *not* fair. In seeking out a white woman I had turned my back on the race, on them. I had committed a blood and bone sin, had thrown at them the ultimate rejection. Or so they reasoned.

I found myself retreating to the bus, to the tunnel, to the comfort of its dark.

You don't understand the eternal fitness of things. There was no way to make it up, there was no way to take it back. My act was irretrievable. Its effects would follow me wherever I went, no matter what I did. I was eternally cursed as unfit. I could never be right again.

The young woman next to me looked up from her book, out the window, spoke softly, "Are you all right?"

"No, I—I mean yes, I'm fine." I wondered if I had been mumbling. I held the newspaper at an odd angle. I righted it.

"Traveling far?"

"Rockville Centre. I don't think it's far. And you?"

"That's just a couple stops from here. Patchogue." Her voice had song in it.

"That's the end of the line."

"How did you know? You're not from here."

You're not from here either, I thought, remembering the newspaper vendor, his hair and coloring like hers.

"I saw it on the first car."

She turned back to her book. I returned to my newspaper,

fumbling its folds. Rising when Rockville Centre was called out, I told her, "That's a long way. Safe journey."

"You too," she smiled, showing perfect teeth. But what I remember most is her eyes, large, with heavy brows, and very open.

"Watch yer step there," the conductor warned, as I was a little shaky leaving the train.

EPILOGUE

I am because we are;
Because we are, I am.

—Ibo saying

Genius is community.

—Albert Einstein

Reflections on What Didn't Happen and What Might Have Been

Lines to Her
They never let us finish that conversation
we started. What did happen to you?
Who were you, really? Those few times
we talked, about nothing, really, yet
we hit dissatisfaction at our cores:
"That dime store job," "Tied to this last."

Had we community such that our
genius could flower, for you had genius,
genius I saw in the quickness of your
mind, the lightness in your walk,
what else would you have said to me?

Epilogue

What did happen to you? What questions
were you forced to answer? By your
manager, by the Law? Your parents
when you got home?

Did they try to link us in some way?
Say we had things we had been hiding?
We had no such things. My seven-word note
should have shown them that. *"I would like,"*
not, "What we have done."

"To know you better," was what I asked.
I wanted to tap that genius, watch it flow,
share, glowing as your smile.

They would not let us. They would not
even let you answer me.

Would you have answered?

Do you, like me, carry a scar?
Did you marry, let children come?
Where are you now? This question
has been open for me all my life.

What did happen to her? I know
what happened to me. Questions.
Jail. Exile. The wandering.

For fifty-seven years I told
no one. I told no one. No one.

An unopened wound kept
festering, never exposed
to the healing power
of sun.

Epilogue

The longer a secret is kept,
the harder it is to reveal,
the more painful to conceal.

It was all those years, remember?
All those years. Of moving,
moving, moving even when

I stood still. My life ran on a
double track. As I aged, I found
it harder to stretch and keep
my balance.

Then one day, after bucking
wind and snow, I screamed, "No more
of this." I stared at my laptop.

I sat.
My first words out were,
I hurt. I had said it. I had
sliced open an internal storm.

I could admit the questions,
dialogue with myself.
Who knows, maybe I could
begin the return.

I returned, and saw under the sun, that the race is not to the swift, nor the battle to the strong, nor yet bread to the wise, nor riches to men of understanding, nor favor to men of skill, but time and chance happeneth to them all. (Eccles. 9:11)

ABOUT THE AUTHOR

Adam David Miller has worked in northern California in the arts
for four decades, as teacher, writer, poet, editor, publisher, and
radio and television producer. His *Dices or Black Bones* won the
1970 California Teachers Association Award for best anthology. He
traveled in West Africa as a National Endowment for the Humanities
Fellow for 1973/74 and has been invited to read, lecture, and present
workshops in schools and universities throughout the United States
and elsewhere.

Heyday

HEYDAY INSTITUTE

Since its founding in 1974, Heyday Books has occupied a unique niche in the publishing world, specializing in books that foster an understanding of the history, literature, art, environment, social issues, and culture of California and the West. We are a 501(c)(3) nonprofit organization based in Berkeley, California, serving a wide range of people and audiences.

We are grateful for the generous funding we've received for our publications and programs during the past year from foundations and more than three hundred individual donors. Major supporters include: Anonymous; Anthony Andreas, Jr.; Barnes & Noble bookstores; BayTree Fund; S. D. Bechtel, Jr. Foundation; Fred & Jean Berensmeier; Book Club of California; Butler Koshland Fund; California Council for the Humanities; Candelaria Fund; Columbia Foundation; Compton Foundation, Inc.; Federated Indians of Graton Rancheria; Fleishhacker Foundation; Wallace Alexander Gerbode Foundation; Marion E. Greene; Walter & Elise Haas Fund; Leanne Hinton; Hopland Band of Pomo Indians; James Irvine Foundation; George Frederick Jewett Foundation; Marty Krasney; Guy Lampard & Suzanne Badenhoop; LEF Foundation; Michael McCone; Middletown Rancheria Tribal Council; National Audubon Society; National Endowment for the Arts; National Park Service; Philanthropic Ventures Foundation; Poets & Writers; Rim of the World Interpretive Association; River Rock Casino; Riverside-Corona Resource Conservation; Alan Rosenus; San Francisco Foundation; Santa Ana Watershed Association; William Saroyan Foundation; Sandy Cold Shapero; Service Plus Credit Union; L. J. Skaggs and Mary C. Skaggs Foundation; Skirball Foundation; Swinerton Family Fund; Thendara Foundation; Victorian Alliance; Tom White; Harold & Alma White Memorial Fund; and Stan Yogi.

For more information about Heyday Institute, our publications and programs, please visit our website at www.heydaybooks.com.